The Kingdom *of* Golf *in* America

The Kingdom of
GOLF
in America

RICHARD J. MOSS

University of Nebraska Press
Lincoln & London

∞

Library of Congress Cataloging-in-Publication Data
Moss, Richard J.
The kingdom of golf in America / Richard J. Moss.
p. cm.
Includes bibliographical references and index.
ISBN 978-0-8032-4482-5 (cloth : alk. paper) 1. Golf—United States—
History. 2. Golf—Social aspects—United States. 3. United States—
Social life and customs. I. Title.
GV981.M67 2013
796.3520973—dc23   2012047430

Set in New Baskerville by Laura Wellington.

Contents

Acknowledgments

This book is the product of a long life in golf and a scholarly life that turned out better than I deserved.

I grew up in Jackson, Michigan, a great golf town. Much of what I have said in this book is shaped by my early life in a town that took golf very seriously. Teaching pros Chuck Smith and Ken Douglas gave free lessons. There were courses on which I could play all day for fifty cents. People for whom I caddied passed on free balls, paid my way to tournaments, and became range buddies. One older gentleman, in particular, convinced a callow teenager that the game posed philosophical, even religious, questions. After that I could never think of golf as merely a silly game.

At Michigan State University Douglas Miller and Russel B. Nye allowed me to think seriously about the history of popular culture. In recent years several individuals have eagerly provided support and the best sort of criticism. Bradley S. Klein of *Golfweek* has made this book better in countless ways. His thoughtful readings of this and earlier manuscripts have been invaluable. Orin Starn and Jim Dodson have provided encouragement and have served as examples of people who take golf seriously. I owe a considerable debt to the United States Golf Association. Research into the history of golf would have been virtually impossible without access to their library and research services provided on the Internet. The most immediate guardian of the collection, Nancy Stulack, has been unfailingly helpful on numerous occasions. The USGA has also conducted a series of symposiums at which I was allowed to try out ideas and at which I learned much from other historians. I would like to thank David Normoyle, once at the USGA and now on his own, for his friendship and for the discussions of golf that helped me sort out what I actually believed. I also need to thank my wife, Jane, for her bottomless patience with my golf obsession and my desire to write books about it. Family friends Pearl Rose and Georgia Katz have been there when I needed them.

My fondness and respect for reference librarians is boundless. At Colby College and at Duke University these selfless souls invariably understood my vague needs and directed me to the resources, often obscure, which are central to this book. Sarah P. Ward was a pal and the best person to translate my scrawl into a workable manuscript. Karen Brown was my dream copyeditor; she sanded off a lot of junk and made the remainder shine.

It has been my privilege to be a regular on a golf discussion show on WEEB Radio in Moore County, North Carolina. The others on the show—John Derr, Pat McGowan, Tom Stewart, Rich Mandell, and the creator of the show, Les Fleischer—have created a neat little world where the game is taken seriously every week. On the show I have had a chance to listen to smart people like Ben Crenshaw and Richard Coop talk about golf from their own extensive experience. Being part of the show has deepened and widened my perspective on the game.

I have played golf with thousands of people over the last sixty years and I have learned something from each of them. My play in the scrambles at Waterville Country Club in Maine and in the Monday Group and the Tuesday Golf Society at Pinehurst has profoundly enlivened my sense of what the game means to people. From this vast group of golfers let me dedicate this book to two of them. Let it be a small tribute to Dale Brown and Tim O'Day, princes in the kingdom.

Introduction

My once-or-twice-a-week golf games have been islands of bliss in my life, and my golfing companions, whose growing numbers now include a number of the dead, are more dear to me than I can unembarrassedly say. Somehow, it is hard to dislike a man once you have played a round with him. —John Updike, "The Bliss of Golf," 1982

Golf has always been a part of my life. There once existed a photo of me, now lost, taking some of my first steps aided by my father's hickory-staffed brassie. I cannot remember a time when I did not care about how I was playing and when I would play next. In the last fifty years I have developed a profound fondness for a number of golf courses, both public and private. I feel more comfortable on a golf course than I do in my own bed.

So I find it difficult to think of golf as a hobby, a diversion, or a consumer choice. I do not like the idea that I am a small part of a big sport industry. Golf is not a commodity unless you think it is. Golf, as I have experienced and studied it, is a physical and mental place to be — in other words, a community.

I have tested this idea with some of my fellow golfers. The question put to them was, do you feel like you belong to a golf community? As an academic playing golf with nonacademics, I am subject to considerable suspicion when I ask such questions. Most, however, readily agree that they belong to a golf community. Most belong to a private club or have a membership at a public course, and this obviously creates a sense of community, a sense of belonging. One went further and called this community "the kingdom of golf." In this kingdom you are, he said, restrained by a set of rules and traditions. You are provided a slowly growing set of heroes. The kingdom has a founding, a history, internal divisions (parties), and a generally agreed-upon set of values. The official language is English but with a highly specialized vocabulary that can bewilder noncitizens. Obviously, the golf community offers several levels of citizenship. There are those who care deeply and make golf one of the most vibrant parts of their lives. There are many who only occasionally pass through the kingdom — transients of a sort. Oddly, there are those who watch others play but do not play themselves. Like all communities, the kingdom of golf has a hierarchy. It has developed a politics with leaders who claim the authority to protect and regulate the game. They pass laws that provide order in the kingdom. These laws generate controversy and are not always obeyed.

Finally, the golf community has a literature. It is a complex pile. At the bottom are national, regional, and local magazines. They began to appear almost as soon as golf, the game they chronicle, began to be played in America. They convey news and opinion; they do much to hold the community together. As we get nearer the top of the pile, golf literature gets more literary and philosophical. Works on heroes and great moments are common. At the very top are a small number of works that attempt to define the game's essence and to place it within the larger history of sport and the nation.

This book is a history of the golf community in the United States. This history began in the 1880s and continues, of course, to the present. For 130 years, the kingdom has waxed and waned in response to larger historical currents. In the most general sense, the people who founded the golf community were responding to modernization. By modernization, I mean a set of forces that arose most clearly after the Civil War. For golf, the most important forces were urbanization and suburbanization operating in tandem. By 1890 Americans were confronted with what might be called the new city. Golf was part of the adjustments that Americans (mostly affluent) made to the new city. The rise of the new city eroded the sense of community that most had felt prior to 1870. It also detached them from nature and plunged them day after day into a rapidly declining cityscape. Golf was just one of the many ways that people sought to reconstitute community, to revive a sense of belonging. It was also one way that Americans sought to reconnect with nature.

There were other modernizing forces that shaped the kingdom of golf. Technology was crucial in making the game more accessible (playable) for more people. Also crucial was the fact that Americans over the last 130 years have had more free time and money to spend on nonessential items. This is such an obvious fact that we often forget that people had to react to it. It is only recently in the grand sweep of history that average people have been confronted with the choices created by the existence of expanding discretionary time and income. Becoming a golfer was one of those choices.

Today the golf community is huge. It occupies a great amount of space and it has millions of citizens. Its growth in the last sixty years has been rooted in the spread of affluence and certain technological advances. As an economic reality, it is intensely complex. Just one aspect of this complexity is the split between golf as it is played and golf as it is watched. Huge corporations rely on the health of the golf community. On the other hand, owners of nine-hole courses in rural areas can envision opening for the season and no one shows up. Many people need the golf community to be big and healthy. The point of this book is to tell the story of how it got that way in the first place.

This book is not an exhaustive history of golf in America. I am sure that every reader will note an omission they view as tragic. Maybe I haven't given Sarazen his due. Maybe their favorite course designer fails to appear. There is no desire on my part to write a golf encyclopedia. Instead this book traces the growth of golf as a community with a complex set of parts, a community that has thrived inside the much larger American community.

From Nothing to Something

In March 1889 the *Philadelphia Dispatch* published a description of golf that provided a sense of what Americans knew about the game. This report began with the claim that "golf is played only by people accustomed to Scottish sports and Scottish scenes." The game was played in Canada, but "even there it has not assumed the importance of a regular department of sports." The newspaper stated that "no man should attempt to play golf who has not good legs to run and good arms to throw with." The game is played from hole to hole on the dead run and there are no codified rules according to which the game is played, except that "an inviolable rule" forbids a player from touching the ball with his hands.

Approximately five years later, James P. Lee, in one of the first books about golf in America, provided a better description:

> The general idea is easily stated. Starting from a given point with a small gutta-percha ball, it is the object of the play to show which of the competitors takes the fewest strokes to get his ball in a hole, let us say 400 yards distant from the starting point. He who does so is the winner. A full course consists of eighteen of these holes. The winner of the majority of them is the winner of the match. This certainly sounds simple; but there is much more to the game than would appear from such a statement.

Exactly. In five years golf in America had gone from very nearly nothing to something. Joseph Lee's description, and particularly his notion that golf seemed simple but that this simplicity was an illusion, captured the essence of golf's early years in the United States. Golf was going through a process of birth and growth, and to understand that process requires that we understand not only the nature of the game in the late nineteenth century, but also the complex history of the years in which golf migrated from Scotland and England to the United States.

In the early days, golf in America was very much like a colony. The homeland was Scotland, England, and, to a much lesser extent, Europe. Affluent American males with Scottish backgrounds or the leisure to travel in Europe were the main agents of colonization. These men transferred the game to the United States by founding clubs that had as their basic purpose the construction of a course upon which to play golf.

The first lasting, important club was St. Andrew's Golf Club in Yonkers, New York. The animating force at the heart of this club was John Reid, the manager and treasurer of the J. J. Mott Iron Works at Mott Haven, New York. Reid was a Scot to his soul. He loved to drink Burntisland Scotch Whiskey and to sing Scottish ballads. Early in 1888, Reid and John B. Upham demonstrated the game of golf to a group of friends. Reid and Upham used a set of clubs that Reid's friend Bob Lockhart had sent from Scotland. The demonstration succeeded and Reid and his friends set out to find a place they could play. They ended up on a twenty-acre pasture owned by a butcher named Shotts. By November of 1888 a club had formed; it was called St. Andrew's Golf Club of Yonkers-on-the-Hudson. For four years the club was content to play on the tiny meadow near their home.

In 1892 the town of Yonkers needed to extend Palisade Avenue through their course. This forced the group to find a new home. They moved to an apple orchard nearby, thus giving birth to "the Apple Tree Gang." The "gang" established six holes among the apple trees and elected one particularly ancient tree as a clubhouse of sorts—there they hung their coats and lunch baskets. The golf club began to draw members from a local city club (the Yonkers Club). Of the thirty-three original legendary members, most belonged to both organizations.

Soon it became clear that St. Andrew's was falling behind newer clubs that began to appear on the margins of New York City. The members decided to buy the Odell Farm in Grey Oaks. The land came with an ancient clubhouse that some thought was haunted. With this move the club began to look and act like a modern golf club. They hired a pro from Scotland, Samuel Tucker, and on April 14, 1894, they finally incorporated. In the incorporation documents they stated that the club's purpose was "to play the game of golf and provide proper ground for so doing."

When St. Andrew's incorporated in 1894, there were, according to Joseph Lee, about seventy-five golf clubs in the United States, most born "within the last year or two." Perhaps the most important of these clubs, and the first to incorporate, was Shinnecock Hills Golf Club. The idea for Shinnecock Hills was in fact born in Europe. Samuel L. Parrish, who was deeply connected to the club and to the early history of golf in America, describes, long after the fact, the way in which Shinnecock Hills got started:

> While traveling in Italy in the spring of 1891, I received a letter from Biarritz, France, from my friend, the late Duncan Cryder, a summer resident of Southampton, in which he stated that he and our mutual friend, the late Edward S. Mead, were passing the winter in Biarritz and that they had both become greatly interested in a game called "golf" (my first introduction to the word) which they thought might be successfully introduced at Southampton, and played, possibly, on the Shinnecock Hills.

Cryder and Mead infected others when they returned to the States. They obtained advice from the Royal Montreal Club (founded in 1873). The pro at the Canadian club, a Scot named

Willie Davis, visited Southampton and passed along a load of clubs and balls for the new golfers. Two men, George R. Schieffelin and General Thomas H. Barber, made it their job to raise money for the new club. There was a meeting at Mead's house. By the fall, forty-four members of the Southampton summer colony had purchased shares in the venture. Several were women; unlike St. Andrew's, Shinnecock never nurtured a tradition of excluding women.

The building of the course and construction of the clubhouse proceeded swiftly. Willie Dunn, another Scot, designed a twelve-hole course and the noted architect Stanford White was commissioned to design a clubhouse that was completed in June 1892. The women organized the first event, a "grand golfing rally," in September 1891.

The original twelve-hole course quickly became congested. The club constructed a nine-hole course for women only. Samuel L. Parrish remembered that this "created a certain amount of dissatisfaction," and the nine-hole course and the original twelve-holer were abandoned and replaced by a single eighteen-hole course. In 1892 the club had seventy members and a long list of regular players labeled "season subscribers."

Until 1892 the activities at Shinnecock attracted virtually no interest outside the society pages of the local Southampton papers. It was Parrish's memory, however, that from 1893 onward "a veritable craze swept over the country, and the Shinnecock Club became the mecca for golfing pilgrims from other sections of the country seeking information before starting in to constructing their own links."

The birth of a third club, the Chicago Golf Club, illustrated not only the profound connection between golf in America and Scotland, but also the spread of the game outside New England and the Northeast. This club was the child of Charles Blair Macdonald, a crucial figure in the early history of golf in America. His father had sent him to Scotland and St. Andrews University in the early 1870s. Charles returned to the United

States with a fine education and a lifelong passion for golf. No one in the early years of golf in America had stronger opinions about courses, competition, and the meaning of the game. No one was more willing to force his opinions on anyone willing or unwilling to listen than Charles Blair Macdonald.

The years after his return from Scotland were filled with frustration. There were no courses upon which he could play. Macdonald tried for years to interest his friends in the game, with no luck. He claimed that the Chicago World's Fair in 1893 was the event that led to golf's birth in the Midwest. The fair brought many Scots and Englishmen to Chicago who wished to play golf but were frustrated by the lack of courses. Pushed by the demands of these visitors, Macdonald was persuaded to lay out a very rudimentary course on the Lake Forest estate of John B. Farwell. This experiment led to the founding of the Onwentsia Club in 1895.

The members of Macdonald's city club were also bitten by the golf bug. MacDonald claims that he actually passed the hat at the city club and thirty men contributed ten dollars toward the construction of a course. It was built on land owned by A. Haddon Smith in Belmont. Smith was from Musselburgh, arguably the birthplace of golf in Scotland. By 1893 Macdonald had produced an eighteen-hole course. That same year, Illinois chartered the Chicago Golf Club. This charter was signed by seven men, only two of whom were American citizens. By all accounts, the club was a rude affair, much like St. Andrew's of Yonkers during its early days. However, golf had taken root and the membership grew rapidly.

Always ambitious, Macdonald led the effort to find land upon which he could build a real course that would compare with the finest courses in the world. He found a two-hundred-acre parcel near Wheaton, about twenty-five miles from Chicago. In 1894, as Macdonald was crafting his course in Wheaton, golf clubs began to sprout elsewhere in the Chicago suburbs. Soon there was an impressive list: Onwentsia, Belmont, Midlothian,

Exmoor, Glenview, and Skokie. Chicago was undergoing a revolution of sorts. Its citizens were escaping the heart of the city for the suburbs, and when they arrived they built a golf club as part of the process.

A fourth golf course was founded in the mid-1890s that was very different from the courses at private clubs. In 1895 the city of New York built a course in Van Cortlandt Park, in the Bronx. Established in 1888, the park was on land that was once the estate of Oloff Van Cortlandt, a wealthy Dutchman and patriarch of an influential New York family. The course owed its existence to a group of affluent gentlemen from the Riverdale area on the Hudson River. They clearly wished to have the city build them a public course that would, in fact, be largely private. The Riverdale group formed the Mosholu Golf Club, which exercised extraordinary control over the course in the years prior to 1900.

The course was the scene of the first public golf tournament in the United States, conducted by the St. Andrew's Golf Club in Yonkers and open to players who were not members of a private club. An article in *Golfing*, in 1896, claimed that the course had as many as one hundred players on Saturday and holidays. The article also claimed that "a half dozen private clubs" made Van Cortlandt their home course. This suggests that America was adopting a pattern common in Scotland whereby clubs of golfers shared a single course. Several of these clubs lasted well into the twentieth century. But the idea that a number of private clubs could share a single public course, as they do in Scotland, never really took hold in the United States.

This pattern also evoked much criticism. By the turn of the century, the clubs like Mosholu were driven from the course, and informal private control of the links evaporated. The usefulness of this first public course was reduced by a law that required it to be closed on Sunday, the only free day for most of the players who wished to play. Yet it hung on and eventually flourished. The course was expanded to eighteen holes in 1899 by Tom Bendelow, who became the greenkeeper between 1899 and 1901. With Van Cortlandt Park as something of a model, most large American cities would eventually establish public courses as an alternative to the private clubs.

Golf first came to America, then, in the form of courses paid for or instigated by affluent men who wished to play golf. In every case there was a connection to the Old World, and to Scotland, particularly. These men also believed that an organization was needed to control the game in America. The early history of the United States Golf Association (USGA) is well known. Both St. Andrew's and the Newport Golf Club held what were billed as national amateur championships. The Newport event was held in September 1894, with twenty golfers in the field, playing a stroke-play format. Only eight men survived. William G. Lawrence defeated Charles B. Macdonald by a single stroke. Lawrence's total for thirty-six holes was 188. The quality of play was not high. Macdonald, who seemed to live his life near the boiling point, was sure that he was the best player in America and that he lost because of an improper hazard on the Newport course. His ball had come to rest near a stone wall, and the strokes required to extract it cost him the tournament.

A month later Macdonald had a second chance to prove his superiority. St. Andrew's sponsored a match-play event, and Macdonald lost again. These two controversial events were enough to get Macdonald and others thinking about establishing a national organization to conduct championships and establish rules.

Henry O. Tallmadge, a crucial figure in the organization of St. Andrew's, sent out invitations to St. Andrew's, Newport, Shinnecock Hills, The Country Club (Brookline, Massachusetts), and the Chicago Golf Club. On December 22, 1894, representatives of these clubs met over dinner at the Calumet Club in New York City. There they founded the entity that would evolve into the United States Golf Association. They elected the richest man at the meeting, Theodore A. Havemeyer, the Sugar King, as president. Like all such organizations, they created committees and set out to write a constitution and by-laws.

It is too simple to think that the USGA came into existence because Charles B. Macdonald wanted national championships he could win. Joseph Lee, in his book *Golf in America*, gives us a hint about what was actually at stake. He admits that the USGA was founded in part to end the confusion about national championships. However, he goes on to quote approvingly the English magazine *Golf* on the value of what the Americans had done. The English journal thought that the Americans had

> unerringly . . . diagnosed the weak spot in the government of golf. They have seen that golf . . . is an unwieldy, incohesive congeries of clubs without any central guidance. Everything in golf is haphazard and capricious. The rules have been altered and remodeled, not to suit the average convenience of the greatest number, but to suit the playing exigencies of one green.

Indeed, the USGA was designed to provide order and discipline for a sport that could easily have become chaotic, with individual clubs or local organizations each pursuing their own idea of what golf should be. This was most clearly evident in the voting rules established by the USGA. The constitution created two classes of member clubs — "associated" and "allied." Associated, or full membership, was granted only to courses and clubs that were "representative." Clubs were admitted to this full membership only by a four-fifths vote of the executive committee. This provision gave the full members absolute control over which sorts of clubs could have real power in the organization. Allied clubs had little power and few rights beyond the right to pay dues and to call themselves a USGA member.

Charles B. Macdonald suggested what lay behind this division of clubs into associated and allied. He stated, "I firmly believe the ruling of any sport by an intelligent autocratic body is infinitely preferable to mob rule, which always lowers the

8

morale of games." This kept clubs with "courses laid out in any old place" or "hotel courses" from having a voice in the future of the game. This voting arrangement was hotly debated over the next thirty years (especially in 1905) but it was not changed until 1927.

The USGA, with a few elite clubs firmly in control, set about to establish key definitions central to golf competition. Many thought that the most crucial job was to define the term "amateur golfer." This issue bedeviled the USGA for years. The men who controlled the organization into the 1920s sought to eliminate commercialism, the taint of money, from the concept of amateur. Anyone who had played for money, had given lessons or demonstrations of golf, had caddied after age fifteen, or had designed, administered, or built a golf course was banned from amateur competitions. As established in 1897, the definition of amateur also excluded anyone who "played the game or frequents golf courses for the purpose of exploiting his business." The USGA made member clubs the agents in charge of keeping nonamateurs out of its competitions. All entrants in USGA-sanctioned events needed a document from a club secretary vouching for the fact that the player was a member of an approved club and an amateur according to the USGA definition.

It is easy to view the USGA in its early days as solely a small group of elitists attempting to control the game and limit play to the wealthy and socially prominent, but this would not be accurate. From the start, there was a struggle for the heart of the organization between an aristocratic and a democratic impulse. This struggle has continued to this day without a convincing resolution.

In fact it was the richest and most prominent figure in the early days of the USGA who gave voice to the democratic, austere, egalitarian point of view. Theodore Havemeyer, who made a fortune monopolizing sugar, thought golf could be a sport for the people. The USGA created a magazine called *Golfing*, and it took up Havemeyer's ideas about the game. In a series of un-signed editorials it praised Havemeyer's view that people were spending too much on clubhouses and not enough on cours-es. The magazine claimed that golf could be relatively inexpen-sive, just as it was in Canada and Great Britain.

The USGA and Havemeyer, again in the pages of *Golfing*, were in favor of public courses. It stated that "those who wish to keep the game as the exclusive property of the wealthy who belong to clubs are not carrying out the ancient and honored tradi-tions. In the old country, it is possible for everyone to play and no one has ever objected to this." *Golfing* also crusaded against the ban on Sunday play. It argued that golf was not a disorder-ly game and that average working people, who had only Sun-day free from work, should be able to use the day for golf if they wished. In taking this position, the USGA faced off against pow-erful conservative, Christian forces that fought to keep Sundays free of all play.

Havemeyer's egalitarian tendencies had their truest test at the 1896 USGA Open Championship held at Shinnecock Hills. The U.S. Amateur Championship was also held there and went off smoothly. The Open Championship, even before it began, was enveloped in controversy. The problem was the entries of John Shippen and Oscar Bunn. Shippen was the son of an African American minister who had come to the area from Jamaica. Bunn was a Native American, about whom little is known. Both had been caddies at the club and had learned to play. Willie Dunn, the club's pro, had given them both lessons, but Shippen was the most promising of the two. Dunn allowed him to give lessons and made him an assistant. Apparently some members urged both men to enter the Open in 1896.

When the other professionals arrived they met and threat-ened a boycott if Shippen and Bunn were allowed to play. Have-meyer's response was quick and sure. He told the pros that the event would be played with or without them. There remains much doubt about what was said but Shippen and Bunn competed. Shippen played very well. The event was thirty-six holes of medal play; Shippen played the morning round with none other than Charles B. MacDonald and Shippen's seventy-eight had him tied for the lead. Shippen's chance for victory was crushed when, in the second round, he took an eleven on the thirteenth hole. He finished seven shots behind James Foulis, the eventual winner. Shippen played occasionally in Open Championships after 1896. His last appearance was in 1913. Shippen, however, made one other appearance on the golf record. On September 29, 1897, he played an exhibition against Valentine Fitzjohn, a "Scotch professional." Shippen, in the *New York Times* report, was referred to as the "colored lad." The contest was held at the Ardsley Club; Fitzjohn won easily.

By 1896 golf had come a long way since the game arrived as an infant in an apple orchard in Yonkers. Something like a community had clearly appeared. There were citizens, mostly members of approximately seventy-five private clubs. Of these clubs, forty-three were allied or associate members of the USGA. This list of clubs suggested how localized golf was in 1896. Of the fifteen associate clubs, twelve were in New York, Massachusetts, Rhode Island, or New Jersey. Only two—the Chicago Golf Club and the Washington DC Golf Club—were outside the Northeast. Of the twenty-eight allied clubs, twenty-three were in New York, Massachusetts, New Jersey, Connecticut, or Rhode Island. New York possessed seventeen member clubs, the most of any state. Only three clubs were located in the South—one each in South Carolina, Maryland, and Washington DC.

A political organization had appeared. The USGA sought to take control of the game in America. Essentially an organization of clubs, the USGA established hierarchies of several sorts. Clubs themselves were arranged according to their "worth" and reputation. Amateur players were defined and set off against professionals. Officials of the USGA began to discuss what was proper and improper when it came to golf. An endeavor that would grow as the years passed.

The USGA had a small part in developing the means whereby golfers could learn more about the game they had embraced. The USGA founded a journal called *Golfing* to communicate news and information about the game. Its central function was to publish actions by the organization and to establish the USGA as the voice of golf.

In 1895 a magazine called *The Golfer* also offered itself to American golfers. In a "Publisher's Statement," *The Golfer* (November 1895) made it clear that it sought an elite audience anxious to do things correctly: "Golf is the greatest game of this country. It is the leading game of high social life; it is at once picturesque and scientific. Form is essential, costumes and equipment require the closest attention possible. *The Golfer* meets the call for an authority on the game and correct form."

The existence of an evolving golf community was clearly evident in these pre-1900 golf journals. Beyond telling readers how to swing a club, these periodicals also told their readers what to wear and how to act properly on the course. Furthermore, if one examines the advertisements in these early magazines, one finds an amazing array of enterprises seeking to do business in some way with golfers. Among the advertisers were sellers of golf clothing, makers of clubs and balls, printers of club books, financiers looking to lend to new clubs, real estate agents with properties to rent on golf courses, publishers with instructional books, and trophy makers.

In 1898 *Golf* began to publish a "Wanted" section where people looking for work in the golf business could make their availability known. It contained notices from professionals, caddies, and club stewards looking for a position. There were a number of ads placed by professionals who were looking to hire club makers. The magazine also published an ad for a "Golf Information Bureau" that supplied free information about golf at hotels, arranged golf tours in Europe and America, and claimed to "have special information respecting the state of greens."

In less than a decade, golf in America had become a significant part of the American landscape. Why did it take root so quickly and firmly? There were grumblings that it was just a fad and that it would burn itself out. By 1900 it was clear that golf was no fad.

For some modern-day commentators, the reasons behind golf's rapid rise are clear. They define golf as an elite sport, a game for the rich, and see its adoption as one way the wealthy could maintain their status atop the American social structure. Donald J. Mrozek, for example, states that

> by the very sporting ventures they chose, the American rich set patterns of behavior that distinguished them from the masses and even from much of the respectable middle class. Infected with a desire to set fashion and keep pace with its mercurial changes, the wealthy elite often opted for customs of the British upper classes—a phenomenon that showed itself in the sudden vogue of tennis and golf and invited satire in the rise of fox-hunting.

More simply, Kenneth T. Jackson, in his study of American suburbs, contends that golf has been the "aristocratic pastime *par excellence*." Such views have some truth to them, but, for the most part, they miss the complex reality that actually explains the adoption of golf in America.

In the first place, golf cannot be lumped together with yachting, polo, or foxhunting. Also, the idea that the American rich were copying the habits of the British upper crust is similarly off base. Golf came to America as a Scottish sport that had only recently been adopted in England. For the vast majority, golf was democratic and egalitarian. American commentators repeatedly made the point that golf reflected what they saw as the Scottish character, and this character was democratic, simple, and austere. A point never made about yachting, foxhunting, or polo.

It is obvious that affluent Americans took up golf for reasons that extended well beyond a desire to maintain their class status. It is also obvious that, by 1900, there was a conflict between the desire of some Americans to make golf solely a game for the elite and the game's tradition of egalitarianism and accessibility—a conflict that continues to define the game to this day.

The adoption of golf was not solely the product of class feeling or status anxiety among the rich. Its adoption was contingent upon a cluster of developments that made golf attractive to many Americans. They turned to golf and made a sizable investment privately, publicly, financially, and emotionally because a number of factors came together to make golf something Americans wished to make a part of their lives.

The first of these factors was technology. A number of prosaic technological developments made golf more attractive or made it possible for more people to play. Certainly golf would have made little headway in America if not for the introduction in Great Britain of the gutta-percha ball in 1848. Prior to that date golfers in Great Britain played with balls called *featheries*. These objects were constructed from two small pieces of leather stitched together much like a tiny baseball. However, the process was somewhat more complex than the making of a baseball. For one thing a small hole was necessary through which the maker stuffed wet feathers using great force to create a hard sphere that would compress and stay round. Makers also used the hole to turn the leather inside out so the raised stitches would end up on the inside.

Featheries were expensive. They did not fly as far as the new gutta-percha balls and they became out of round more easily and flew in unpredictable directions. They also took on moisture and became soggy. One hit with the edge of an iron club simply ruined the thing.

Gutta-percha was a natural product of several types of tropical trees. It is a milky latex sap that was first used for insulating cables and waterproofing. Whoever discovered that it could be used as a golf ball remains unknown. The new-style ball flew erratically until makers discovered that markings gouged into the surface made them fly straighter. Between 1848 and the 1880s the markings were applied by hand, and after that molds were used.

The "guttie" changed the game dramatically. They were cheaper and virtually indestructible. In very cold conditions, however, they could dramatically shatter. Its introduction clearly set off a golf boom in Scotland and England—a boom that Americans saw when they traveled to Great Britain. Of course, the "guttie" was replaced by the rubber-cored or Haskell ball, just after 1900. In short, advances in the nature of the ball made the game more fun and much cheaper. Robert Browning, the golf historian, has concluded that the dramatic evolution of the ball between 1850 and 1900 "made golf a different game," especially for older players, women, and children, who lacked the strength to muscle a feathery around the course. The rapid changes in the ball made the game easier for more players; it made it more inclusive.

Other technological advances helped golf take root. The construction of urban railroads and electric trolleys in most large urban areas made getting to the newly built courses possible. It also allowed many to escape the city and set up a new kind of life in the suburbs. Very often golf clubs had their own stations where transportation to the clubhouse was available. Of course, this was only a small step in the history of mobility. By the mid-1920s, the automobile would do much more to bring the rural golf club within easy reach.

Increased mobility was both cause and effect in the rise of suburbs. Certainly suburbanization preceded golf in America, but the suburb and golf were a virtually perfect match. As Americans rode the trains and trolleys into the suburbs, they left behind the social institutions of the central city. Golf and the golf club were perfect answers to this problem. They replaced in part the city club, the saloon, and the ladies group.

Golf, and particularly the golf club, was the answer to the new suburbanite's persistent question: Will we have a social life out here?

In equally important ways, golf was a response to growing antiurban and anti-immigrant sentiment. In simple terms, American cities at the end of the nineteenth century were becoming unlivable for many. People remembered the preindustrial city with a certain nostalgia. There was a sense that something important had been lost. This reaction was not solely rooted in the Northeast—it was general. Booth Tarkington, in *The Turmoil* (1915), could write about Indianapolis in clearly nostalgic terms:

> Not quite so long ago as a generation, there was no panting giant here, no heaving, grimy city; there was but a pleasant big town of neighborly people who had an understanding of one another, being, on the whole, much of the same type. It was a leisurely and kindly place—"homelike," it was called. The good burgers were given to jogging comfortably about in phaetons or in surreys for a family drive on Sunday. No one was very rich; few were very poor; the air was clean, and there was time to live.

Is it any wonder that people who shared this sentiment found in the suburban golf club a solution to their anxiety about the transformation of American cities? It was crucial that Tarkington's image of the old city was populated by people "on the whole, much of the same type," for it was immigration as much as industry that changed the cities. In virtually every city, a massive tide of newcomers from new places was a compelling reality. In the 1880s approximately five million immigrants came to the United States, about twice the number seen in any prior decade. There were "new" immigrants who came from eastern and southern Europe—not northern and western Europe, where previous arrivals had originated. The number of Jews coming to America soared. Many cities, by 1890, had populations that included between 30 and 40 percent foreign-born residents.

And the rush of new immigrants was only part of the problem. Between 1850 and 1900, cities like Boston had become divided. There were a few expensive homes in the Back Bay, but for the most part, the inner city was dominated by work places and low-income housing. In contrast, there was an outer city of middle- and upper-income homes. People in these homes traveled to and from the inner city on a newly built street-railway system. This outer city was the product of economic prosperity and the desire of affluent Boston families to live in safer, cleaner, and more natural places.

The division of cities like Boston into inner and outer cities spawned the rise of the problems we still associate with modern urban life. House buyers flooded into the suburbs. Their sudden departure from the inner city destroyed old neighborhoods. Sam Bass Warner Jr., in his book on the Boston suburbs, summarized the outcome: "With the new metropolis and all its changes the ancient problems of large cities once more came to life: the individual members of urban society became isolated within a physical and social network which had passed their comprehension and control."

In these circumstances, two compelling desires drove those who had the means to leave the inner city. The first was a desire to escape a situation beyond "their comprehension and control." The second was to form associations that would re-create a sense of community. The end of the nineteenth century saw Americans literally go nuts over associations. Sport was a fertile area for association. Existing organizations like the YMCA and YWCA turned to sport and exercise as a new central focus of their endeavors. Almost every sport rode this tide of organization. With community of the older sort—the kind that Tarkington thought had once existed in Indianapolis—in shreds, people sought to rebuild it around sport. Certainly this desire for community was crucial in the rise of spectator sports in the last quarter of the nineteenth century. Commitment, even passion, for the town team brought people together.

Golf, as a sport, was in many ways a perfect solution to the desire for reconstituted community. It seemed to *require* that you form a club. It came with an exotic language that, once learned, gave the faithful a sense of belonging. It had an ancient tradition that created the sense that you were joining a community deeply rooted in the past.

But for golf to thrive, for it to be accepted at all, two final and related historical developments had to occur. The first was the rise in both discretionary time and money. Tracing the growth of discretionary or free time is difficult because it increased at different rates for the various classes and occupations. But the six-day workweek was, in the 1890s, reduced by the arrival from Great Britain of the idea that Saturday should be only a half workday. The five-and-a-half-day workweek became particularly common during the summer months. This was the beginning of the modern weekend. The forty-hour week would not become standard until the 1930s, but the direction was set before the turn of the century. This was one of the factors that profoundly shaped modern existence. The hours worked fell in the last century by 50 percent, while productivity soared.

This productivity translated into more money for personal consumption, money that went to things beyond food and housing. In 1900, one hour of work produced fifty cents for personal consumption (adjusted to 1982 prices). In 1990, the same hour produced $9.75 in personal consumption. Of course, people used this income for essential improvements. They purchased better food, indoor plumbing, hot water, electricity, medical care, and bigger, safer homes. However, there was considerable money left over to sweeten life. Recreation or play was one way to spend this money.

The other historical development contributing to the acceptance of golf involved the changing American attitude toward the pursuit of leisure activities. Slowly, over the last century, the attitude toward play began to change as discretionary time and income increased. There was no official American attitude toward play prior to 1890, but prior to the Civil War, it is hard to find an advocate of unproductive play. Indeed, work and plenty of it was deemed the moral core of life. Recreation or play was only useful as a refresher, as something that allowed you to return to work, even more dedicated to labor. Golf in its first two decades in America benefited greatly from this idea. Golf was celebrated as the perfect antidote to overwork. H. C. Chatfield-Taylor testified "that the businessmen of the Middle West are no longer shallow dyspeptics who toil from 8 A.M. to 6 P.M. Golf has made their blood flow and color come to the cheeks."

What does he mean when he uses the term *businessman*? Surely he does not mean the super rich. In almost all the discussions of golf that appeared in America prior to 1910, it is very difficult to find a connection between the very wealthy and golf. It was not their sport. It was not yachting or polo. Yet clearly, it was not pictured as a sport for the poor. Golf was adopted and promoted by a class of men and women that is hard to name. Upper middle class will have to do. It was a class dominated by middle-level businessmen who worked hard and moved to the new suburbs financed by their modest but growing success. Once there they sought a diversion. Gustav Kobbe, in 1901, described what happened:

> To live in the country once simply meant to sleep there. The balance of the suburban resident's existence was divided between express trains and the city. But with the introduction of sport as a feature of country life — and especially of that sensible, democratic, and reasonable economical sport, golf — and the general adoption of the Saturday half-holiday it is remarkable how much time the country resident can give to healthful outdoor exercise and social recreation. The Nation is beginning to find as much fascination in driving a golf ball as in driving a bargain.

Golf Literature

Imagine an American male, in 1897, interested in becoming a golfer. He has never seen a golf ball or golf club. He has, however, heard about the game; perhaps he has been invited to join a newly founded golf club. Maybe he had just moved his family to a suburb of Boston, New York, or Chicago where there was an established club. He was already taking Saturday afternoons off in addition to all of Sunday. His income was rising. He has several books about golf written by Englishmen or Scots. His wife has brought home something labeled "an official guide to golf." But most important, next to his chair, he has a stack of monthly magazines. These were the television and the Internet for turn-of-the-century Americans. They contained "golf literature."

From this literature, one quickly learned about the clubs and the balls and the nature of the game. The books from England and Scotland explained the game clearly enough. A book by an American was just as good as the foreign stuff. The book was *Golf in America: A Practical Manual* (1895) by James P. Lee. The books by Englishmen had more humor and more technical instruction. The one by Horace G. Hutchinson included a section called "The Miseries of Golf," which was odd. There were parts of the game that apparently made you miserable. One of these was "being asked by your opponent, just as you are starting, whether you have any objection to his wife and sister-in-law walking around with you, as he wishes to introduce them to the game."

From Hutchinson, our beginner also learned that there was a great deal of debate on how one was to hold and swing the club. Oddly, the Englishman stated that "you cannot learn golf from a book" and then proceeded to teach technique in his book. This instruction included the following: "The proper line of motion can only be given to the club-head by grasping lightly with the right hand, and keeping the right shoulder down and its muscles loose. The right shoulder down, and loose, I believe to be the prime great secret for striking the ball as it should be struck." Little did our beginner know that this "great secret" was among the first of thousands to be revealed over the next century.

Another book by a Scot was helpful because it had photographs of the proper style. It was apparent that everyone developed "a style," which was the term used to mean your swing. This Scot, Sir W. G. Simpson, also warned about people who offered a secret path to a great golf swing: "That there is some secret which, if discovered, would make driving [a golf ball] infallible, is a belief that dies hard. Nostrum after nostrum is tried day after day. Hope is quickly followed by despairing desire to break the whole set or spitefully to present them to a friend, so that he too may suffer."

This all made golf seem like some sort of lifelong quest, a mixture of pleasure and pain, exultation and despair.

Our potential golfer has a wife who in the years just prior to 1900 had begun to act strangely. From the husband's point of view she seemed to be in mild revolt against some sacred rules that had structured her life. She complained of "nervousness." She often remarked about the unfairness of the restrictions on her dress and her behavior and the attitudes that society imposed on her. Her friends were just like her. They had come to hate "Mrs. Grundy," the imaginary woman who enforced these rules.

The husband has a hunch that golf might help his wife. He had read an article in an old copy of *Outing* that suggested that golf was like medicine—the right kind of medicine—for women because it, unlike all other outdoor games, was "a game of competition only and not of antagonism." The players do not resist, delay, or even contact their opponents. Golf will ensure to the modern woman "at once health-giving exertion of the most valuable nature, for the necessities of the locality will ensure the links being placed at a distance from the residential center." The husband thought that golf was what they both needed. They needed to get out of the city and stay out.

His wife, he was sure, had been waging a not-too-subtle campaign to get them to join a golf club. A couple down the street had joined and the neighbor's wife and his were always plotting something. They had both come home with several "guides to golf." One had been produced by Brooks Brothers and the other was a volume in the Spalding's Athletic Library. Our would-be golfer had always associated Spalding with baseball but, apparently, they also promoted golf. The guide called the game "a manly and healthful recreation."

He and his wife learned a lot from these guides. They reprinted the rules of the game and explained the "etiquette" required of all golfers. You had to be quiet and generally treat your opponent with excessive respect. You had to play along at a good pace or groups behind could pass you by, and you "must replace turf cut or displaced by a stroke." The United States Golf Association (USGA) had made these etiquette rules as binding as all the other rules. It was in one of these guides that our beginner found a clear definition of "Colonel Bogey." Apparently he was a fictitious person who "is an imaginary opponent, against whose arbitrary score each competitor plays by holes." Soon he would become "par."

The guides were confusing when it came to the subject of golf clothes. The Spalding book said that "there is nothing about Golf which compels its votaries to wear any particular costume."

For the ladies, "golf admits of an endless variety of dress." The Spalding guide concluded "Wear what you are most comfortable in that's nice and loose . . . under no circumstances sacrifice comfort to looks." The Brooks Brothers guide, however, did not mention comfort. They had for sale "red golf coats and sweaters with club collars." They also offered to "make up special designs and insignia for golf coats." There was also a big section on Scotch tartans. Apparently at some clubs the swells had special clothes to play in, but everyone else could wear what they wanted.

From the Spalding guide the husband learned about clubs and balls. He was sure that Spalding was trying to get him to buy their products. He read that in golf there was much controversy over what were the best clubs and balls. The guide said that a player "often attributed good play to the merits of the tools he is handling." The wooden clubs seemed to provide the most variety and the most debate over what was best. Shafts could be made of orangewood, lance wood, blue mahoe, greenheart, and, the Spalding people stated firmly, "last and best, hickory." Wood clubs could have heads of pear or apple but beech was the best and by far the most common.

There were lots of ads in the guides. They provided much information, but our husband and wife had grown accustomed to advertising even though it was relatively new. The husband was attracted by two kinds of ads. The ones that notified him of hotels and resorts in the South were particularly interesting. Golf had vacation possibilities. You could get out of the northern winter and play a little golf while your friends were wallowing in the snow and ice. He also liked the ads for golf gimmicks. There was an ad for a device called the "Linka." It was about the size of a dinner plate. You nailed it to the ground in your yard. A thin piece of rope came out the side to which was attached a golf ball. The rope was connected to a spring and a meter so that a dial on the top told how far your shot had flown. The husband found such devices irresistible.

The guides were helpful and people looked forward to their appearance each year. The best golf literature, however, was in the glossy monthly magazines. There was a great deal about sport in these periodicals. *Outing* had always been about sport, and by the late 1890s they were doing a lot with golf. There was a regular column with golf news from around the country. The other magazines like *Scribner's, Collier's,* and the *Atlantic Monthly* featured articles on weighty political and economic subjects. That they printed essays on golf gave the game respectability. These magazines laid around the house forever and people passed them along to friends. They lasted.

Our potential golfer's favorite piece was called simply "Golf," and it appeared in the May 1895 issue of *Scribner's.* It was by Henry E. Howland, and it also contained great humorous drawings by A. B. Frost. Howland talked about the game in a very serious way. The drawings by Frost seemed to make fun of players who became overly emotional or took the game too seriously.

Much of what Howland had to say had a defensive tone. Apparently golf had its detractors, people who were labeled "scoffing on-lookers," who thought the game too simple and genteel, who thought it a game for swells and sissies. Howland thought that these critics were people who had never played, because once you gave it a chance, golf was addictive. He could become effusive about the game's virtues. For example, he portrayed the devoted golfer in terms that seemed excessive:

> His sense of the ultimate purpose and the true proportions of his existence is unruffled, whether he views life from the exaltation of a two-hundred-yard drive on to the hill, or the lowest heel-mark in the deepest sand-pit on the course; while the feelings of momentary success or depression, which so possess the souls of weaker men, pass over him with no more influence than the flight of birds. His soul is so wrapped in the harmony of earth and sky and the glory of the game, that no buffets of fortune can come at him.

Most of Howland's essay was much plainer than this. Several of his better lines stuck in our reader's mind. Here are some of Howland's best:

> The origin of the royal and ancient
> game of Golf is lost in obscurity.

> Redcoats are not becoming to the
> American landscape, and on a warm
> July day are fairly distressing.

> As a teacher of self-discipline the game
> is invaluable.

> Golfers as a rule are an exceptionally
> honest race of men, but uncertain arithmetic
> is occasionally encountered. "I aim to tell
> the truth," said one; "Well, you are a very
> bad shot," was the reply.

> The golfer's expletives must be directed
> against his own lack of skill, or lies,
> or hazards, and the luck and vengeance
> must light, and often do, on the unoffending
> clubs, even to their utter extermination.

> [on the caddie] One of his principal
> qualifications is that he should be
> able to conceal his contempt for
> your game.

> The relation of the fairer part of
> creation [women] to golf varies
> between that of a "golfer's widow"
> and that of a champion.

> There is no Anglomania about this
> game in America.

The game is a leveler of rank
and station. King and commoner,
noble and peasant, played on equal
terms in days gone by.

Our potential golfer liked all of these statements and he started to use them in conversation. When he talked with people
who had taken up golf, they used Howland's language. There
grew the odd sense that golf was a secret society with an ancient set of values and a common language with which to express these values. He liked the fact that people defended the
game as democratic and egalitarian — he was an American after all. People could claim that golf was only for the very rich
but he grew convinced that this was not true.

There were, however, some writers on golf that baffled him.
They seemed to make more of golf than he could understand.
They made it too complicated, too intellectual. Perhaps the
most perplexing of these authors was William Garrott Brown.
Born in 1868 in Alabama, Brown had graduated summa cum
laude from Harvard. He earned a master's degree at Harvard
and was appointed a lecturer in the history department. He was
a Democrat. He wrote essays about the South that our reader
had noticed in many of the finest magazines. He also wrote in
the magazines about contemporary politics and the economy.
In 1902 he published an essay in the *Atlantic Monthly* called,
simply, "Golf." Our imaginary potential golfer was suspicious of
Brown because he was from the South and was clearly a Democrat.

Brown had some very odd notions. For one thing, he claimed
that in 1902, "any company of reasonably alert and well-to-do
Americans" was talking about three subjects that had not existed a decade earlier. The first was the power of "money as a social
and economic force." Americans were entranced, in other words,
by the rise of "trusts" that amassed billions of dollars and with
it commensurate and frightening political power. The second

was the sudden appearance of the United States as a colonial power. The country, largely thanks to the Spanish-American War, had become an empire. Equally interesting was Great Britain's decline. Was America about to replace her former mother country as the greatest power on the planet? The third subject was golf. Brown did not appear to be joking. The rapid acceptance of golf was important because it signaled that "from our passionate absorption in work we have somehow passed into an equally passionate absorption in play." Brown noted that of the three, only the trusts were actually new. Golf and empire were old and he limited his essay to these two topics. The trusts he was willing to leave to the Supreme Court.

Actually Brown spends most of his energy on golf. He admits that some play it because it is "the fashion" to do so. For these people he had nothing but contempt; such a follower of fashion "should be a butler, a hired mourner at funerals." But the game is more than just fashionable. It will persist because Americans can play it well and they genuinely like it. The game will spread to California and Florida where the climate will allow year-round play and this will produce world-class players.

While admitting that golf took root among the older, more affluent element, Brown argues that now (in 1902) there are signs of general acceptance. Towns are building public courses and he claims that the number of cheap, small, village nine-hole clubs is growing fast. There exists an antiextravagance movement, and he thinks that it will crush "anything like display in dress." America, at first, took to red coats and other costly golf costumes but now "we seem to be rid of the people who thought they found in golf a new sartorial opportunity."

Brown thought that Americans had gone through a brief period when people played golf because of the clothes and fashion. By 1902, however, this period was over. Americans took up golf after that point because they liked it. So what was there to like? Golf was appealing for two reasons. It made "demands" on the player and it also dispensed "compensations" or benefits.

In simple terms Brown claimed that golf demands "work." It requires more "deliberation" than other games. A player must understand the nature of the shot confronting him, the state of the match, the weather and one's own level of competence. There is plenty of "time" for the player to do this work. Brown had put his finger squarely on what made golf different from all other American sports. Baseball, football, and all the others were based on the quickness of the action, on the instantaneous nature of the actions and reactions required. Golf was deliberative.

At an even higher, more intellectual, level the game puts heavy demands on the player's moral fiber. There is no game with more room for cheating or willfully misinterpreting the rules. Golf demands "virtue"; it demands patience, good temper, and courtesy.

Brown's heavily moral view of golf was rooted in the unique nature of the game. In golf, every course has a posted standard of good play. Brown calls it the "Bogey Score"; we would call it par. For him a golfer is always in two matches, one against your opponent and one against par. When a duffer battles par, he or she in fact confronts "a clear though unattainable ideal." The game demands that "with every stroke we assail an ideal."

At this point, Brown's moral view of golf subtly becomes religious. A golfer, as he plays, constantly faces a moral or religious challenge to live up to an ideal, to "the moral law of golf." If granted this view of the game, then "a golfer's mistakes . . . are sins—nothing less; he will writhe under them ere he sleeps." Thankfully, there is one mitigating element in what seems like an impossibly unhappy situation and that is the existence of handicaps. But, for Brown, this only creates a context for the striving after the ideal (perfect play) that is the very heart of the game. Golf was play but it was addictive because at the same time it was both actual and moral work that sought a visible but unattainable goal.

I am sure that readers probably agreed when, at this point,

Brown states that "this is growing a trifle serious." He turns to what golf gives—its benefits. His analysis is again more intellectual, more penetrating than anyone else writing about golf. He is one of the first people to state that golf gives "mere bodily delights," that hitting a golf ball (well?) is a true pleasure. Once a player learns to play, golf provides "a sense of effectiveness, of competence." Golfers also develop solid friendships with their fellow players, even their opponents. Given the long spaces between shots, golf is the "best method of beginning an acquaintance."

Golf allows Americans to return to nature. This, of course, assumes that Americans were once more in contact with nature. Briefly, Brown suggests that players develop a unique relationship with their course, their own little nature preserve. Certainly the history of golf illustrates how central the love of one's course became in the twentieth century. This contact with nature was the doorway to a better mood or temper. Brown states that golf is a sport that "one can actually play dreamily." A mood that he claims allows one to play better.

The game can also produce "serenity and tranquility," something that, Brown thinks, Americans badly need. It is, in short, a perfect game for Americans "who because they are so busy and hurried, will not take the time for it, but prefer instead some sort of rapid transit through their diversions and would have their relaxation without relaxing and bolt their nature like their luncheons."

At times Brown's essay seems like a subtle critique of the American character. Or maybe he was offering a critique of the northern business culture from a southern perspective. This emerges most clearly when he describes his "most annoying" golfer; he was

a little man, all nerves and energy and alertness to opportunity, who cannot for the life of him move over the course at any fixed and deliberate pace; who cannot, indeed, walk at all, but alternates from lingering, leashed by courtesy, at the side of his partner, to bouncing after his ball. If through golf such Americans should come into the practice of a pace that is neither hasting nor delaying, it will prove not the least valuable part of the education of our masters.

Brown, more than any other writer on golf, sees the nature of the game at odds with some American habits. The rushing, pushing, urban American needs the slow and serene pace of golf to keep him from burn out and an early grave. Golf demands a slow, dreamy, and deliberate approach to time. In 1902 Americans, in almost all the other areas of their lives, especially business, had learned that time was to be filled in a panicky, nearly hysterical way with great efforts, with exhausting attempts to push oneself forward, to create in some vague way progress or success. Golf was one diversion created to hold this spirit in check. Golf, Brown clearly implies, is not for the ultra rich. Instead he suggests that midlevel American businessmen caught between the plutocrats above them and poor below him might find in golf something like salvation.

Brown concludes by drawing a parallel between the British and the Americans. He notes that as we take over their empire we seem also to be taking over their sports and diversions. He does not pursue this thought beyond suggesting that Americans have much to learn from the British experience. But he does suggest a connection between empire and golf, an idea worth pondering. For wherever the British Empire had traveled, golf had gone along on the trip.

Among golfers Brown was clearly not as well known as Arnold Haultain. Born in India, in 1857, Haultain lived most of his life in Canada. Like Brown, he wrote on many other subjects besides golf. He produced books on walking and hiking and a book on the nature of love. Haultain's book on golf, *The Mystery of Golf*, was preceded by two short essays, one in the *Atlantic Monthly*, that were warm-ups of a sort for producing the book, which appeared in a limited edition in 1908. In 1910 another publisher released a much larger edition. Like Brown, Haultain sought to create an intellectually complex and penetrating analysis of golf. He succeeded. However, while many collect copies of his work, one wonders if golfers in 1908 were compelled by *The Mystery of Golf* to buy clubs and take up the game.

Haultain begins by creating a "scoffing onlooker." This is a gentleman who has joined a golf club for the social life and spends much of his time there mocking those who play. Once he gives the game a try, however, Haultain tells us, "then indeed did the scales fall from his eyes. He discovered that there was more in golf than meets the eye—much more."

Most of the book is an attempt to define this "much more." Haultain repeats much that was usually claimed for golf. For example, he claims that the game is somehow inherently Scottish, it "is self-reliant, silent, sturdy. It leans less on its fellows." In short, it is a game for individualists.

But this is mere prologue to Haultain's main position. He is a Darwinist. For him sport is friendly combat, and success in sport is a symbol of success in the struggle between individuals and the larger conflict between the individual and nature. Sporting success lets us see an individual's true worth, it reveals a person's "real and inner self."

Haultain was a big thinker. He could go off on flights of fancy about what most saw as a simple game. For example, "In golf we can see a symbol of the history and fate of human kind careening over the face of this open earth, governed by rigid rule, surrounded by hazards, bound to subdue nature or ere we can survive, punished for the minutest divergence from the narrow course."

Haultain's attempt to make golf part of a Darwinian struggle is a failure. Most readers will automatically view golf as markedly different from other "combat" sports. People who passionately play golf have usually explicitly rejected the combat sports.

His strongest argument is not about Darwinism or the struggle to survive. It is about the value of golf as a means of getting back to nature. Like Brown, Haultain extols the connection between the player and the little bit of nature he or she calls their home course. All talk of struggle with nature ceases and the golfer finds, instead, serenity as he enjoys his little piece of nature. When he plays Haultain contemplates nature: "There are nooks, and courses, and knolls, and sloping lawns on which elfish shadows dance. . . . I seem to be listening to some cosmic obligato while I play; a great and unheard melody swelling from the great heart of Nature."

Nearly equal to the pleasures provided by nature are the pleasures provided by the clubhouse. Haultain argues that after play the clubhouse serves up "spacious verandas and arm chairs, shower-baths; teas and toast; whiskey and soda; genial comradeship; and the ever delectable pipe." As important as these pleasures are they are secondary to the comradeship, the sense of community that one finds at a golf club.

Much of Haultain's little book, however, borders on the incomprehensible. At times it seems that he is determined to apply everything he has read to golf. So we get bits about the physiology of the eye, Neoplatonic philosophy, and the psychology of the subconscious. At certain points, he states his case in ways with which every golfer can agree. The contact with nature, and the love of the course as one's own little plot, is certainly one of golf's enduring attractions. With qualifications, Haultain is also right to see golf as a struggle and to see this as a virtue, but his attempt to haul Darwin into the debate is a failure.

William Garrott Brown has a much better view of this idea that somehow we are attracted to golf because it is a struggle. Brown sees the struggle to be against an ideal like par or "your best score ever." Americans have a much deeper faith than other peoples in eventual perfection, or at least the moral necessity of constant progress toward perfection. Golf, more than any other game, neatly fits this faith. It has a concept—par—that creates a goal for all and serves to sort out all honest players along a continuum. A handicap system exactly places an individual on that continuum and allows an honest player to monitor his or her progress with numerical exactness. This may be one reason Americans have been so fond of medal play and the quantifiable aspects of the game. Golf at *match play*, where one plays an opponent hole by hole, is very different from *medal play*, against a field of opponents each counting every stoke. It may also explain why we have divided golfers by gender and age so that one can measure one's progress against one's peers.

Golf literature had some impossible-to-measure impact on the growth of golf before World War I. It provided golfers with a language to speak and jokes to tell. It conveyed golf's long history. It answered the game's critics. Most important, early golf literature tried to explain why people became obsessed by the game. This literature created the sense that with golf you were not just taking up a game, you were joining a community.

Fiction played almost no role in explaining golf to Americans. Instead, stories about love, romance, and marriage, which could have been set anywhere, were merely transferred to the golf club. The fiction that was produced told us more about the country club than about golf.

After 1915 golf would continue to develop a significant literature. This literature would, however, never have the purpose that the pre-1915 works exhibited. Before the war, writers took up the job of telling Americans about a game that was new to them. Slowly writers turned away from that job to the task of describing what was going on in the golf community. They turned to recording results and to creating heroes.

CHAPTER THREE

Clubs and Courses

G olf in America has always been about land use. After
1888 some portion of the American population decided
to devote a not insignificant portion of their land (old
farms, declining estates, seaside sand barrens) to golf courses.
Until World War II, the majority of these courses were created
and operated by private clubs. It is a fact that many of golf's sacred places were the product of affluent Americans banding together into voluntary associations that stated as their purpose
the advancement of golf.

There was nothing simple about this link between private
clubs and golf courses. Some clubs were the products of rich
people looking to enhance their grip on high social status. Others were the product of modest Americans looking for a sporty
game and a breath of fresh air. The clubs used a variety of methods to finance their endeavors and to create a membership to
foot the bill. For some there was a profit motive; for most the
idea of profit was secondary to their collective purpose. They
thought that, as a group, they could create something that they
could never have as individuals. People could use the words "so-
cialism" and "utopian" to describe their efforts.

The evidence indicates that club and course building went
through a two-stage process between 1890 and 1915. The first
stage was dominated by upper-class types in the Northeast.
Shinnecock, St. Andrew's, Baltusrol, and others were typical

of this period. If the founders of these clubs believed that they could keep golf for themselves, they were mistaken. By 1898 something called "the country club idea" had begun to infect the middle classes. Clubs and golf escaped the Northeast (and Chicago) and, by 1915, the country club–golf club idea had spread everywhere a middle class proud of its city existed.

By 1900 a second stage of club and course creation was clearly under way. Americans moved away from the Scottish model and, in essence, redefined the golf course. Americans would begin to spend dramatically more on clubs and courses. The courses would differ markedly from the Scottish models. They would be more expensive, more private, and they would be greener.

Both stages of club creation employed the distinctive American institution: the voluntary association. America, lacking the clear-cut class distinctions and occupational guilds of aristocratic Europe, had made use of voluntary associations for a number of purposes. For three centuries, many Americans thought of a proper church as a voluntary association. This they saw as the antidote to tax-supported national churches and, most clearly, to Catholicism. In the early nineteenth century, reformers made use of voluntary associations to gather people into groups that pursued reforms that ranged from the abolition of slavery to women's rights to diet reform. The stock corporation, central to the growth of capitalism after the Civil War was, in effect, an elaboration of the voluntary association.

In the 1890s and the first decade of the twentieth century, Americans of all types created a vast array of associations. Groups were founded for occupational reasons, to promote political and social causes, to engender ethnic solidarity, and to advance any number of special purposes or causes. The national professional associations (for doctors and lawyers among others) date from this period. Increasingly people came to believe that as individuals they were growing powerless. Associations allowed the Americans who joined them to feel they were part of a community that could deal with this sense of powerlessness. As society became more a mass society, associations became more important.

The groups that formed golf clubs chose widely varied structures. Most, however, moved very slowly and committed to expend money or take on debt only after the club was on solid ground. St. Andrew's, the first club, was an example. John Reid and his fellow founders reluctantly moved from leased land to a permanent location at Mount Hope. They financed the move by issuing bonds that raised twenty-five thousand dollars. Several members made substantial purchases of these bonds. Theodore A. Havemeyer, president of the United States Golf Association (USGA), was one. The club's ability to settle at Mount Hope was greatly aided by a mortgage on the property held by Andrew Carnegie. From the apple orchard days the club, step by cautious step, moved to new quarters with eighteen holes and a fifty-thousand-dollar clubhouse (the plans called for a more expensive clubhouse but John Reid vetoed it).

The organization of Shinnecock Hills Golf Club was based on the simple sale of stock. But before the stock was sold, a small group of men set out to raise three thousand dollars that would go to clearing the land, putting in greens, and constructing a rude clubhouse. In August the money was raised and some sort of start on a club and a course was made. At that point the group of golf promoters sold stock to members of the Southampton summer community. People were asked to come to Edward S. Mead's house on August 22 in the afternoon. Someone no doubt explained what had been done and what the future plans were. The land was leased for five years with an option to purchase. Shares sold for one hundred dollars.

This meeting also adopted a constitution and elected trustees. At a second meeting of the newly elected trustees, officers were elected for the new club. Thomas H. Barber was the first president. They also elected a house committee, no doubt to deal with the task of building a clubhouse. By late September 1891, there were forty-four men and women who were stock-owning members. While the invitation to buy stock mentioned leased land, the club changed its plans. One of the first actions of the trustees was to buy approximately eighty acres from an English company. Over time Shinnecock bought more land until, in 1923, it owned 180 acres.

Baltusrol illustrated another method used to get a golf club started. The club was the idea of Louis Keller who created the Social Register. Keller had a lot of nerve. At age thirty, he set himself up as the sole arbiter of social acceptance in New York City. To be listed on the register you needed Keller's approval. In 1895 Keller decided that he wanted to play golf. He belonged to a racquet club but they refused his request to add a golf course. So he decided to create a golf club on his own. He owned five hundred acres in Springfield Township in New Jersey.

In April 1895 he sent a letter to his friends asking them to join a golf club he was creating. He had already installed a golf course on his land (designed by George Hunter, an Englishman). He had also given the club a name—Baltusrol. A friend, Louise McAllister, was given the credit for inventing the name, which was derived from the name of the farmer, Baltus Rol, who once owned the land. He had been murdered in 1831.

The club was a success. In three years the membership grew from thirty to almost four hundred. The club was run by a board of governors of which Keller was the secretary. The club leased the land and clubhouse from Keller. The initiation fee was twenty dollars and the yearly dues were ten dollars. The membership changed, often dramatically, each year. In the fall as many as sixty members would resign to be replaced the following spring. Over the years, however, a core of loyal members developed. The original invitation to join contained a list of women patrons and the club quickly began to produce notable female players like Mrs. William Fellowes Morgan. She was one of the thirteen contestants in the first USGA Women's Amateur in 1895.

Because Keller leased the club at a low rate to the membership, they were able to expand as more members arrived. In 1897 the course was expanded to eighteen holes. Within this course, a "short course" was designed for beginners and women. This structure allowed Baltusrol to keep its dues relatively low. Keller was often quoted in the New York papers about the dues at Baltusrol. In 1900 the club offered lower rates for people who lived a great distance from the club. The dues ran from fifteen to thirty dollars, depending on where you lived. By 1906 the membership stood at 750, perhaps the largest club of its kind in the United States.

Another club with a decidedly upper-class membership was the Tuxedo Club at Tuxedo Park in New Jersey's Ramapo Hills. The park was from the beginning a real estate venture conceived by Pierre Lorillard Jr., the great-grandson of the tobacco tycoon. He may have been attempting to create a community that would challenge Newport as the ultimate seat of fashion. Like Keller, Lorillard owned a vast tract of land. In 1885 he ceded five thousand acres to the Tuxedo Association, which built a clubhouse and, in turn, leased it to the Tuxedo Club. The association constructed a fourteen-strand barbed-wire fence around the compound. There was a clear emphasis on preserving nature and allowing the owners of "cottages" to experience nature directly. At first the main activities were hunting and fishing. As for the clubhouse, a visitor in 1891 claimed there was "an aggressively English air about the place." He thought it evoked "the English country house and the life peculiar to it."

Getting into Tuxedo was a two-step process. If one wished to buy land, a contract was drawn up. The second step was an examination by the club. If one failed this exam, the contract was voided. A second form of membership was available to nonresident members, who could stay at the club for limited periods.

The club built a crude six-hole golf course in 1885. A nine-hole course designed by a transplanted Scottish engineer, Henry Hewat, opened in 1892. In 1895 an improved nine-hole course appeared. Golf has always shared the spotlight with other sports—tennis, hunting, fishing, and sailing on Tuxedo Lake. Unlike most clubs, Tuxedo was clearly a capitalist enterprise and, as such, was an early experiment in selling real estate and in creating a socially exclusive gated enclave in a community based on access to sport and nature.

Tuxedo's main competition for social ascendancy was Newport. The establishment of a golf club there illustrated other aspects of the early clubs. Members of the Newport colony began their golfing on rented land in the Brenton Point area. The inspiration behind this tentative beginning was none other than Theodore Havemeyer. Havemeyer had seen golf played at Pau, France, on a course built for English and Scottish tourists. In January 1893, the course on Brenton Point had attracted enough interest to convince Havemeyer that a more formal, ambitious club was needed. A group assembled at Havemeyer's home in New York City and over several meetings elected officers and established a constitution and by-laws. The membership was limited to seventy-five. The group agreed to erect a suitable clubhouse on the ground rented for golf. On March 1, 1893, the club was incorporated under the laws of Rhode Island. They hired William F. Davis as professional and greenkeeper away from his position at the Royal Montreal Golf Club.

This was a very timid start by people with enough money to take a more reckless plunge. They played on forty acres of rented land with numerous stone walls and fences that they could not remove. The club did not immediately build a clubhouse; instead they leased the nearby Bateman Hotel as a headquarters. Even so the course and club quickly became the site of lavish social events during the 1893 season. The club put up a purse for a match between Willie Davis and Willie Dunn, from Shinnecock Hills. Dunn nipped Davis by a shot, carding a 45.

By the end of the first season, the founders were convinced that the club would be a success. There were seventy members and seventy-eight seasonal subscribers. For the next season, the initiation fee was set at one hundred dollars and annual dues at thirty dollars. The club made an attempt to buy the Bateman Hotel, but failed.

In October 1893, Havemeyer, sure that the club would prosper, created a syndicate to buy land for the club. It was an impressive syndicate. The group included Cornelius Vanderbilt, Perry Belmont, John Jacob Astor, and Fred W. Vanderbilt. They paid eighty thousand dollars for a 140-acre parcel called Rocky Farm. This syndicate leased the land to the golf club for $3,500. In the spring of 1894, Willie Davis was hard at work laying out two new courses on the new site. The result was a nine-hole course for men and the better women players, and a six-holer for beginners, women, and children.

In August, at the end of the 1894 season, the syndicate sold the club land to a newly incorporated entity called the Newport Country Club. This created two stable groups, the country club, which owned the land, and the golf club, which leased the land. This relationship lasted until 1917, when the two merged. This new development in 1894 apparently set off a growth spurt. The membership was increased from 75 to 275.

The Newport Country Club was a land development corporation. Most of the original syndicate members agreed to buy fifty shares at one hundred dollars each. This raised $150,000 in capital. There were fourteen stockholders, and the country club remained a closely held company until 1917. It was an example of a structure that many golf clubs would adopt. It might be called the two-level approach. The upper level was an individual or group who owned the property, took on the risk, and garnered any appreciation. The lower level consisted of a membership who paid the various fees and dues that paid the rent and yearly expenses.

This arrangement worked well enough at Newport. Magazine articles that appeared after 1900 about establishing a club often recommended this two-level approach. However, in 1897, Havemeyer's death shook the club and the corporation. Amazingly, he died intestate and his stock was not turned over to his heirs until 1908. Actually, Havemeyer's death was quite the event. People talked about the lack of a will, but were even more astounded by his death-bed conversion to Catholicism.

The early affluent clubs took a variety of paths to the creation of private golf clubs. Some were simple corporations with stockholders; others were complex multilevel affairs. Real estate speculation was part of the process for some, and was absent for others.

However, this brief survey does suggest something that unites all the early (pre-1895) clubs. They were all timid about building their courses. Few clubs simply spent the sums necessary to have a fully realized eighteen-hole golf course. After 1895 most of the early clubs expanded their operations and took on debt in order to build grander and grander courses.

There were two reasons for this timid approach. The first is relatively obvious. The clubs were waiting for their memberships to grow. The membership numbers in the first year were small; sometimes there was only a handful of committed members. But in each case, memberships grew rapidly. It was easier to spread a big debt, a big commitment in land and money, over four hundred members then it was to get thirty pioneers to take the plunge.

The second reason is also obvious and requires some basic knowledge of the period between 1888 and 1894. It was a time of acute financial anxiety. There was a bitter debate between prosilver and progold forces over the proper way to back currency. There was an intense conflict between debtors who wished to use silver to inflate the currency and creditors who wished to be paid in gold-backed dollars. In 1893 a London banking house, Baring Brothers, collapsed, setting off a worldwide depression. This was the sharpest economic downturn that Americans had seen to that point. During 1893 and 1894 many Americans thought their world was about to collapse. Farmers and industrial workers staged frightening protests. The Populist Party organized this discontent into a formidable political force. An "army," led by Jacob S. Coxey of Ohio, marched on Washington demanding radical solutions to the nation's economic woes. This all led to the dramatic election of 1896 in which "radicalism" (William Jennings Bryan) faced off against "conservatism" (William McKinley). It was, to be a bit flip, a lousy time to start a golf club. Looking back it is astonishing what the clubs did accomplish in an era that made everyone cautious about the future.

Golf also made its way in the United States without the aid of a newly created private golf club designed expressly to build a course and advance the game. For example, existing clubs that were devoted to other sports such as polo, hunting, and cricket found it easy to add a simple golf course. Notable examples were the Myopia Hunt Club and the Philadelphia Cricket Club. The Agawam Hunt Club in Providence, Rhode Island, apparently caught the golf fever in 1895. They installed a course that an 1897 issue of *Golfing* called "very sporty." The first hole was called "Railroad" because the main hazard was, well, the railroad. In addition, on the same first hole, players encountered two split-rail fences, a roadway, and an orchard. Shots "lofted too much" often hit one of the telegraph wires.

The Philadelphia Cricket Club installed a course in 1896. The November issue of *Golfing* gave a full account of the club's adoption of golf. The course cost $3,400, but the club was looking for more funds to lengthen several of the holes. An official admitted that the course had increased the cost of belonging to the club, but this was offset by a dramatic increase in the membership. He stated that the increased costs "had been amply repaid to the organization in the enormous increase of activity it has caused in the Club." Before golf was added, the club always shut down for seven months. After golf the clubhouse remained open except for a few weeks in the dead of winter. Golf, the official stated, had clearly assured the club's future. The outgoing board requested that their replacements "make every effort to do all that circumstances would permit to improve the links and foster the game . . . as a most valuable adjunct and part of the club."

Both the Myopia Hunt Club and The Country Club in Brookline existed prior to the arrival of golf. Both eventually created notable courses. However, their approach to adding golf was cautious. The first course installed at Brookline cost fifty dollars to build.

Like hunt and cricket clubs, hotels and resorts saw fit to add courses as an attraction that would draw more business. A story, perhaps fictitious, is often repeated about the birth of golf at the Wentworth Hotel in Portsmouth, New Hampshire. The owner in the mid-1890s was Frank Jones. He was at the front desk when a guest who was to stay the whole summer arrived. The guest asked if there was a golf course at the Wentworth. When told there was not the guest decided he would only stay a week. Within days, the story goes, Jones had leased a thirty-acre site and had hired Alexander Findlay to supervise the construction of the course. Something like this occurred at a number of hotels and resorts. Owners responded to the demand by guests for golf. This was exactly how golf began at Pinehurst in 1898.

In a somewhat opposite development, clubs sprouted without courses on which to play. Many schools and colleges sported such clubs that played where and when they could. One example was the golf club at Wellesley College. Formed in 1893, the club had no course on which to play. In 1894 something like a practice range was built near Lake Waban, on the campus. Later a course was established that ran through the campus. It was not until 1900 that the club had a real course. In 1927 this course was renamed Nehoiden, the name it bears today.

The devotion to golf at Wellesley was part of the school's founding philosophy. The college held that part of a young woman's education should be physical. Golf seemed like an ideal sport or game to put this philosophy into practice. Other schools and colleges also founded "golf clubs" to encourage healthy physical activity among their students. The Harper's *Official Golf Guide* for 1899 listed twenty-three schools that had such golf clubs. While many (fifteen) were in the Northeast, a surprising number of them were outside New England and New York in places like North Carolina and Ohio.

All this suggests that by the mid-1890s golf clubs were cropping up in good numbers, but it suggests nothing about golf courses. Mirroring the timidity of the clubs that were created, course construction was modest, to be polite. It was apparent that the first courses were, with a few exceptions, simply thrown down on the land. They often shared space with railroad tracks, fences, walls, and telegraph poles and wires. Geoffrey Cornish and Ronald Whitten in their history of the American golf course bluntly state that "woeful courses were appearing everywhere."

A central task in creating these woeful courses was clearing the area of rocks and stones. They were piled and covered with earth and thus "the chocolate drop" was born. These mounds were probably the only hazards actually created to be a hazard. The early courses also had nothing like a modern golf green. The "green" was usually indistinguishable from the fairway. The layouts of the early courses often featured holes that crossed, creating interesting traffic problems.

By 1898 things were beginning to change. The economy was much improved and clubs felt more secure investing in their courses. But more important, the golf club began to slide down the class structure, becoming more attractive to the middle class. As this was happening, a number of factors coalesced to bring about the rise of the professional golf architect and to motivate the construction of more expensive courses.

In 1909 and 1912 two magazine articles appeared, one in *Country Life* and the other in *Outing*, both with the same title: "Country Clubs for Everyone." The author of the *Country Life* piece, C. O. Morris, tries to explain why country clubs seem to be popping up everywhere. Dues and fees are low, and people create simple clubs at first and then expand as the membership grows. He notes that many towns have come to see clubs as a community resource. Once a club takes root, Morris suggests, it "will be like a snowball rolling downhill. After a few years it will come to be regarded as just as permanent a feature of the town as its library, churches, or town square."

In the *Outing* essay, the author, Edward L. Fox, argues that obsessive devotion to work has received a mortal blow. People in the Midwest, especially, have turned against the six-day workweek and Sundays of rest and boredom. He also claims that the clubs he knows about are democratic and egalitarian. After reporting that at one club the owner of the town's largest store "sat down to dinner with one of his clerks," Fox states, "Sounds like a Socialist farm, but it's true." Middle-class Americans realized by 1915 that they could create collectively the sort of country retreats that aristocrats and the wealthy had enjoyed as individuals.

This sort of enthusiasm was tempered by lessons that may have been learned from the early clubs. In 1915 the advice was to start small and cheaply. The perfect start was on rented land with a patched-up farmhouse as a clubhouse. By 1915 something like "country-club making" had developed its own language. Much of this language was about memberships (full, associate, life) and debt. Apparently, by 1915, the unmarketable country-club bond was already a well-known financial instrument. This flurry of articles was clearly describing developments in club and course building that had occurred in the preceding fifteen years.

The Wichita Country Club (founded in 1900) illustrates many of the points made in these general essays about country clubs. Wichita in 1900 was a classic Midwestern town with a strong booster spirit among the business class. Its citizens liked to refer to their town as the Peerless Princess of the Plains. Golf in Wichita, however, found its first promoter in the person of Dr. J. D. Ritchey, the rector of St. John's Episcopal Church. He had caught the golf bug when assigned to churches in St. Louis and Newton, Kansas. At Newton he had taken part in the founding of a country club. Ritchey found a kindred spirit in his choirmaster, Bennett Cushman. He had played some golf while in Washington DC, working for his uncle who was then a senator from Kansas. These two convinced seven others that Wichita needed a golf club.

It was an audacious idea. They set out to create a club based on a game that almost no one knew how to play. Their first task was to find a site for the club, and their hearts were set on the College Hill area, but they ended up on leased land in a part of town called Fairmount. In September 1900 a few members played the first golf on a simple six-hole course laid out over very flat ground covered with buffalo grass. One of the next steps was to "skin" the greens and soak them with oil.

Play and the organization of the club began at the same time. They adopted by-laws and set out to promote the club. They invited the public to a "tournament" in October. Three twosomes of males toured the course demonstrating the game, as did one female twosome. This went so well and attracted so many new members that the club was able to move to College Hill and a much better site. They leased land and rented a place called Hillside Cottage to use as a clubhouse. A group stayed at the Fairmount course and established the Braeburn Country Club. The group at College Hill began to attract notable citizens such as A. A. Hyde, the inventor of Mentholatum, a remedy that my mother held in high regard. The club was thrilled to discover that a good part of their rent could be paid by cutting the hay on their new course. This 2,548-yard course was laid out by a member, Thomas H. Griffith, who had become the club's president.

The establishment of the club gave a new justification for suburban life. People in Wichita saw that the club could enliven the suburbs, and the College Hill site brought them into contact with cool breezes that somehow never arrived in the city center. The membership expanded to 150 and the clubhouse and the course grew crowded. The club needed to incorporate so it could sell bonds and establish itself as a "real" club on its own land. A stock company was created, selling to the members 320 shares at twenty-five dollars each. With this money in hand they took a ten-year lease on the land and purchased two acres on which to build a clubhouse. This new clubhouse opened in 1902; they had come a long way in a short time.

The club was creating a critical mass. It had become substantial. Caddies began to show up at the club. The membership limit rose to 275. The initiation was set at twenty-five dollars; soon there was a waiting list of people who wished to join. Interestingly, it was only at this point that the club adopted the USGA rules. Previously the members had been playing by their own set of local rules. The club had also created its own "game," called progressive golf. I would like to explain it but the only description I have ever read is totally inexplicable. In 1903 the club installed a four-hole course for juniors, beginners, and women.

The club expanded in unexpected ways. There were a few rooms for rent in the clubhouse and members began to rent them for vacations that stretched to a week or more. During the summer young men pitched tents around the course where they enjoyed the cool breezes and the view of the golf course and the city below them. The club became, as many golf clubs did, a destination. People came for lunch or just to sit on the porch.

The membership knew their lease would run out in 1912 and that they would almost surely be forced out. The land was worth more as house lots, and the owner knew it. So, in what had become a pattern, they raised the membership to four hundred and began looking to buy land.

They sold the old clubhouse and the land on which it stood for a good profit. Armed with this money and the buying power created by a larger membership, they spent forty thousand dollars on land and a new clubhouse. They even included a small pool. John Powell, a member of a golf club in Kansas City, laid out an eighteen-hole course on an eighty-acre site. The greatest effort was put into the course, but the club too had clearly expanded to meet the desires of a large membership. They installed grass greens and a water system to keep them alive in the Kansas summer. They also, in addition to the pool, added bowling, billiards, and tennis to the sports menu. There also seemed to be a great desire to have big comfortable porches upon which one just sat. So the new clubhouse included a dandy porch.

In twelve years the Wichita Country Club had gone from almost nothing to a really grand, complex institution. Good economic times no doubt played a part. Even the sharp downturn in 1907 seemingly had no impact. But as the club had expanded, so had the membership. From the original nine advocates of golf grew a membership of four hundred. Fees and dues from this membership underwrote each move, each improvement. It was not lost on some of the early members that as the club grew it became less exclusive, but they probably just shrugged and saw it as the price of progress. The Wichita Country Club was no doubt seen as a community asset that had helped the town grow by attracting new business. There was nothing like a modern up-to-date country club to give a town a progressive tone. What happened in Wichita happened all over America. By 1912 golf and country clubs had become an accepted part of middle-class life.

In roughly the same period, the courses at these clubs and at all the clubs underwent equally dramatic growth and change. At the heart of this change was the rise of specialization. The first American clubs hired a "professional" who often occupied four positions—greenkeeper, course designer and modifier, teacher of golf, and club maker. In retrospect it is clear that specialization would kill off people who continued to occupy all four jobs. Club making would pass to corporations like Spalding and others. The teaching function would fall to the PGA (Professional Golfers' Association) professional. The greenkeeper

would be overtaken by the trained agronomist and turf special-
ist. The course designer and modifier job would pass into the
hands of the golf architect.

As noted earlier, the courses built before 1900 were not very
good. They were usually laid out by a Scottish professional who
found himself looking at land of a type that he did not understand. In 1895 James P. Lee expressed the common wisdom
when he claimed that "for natural fitness and suitability, no links
in the country can be said to excel those of Shinnecock Hills
Golf Club." This was true because "the ground which one finds
upon links by the sea is always apt to be more favorable for the
game than that upon an inland course." There was also the issue of trees. Seaside Scottish links were usually treeless. Away
from the sea America offered a great mass of land upon which
to build golf courses, but there were trees almost everywhere.

In a relatively short time American golf got over its bias in
favor of seaside golf and its negative view of trees. This process suggests exactly what the golf architect was up to between
1900 and 1916. They were altering nature in order to make it
useful to Americans who wished to experience nature not in
its rawest form but in some ordered and useful form. It is worth
noting that while golf architects (and park designers) were re-
configuring nature for human use, other Americans were demanding that some nature be set aside in its virgin state. During Teddy Roosevelt's administration the federal government
placed 150 million acres in federal reserves. The conservation
movement was born. The movement had two wings. One group
wanted land to use for sporting, recreational, and profit-making purposes. They often used the term "wise use" as a way of
expressing what they wanted to do with nature. Golf courses
were one of these uses. The other wing wanted to preserve nature as it was. They saw great value in wildness and wilderness.
So just as the great golf courses were coming to the fore, the
nation launched a debate that continues to this day about what
people should or should not do with the land.

The golf architect in America was the agent whereby Americans redefined the golf course. They wished to dramatically alter the land for human use. This is a bedrock principle of the golf community. One of its most endearing advocates was Tom Bendelow. Born in Scotland, he came to the States in 1892 and went to work for the *New York Herald.* Soon he took a job with A. G. Spalding and Brothers as, among other things, a golf-course design consultant. Spalding believed that the way to sell more balls and clubs was to build more courses. Bendelow became the nation's first advocate for cheap, simple, public courses for the masses. He controlled the course at Van Cortlandt Park in New York City in the late 1890s, where he added a second nine and stabilized the facility. It became the model for other municipal courses around the nation. He became the master of rapid course design that has been called the "eighteen stakes on a Sunday afternoon" approach. Over time, however, Bendelow became a very good and creative designer. He is credited with the design of the Medinah Country Club (Illinois) and the Royal Ottawa Golf Club in Canada, among many others. The evidence is clear, however, that he never gave up on the idea that simple, challenging courses could be inexpensively built and enjoyed by the masses.

Donald Ross presents a somewhat different story. Like Bendelow, Ross came to the United States from Scotland. During his youth in Dornoch and elsewhere he had become expert in the four areas that defined a golf professional—greenkeeping, club making, teaching, and course design. While at Dornoch he met Professor Robert Willson of Harvard. The astronomy professor and his wife were on an extensive tour of Britain and had come to Dornoch to play the course. Willson was a member of the newly founded Oakley Country Club in Watertown, Massachusetts. While details are scarce, Willson clearly invited Ross to come to Massachusetts and the Oakley Club. In March 1899 Donald Ross, like so many other Scottish pros, sailed to America and a new life.

He immediately went to work at Oakley. He pursued the four threads of a golf pro's life at the time. One of his first tasks was to redesign the Oakley course. He saw before him a clay-soil, rock-strewn course pinched on a site that was too small. He did the best he could. In 1900 he established a connection with the Pinehurst Resort in North Carolina, where he would spend the months between November and April. In 1910 he left Oakley and moved to the Essex County Club, where he redesigned the course and undertook all the other professional tasks. So he had a summer life in Massachusetts and a winter life in Pinehurst. Gradually, this would change. He would remain at Pinehurst until his death. It was his summer life that changed. In his lifetime he would design or remodel hundreds of golf courses. This he did in the summers, traveling like a frantic salesman bringing great golf courses to America.

Certainly Ross's work has been examined by more expert critics. My interest is in the transformation of his life before 1916. Slowly the four threads of a professional's life unraveled and reformed. Ross turned club building over to others, and slowly, mass-produced clubs turned him from a maker into a mere retailer. The day-to-day care of the courses at Pinehurst fell to assistants like Frank Maples. Teaching golf to resort guests was carried out by others. The transition was never as complete as it might seem, but the fact is that by World War I, Donald Ross was most fundamentally a course designer building new courses at Pinehurst and around the country.

Using the lists in Bradley Klein's definitive work on Ross, we learn that he designed or remodeled 399 golf courses. Of this number, 71 came before 1917. He was riding a powerful tide of demand. He worked for resorts like Pinehurst, the Balsams, and Wentworth-by-the-Sea, and he worked for clubs that had money for a designer. These clubs were in places like Muskegon, Michigan, and Cedar Rapids, Iowa.

What exactly was he doing? Course architecture critics have offered any number of reasons for Ross's preeminence between

1900 and 1930. Most have emphasized the elegant naturalness of his designs. But there is a simpler and more profound way to understand Ross's work. Henry Leach, the correspondent for the *London Evening News*, understood it differently. In 1912 Leach was playing at the Essex County Club while Ross was redoing the course, and he submitted to his paper a story titled "Nature Altered to Suit Golf: The Man Who Is Blowing Up America."

Leach was playing the back nine when from the fifth hole came "a great roar and crashing sound." There was a great cloud of smoke and vast amounts of earth and rock were thrown into the air. Leach came to an important conclusion:

> The truth is that golf at Essex, as elsewhere in the country, is undergoing a great and wonderful transformation, regardless of cost, regardless of the magnitude and seeming impossibilities of the task, regardless of everything, but caused by the insatiable desire of the American golfer to have courses as good as they can be. To satisfy this desire he is everywhere pulling Nature to pieces and reconstructing her; doing this most deftly and skillfully, and with a fine eye for pleasing effect.

Leach's pronouncement is crucial for understanding the evolution of the American golf community. Until 1900 no one could have said this about American golf, but in the years between 1900 and World War I a variety of factors came together that called forth Donald Ross and the other great architects of the period. Their charge was simple: take this piece of nature, this forest, this sand barren, this swamp, and make it into a course that golfers will want to play. Plus, make it pleasing to look at.

What were the factors that made Ross and other course designers possible? It is my view that the growth of the country club movement was crucial. More clubs, with more money, equaled more and better courses. There were a number of other factors. The evolution of the Haskell ball tended to make courses designed to be played with gutta-percha balls obsolete — they were just too short. In 1897, at the Essex County Club, the winner of

the long driving contest at the Women's Amateur drove her guttie 137 yards, six inches. In 1907, again at the Women's Amateur, the winning long drive by Margaret Curtis (using a Haskell
ball) was hit 220 yards. By simply discovering that you could
wind rubber strips around a rubber core and cover it with balata, Coburn Haskell had changed the game dramatically. America needed new, longer courses.

Suburbanization also continued to push club and course creation. After 1900 the process was somewhat different. Established suburbs continued to install courses and create clubs
as social centers. As the new century dawned, developers who
wished to attract buyers to their suburb began installing courses
and clubs before the sales push began. A golf club with a course
by a known designer became a key way to promote the growth
of a new suburb.

But in the end, it was the growth of the private clubs that drove
course construction and created a demand for design services.
Spectacular clubs and courses tended to arise together. Clubs
were created for the purpose of building a unique, potentially
famous course. An example that stands as a symbol of the era
between 1900 and 1916 was the building of the National Golf
Links on Long Island and the "club" that financed the job.

Charles Blair Macdonald was a crucial figure in the early history of American golf-course architecture. He wanted to trans-
fer the principles that underlay the great English and Scottish
courses to America. He was a tireless advocate of the idea that
"real golf" could only be played by the sea. Never mind that he
constructed the first American eighteen-hole course in Chicago. He was, however, in the end, a pioneer in establishing the
idea that you could, at vast expense, transform raw nature into
a golf course and that doing so was good business.

Sometime in 1905 he began assembling a group that would finance his desire to build a truly world-class golf course in America. He induced seventy very affluent gentlemen to back his dream.
Each invested a thousand dollars and bought a thousand-dollar

bond. He also took $20,000 in initiation fees from associate members. The total cost of the project—course, clubhouse and miscellaneous expenses—was $177,000. He had raised $160,000 so the club, when it opened, was $17,000 in debt. The two biggest items were land ($45,000) and labor ($65,500). The clubhouse cost $53,000. At about the same time, Wichita got a new course and clubhouse for $40,000. In 1897–98, the yearly expenses for the Chicago Golf Club were $1,944.

The links formally opened on September 16, 1911. It was clear that Macdonald had created a classic, a course that would last. It was also clear that he had had a lot of help. His engineer and surveyor, Seth Raynor, was perhaps most crucial. The layout and design were Macdonald's but he had benefited from advice by Devereux Emmet and H. J. Whigham. The founders took a hand in decorating the clubhouse. Albert Fish contributed an antique clock; R. C. Watson provided a mounted tarpon and a sailfish.

The founders got a very good deal. The bond paid 3 percent. More important, the plan was to eliminate all dues and fees for the founders when the membership reached three hundred. In addition, the founders owned the land not used by the club. By 1911 this land had risen dramatically in value. The list of founders contained men of great wealth like William K. Vanderbilt, H. Payne Whitney, and Henry C. Frick. They did not really need the money but, in the end, their involvement in the club was a good deal.

Macdonald, never bashful, called the course "second to none in the world." It was and is a great course. But its significance extends far beyond its fairways and greens. It was the perfect symbol of the marriage between private clubs and the golf course.

The National and other courses designed by Macdonald were important for another reason. Since he loudly proclaimed his devotion to Scottish golf and to the courses there, it is easy to think that the National was modeled after them. Were not some of the holes replicas of famous holes in Great Britain?

The truth was that Macdonald and the other early architects moved American golf decidedly away from its Scottish
roots. Most of the great Scottish courses were laid out on ideal
sites that required almost no alteration. They were hardly engineered or designed at all. The National was a stark contrast to
such courses. The site was hardly ideal. There was a great deal
of swamp and bog; in its natural state most of the land could
not be explored on foot. Macdonald claimed that the majority
of the holes were natural and he was reluctant to admit the extent to which he had imposed his vision on the land.

Another issue was grass. Macdonald and his crew learned a
lot about grass as they created the National. Scottish courses often came with a fine readymade turf, probably because the soil
contained more loam. The Long Island site was too sandy and
would not produce the sort of turf that Macdonald desired. He
consulted with the United States Department of Agriculture.
He learned that he could not simply plant the mixtures provided by seed merchants. The green sites had to be prepared (by
adding loam and other organic material), and this cost money
and time. It delayed the opening of the course by more than a
year.

An even more vexing problem was summer on Long Island.
The course baked like a Christmas ham. The fairways and greens
became rock hard and the course was close to unplayable. Sometime in 1912, a man (his name lost to history) visited Macdonald at the National. He was from the Boston Sprinkler Company
and he had in his possession the answer to the sun-baked conditions at the National. Macdonald installed a gravity-fed watering system that quickly improved the greens and the approaches. It was a simple but profound revolution. The controlled use
of water would do what nature refused to do.

Macdonald would not simply accept nature as a given. A golf
course could be made to conform to the demands of the golfer. The idea that you simply found a course lying upon the land
would always have its adherents, but they were clearly romantics.

The American golf course, by 1915, had come into its own. It was going to be designed and engineered. It would be known as the product of its designer. These men would become famous—heroes of the American golf community. They would move and shape the land to conform to human need and desire. Rainfall would come from the hand of man. Associations would, in most cases, assemble to pay for it all.

On few occasions, a single individual would become the financial and design force behind the creation of a club and a course. Such was the case with Pine Valley, a place very nearly sacred in American golf.

It was the product of George A. Crump and his desire to build a demanding course that would offer a longer playing season than the Philadelphia courses in 1910. Born in 1871, Crump made his fortune in the hotel business. In the 1890s he became a golf fanatic, belonging to as many as five area golf clubs. A good player, he was a frequent participant in intercity matches and other amateur events. He and his friends were frustrated by the short season in Philadelphia and the constant failure of area golfers to do much of anything in national championships.

In 1910 he sold his hotel interests and set out to build a first-class golf course. First he toured Great Britain and Europe, studying the great Old World courses. While in Great Britain he was more influenced by the new heath-land courses in England than by the ancient Scottish models. He was particularly impressed by Sunningdale, the 1901 design by Willie Park. The courses built on sandy soil in Surrey were also interesting.

Crump knew that he would have to build on sandy soil in the Jersey sands region near Philadelphia. He settled on a 184-acre site fifteen miles south of Camden, New Jersey. It was covered with pine, oak, and brush. Crump moved to the site, pitched a tent, and began to clear the land. It was man versus the trees. At first, the crew kept count of the trees removed, but when the number reached twenty-two thousand they stopped counting.

In the end, as many as fifty thousand were taken out. If we assume that the course covered 150 acres and that the number of trees removed was thirty thousand, then Crump was forced to de-tree at a rate of two hundred trees per acre. Dynamite proved useless in the sandy soil; most of the trees were removed using steam-powered winches.

The project was Crump's personal obsession, but as time passed, others came to his aid. A. W. Tillinghast, a Philadelphia friend, wrote an article for the *American Golfer* praising the project. He noted that Pine Valley was going to be a course for the skilled player; the timid, the duffer, should stay away. Another friend, H. W. Perrin, headed a group that would eventually form the nucleus of a club. The English designer H. S. Colt visited the site and offered his advice. To some extent, the final product was a collaboration between Colt and Crump. Others also came — Walter Travis, Donald Ross, and C. B. MacDonald — and offered their opinions.

In the spring of 1913, Perrin sent a letter to selected Philadelphia golfers announcing the formation of a club to help finance construction of the course. This was the reverse of Macdonald's procedure; he had formed the club, collected the money, and then built the course. Perrin, who would become the president of the USGA in 1917, outlined the nature of the Pine Valley club. There would be two hundred to two hundred and fifty members who had to buy at least one share of stock for one hundred dollars (you could buy more than one share). There would be a small austere clubhouse. Small lots around the course would be available for members to build small "bungalows" but, Perrin claimed, the venture was "not a land scheme." The proceeds from the stock and land sales would go to pay for the land and course construction.

When Macdonald visited the course, he reportedly said, "Here is one of the greatest courses — if grass will grow." Just as at the National, the biggest problem was growing grass. Great design means nothing without great grass. Crump had turned to Carter's

Tested Seeds for seed and advice. The company placed an ad in the *American Golfer* that claimed that their seeds "were used exclusively at Pine Valley." The ad appeared in July; in the fall, the entire course died. The biggest problem was the fairways, which were seeded with fescue grasses. This produced tussocks of grass with large bare spots that washed away after a heavy rain. Overmanuring also hurt because this kept the roots too near the surface and the grass died when hot weather arrived. Crump had installed a watering system for the greens only, leaving the fairways at the mercy of the elements.

By 1916 Crump was totally frustrated. His drive to produce a demanding, world-class golf course had begun in 1910. In six years there had been many changes in the design and costs far beyond anything imagined in 1910. In 1917, when war stopped work on the course, Crump was out of money, or very nearly so. Pine Valley had become too important to George Crump. His wife had died in 1907, he had given up his business, and he had no children—if you do not count Pine Valley. In January 1918 he took his own life. A legend has grown that he died of an infected tooth, but surely this story has its roots in a desire to protect Crump's memory.

Crump's brother-in-law, Howard Street, took over the construction of the course. Without him, Pine Valley might never have been completed. It was not until 1921 that all eighteen holes were complete and in play. The story of Crump and Pine Valley is one of the first great myths of the golf community. In article after article, golfers would read of Crump's great obsession and the creation of the nation's most fearsome and penal course. Like all myths, this is partially true, but it distorts reality. The course was a collaboration. Others contributed to the design, others finished the project, and Crump died at his own hand, not of an infected tooth.

Pine Valley and the National are iconic courses. Yet they were very different—one financed almost completely by one man, the other the product of a single designer supported by an affluent group of backers. Pine Valley was a penal design. Crump wanted to punish all wayward shots. The National was a strategic design, offering several routes to the hole and a much easier experience for all types of players. Pine Valley sported a modest clubhouse, the National's was opulent and featured numerous amenities unrelated to golf.

The two clubs have several important things in common. Both were for men only. This put them in a small group of clubs that excluded women and laid the groundwork for one of the most contentious issues in golf's future. They both illustrate that, by 1915, some Americans were willing to expend large sums to put a course down upon the land. Golf would be played on less-than-ideal sites. Nature would be reconfigured and a golf club and a golf course would appear where men wanted one. (See appendix A.)

As far as clubs and courses were concerned, the golf community was virtually complete by 1915. The voluntary association and the private, exclusive golf club–country club had become the mechanism whereby most courses came into being. Courses were ranked by their perceived worth. Courses like Pine Valley and the National were well on their way to becoming prestigious, almost sacred, models of course design. In the most recent *Golf Digest* list of one hundred best American golf courses, courses from before 1929 occupy nine spots in the top twenty. By ranking, they include Pine Valley (1), Shinnecock Hills (2), Oakmont (5), Pebble Beach (6), Merion (7), the National (13), Pinehurst No. 2 (19), and The Country Club (20).

Along with the iconic, prestigious course came the local country club with an improved course. This was the more important development. For every Pine Valley, there were at least fifty Wichita Country Clubs. The municipal course had also appeared. Many cities discovered that citizens wanted sport in their parks and a modest golf course was often the answer. Finally, hotels and resorts also contributed to the stock of American courses. By 1920 Pinehurst offered four courses to its resort guests and to a small population of seasonal residents in Pinehurst Village.

In 1920, as America emerged from the war, *Golf Illustrated* published a list of the country's golf courses. There were 1,304. Most were private clubs. There were thirty-six municipal layouts, almost all installed in preexisting public parks. As many as fifty were associated with hotels, inns, or resorts. New York had the most courses with 182. Illinois was the only other state with more than one hundred (103). Nevada and Wyoming each listed only one course. (See appendix B.)

By 1920 the rudimentary elements of the golf community were mostly in place. The golf and country club had become an established feature of the American landscape. The golf course as nature modified to fit the needs of a game had arrived. Americans had literally redefined the golf course. Books and magazines had introduced the language, culture, and history of the game. All that was required was to rationalize competition into a marketable commodity. It is to that topic that we turn in the next chapter.

Golf before the War

The United States Open of 1913 seems, from a certain perspective, to have been the most significant competitive event in the nation's golf history. It had everything a golf journalist could possibly want. The winner, Francis Ouimet, was a local boy—an American amateur battling British professionals— and an ex-caddy at The Country Club in Brookline, Massachusetts, where the championship was held. He was young while his main opponents, Harry Vardon and Ted Ray, were older veterans. Most of all, Ouimet could be made to fit the Horatio Alger story of a young boy from poor circumstances struggling upward, gaining his reward for his preparation and sacrifice. His victory could be painted as the product of pluck and luck. In 1913 this was the stuff that sold papers.

Writers on golf have made great claims concerning the impact of the 1913 Open. Somehow Ouimet's victory liberated the game from the clutches of the upper crust and handed it off to the masses. Ouimet's victory, the story goes, democratized the game. After Francis, any young boy could find a place in the game and with pluck, luck, and excellent eye-hand coordination make a name for himself. Of course the one thing this lovely story could not do was to account for Francis Ouimet himself.

Golf journalists have made far too much of Ouimet's victory. Herbert Warren Wind, in his widely read *The Story of American Golf*, titled his chapter on the 1913 Open "The Shots Heard Round the World." The eighteen-hole playoff between Ray, Vardon, and Ouimet, Wind claimed, was "the most momentous round in the history of golf." He also contended that "under the impetus of Ouimet's victory, within a decade golf became an American game."

This has always struck me as more than a bit off the mark. For one thing it fails to account for Ouimet's rise. How did he get good enough to end up playing Vardon and Ray in the rain at Brookline? The fact is that he was a product of the institutional growth of the game. The game had been growing rapidly for two decades and had already become an American game, had already become substantially democratized. Once young Francis fell in love with golf, he took advantage of something like a "system" that had grown up in the previous two decades. The story of that system is infinitely more important (but less heartwarming) than any single round of golf or any single championship.

The system evolved to organize golf competition and identify the best players. Golf can certainly be played alone. In this it is unlike all other major American sports. Golf, more than most popular sports, bears some similarity to hunting and fishing. In the American psyche there is an honored place for the solitary hunter and angler. The golfer out on the course alone also makes sense to us. The image of the solitary football, baseball, or basketball player does not. But playing alone is, and was, only a small element in the world of golf as it evolved after 1892.

Deeply ingrained in most every American (every human?) is a competitive instinct. So it was not strange at all that as the game grew, one of the fundamental tasks was to create a structure of orderly and fair competition to discover who was best. Certainly that was one motivation behind the formation of the United States Golf Association. The early attempts to mount a truly national championship to identify the best male and female amateurs and the best players overall in an open championship were not satisfactory. They remain curiosities in the history of golf for the simple reason that there were so few decent players. Furthermore, the handful of decent players, like Charles Blair Macdonald and others, had learned the game in either Great Britain or Europe.

The 1895 USGA Amateur provided clear evidence that there were few even competent players in the United States. In the eighteen-hole matches that got MacDonald to the final, he simply crushed his opponents. His margins of victory in these contests were 7 and 6, 8 and 6, and 5 and 3. In the thirty-six hole final, he destroyed C. E. Sands 12 and 11. Sands, a fine tennis player, had only recently taken up the game and had entered the event mostly for his own amusement. For most of the 1890s, there simply was not a critical mass of evenly matched, decent players.

Twenty years later, in 1915, this critical mass of competent, relatively evenly matched players did exist. It was the product of a complex set of institutions that accomplished many things, but one of the most important was to create a testing ground for individuals devoted to the game. Without debate it was agreed that competition should be fragmented and that it should take place between individuals by group. Women would play women. Men would play men. Students would play students. Senior golfers would have their own competitions. The real passion, the centerpiece of competition, was reserved for males. For the most part, amateurs would play amateurs. Open competitions, where all could play, brought amateurs and pros together and were generally secondary to the U.S. Amateur. There were very few pro-only events.

Perhaps the most crucial element in the growth of this system was the private club. These organizations served many functions but one of the most important was the staging of local championships. By early in the new century almost every club had established events that were quickly becoming traditional. In the early days these were called "fixtures." Resorts also contributed to the list of annual fixtures. Pinehurst, by 1910, had established

a set of North and South tournaments for male and female amateurs as well as an open event that became a fixture of sorts on
a list of events for professionals. In 1912 *Golf Illustrated* claimed
that in May and June alone of the coming year there would be
sixteen thousand "club and open events" with approximately
one hundred thousand participants.

As the number of clubs grew and the thirst for competition
exploded, private clubs began to organize into local, state, and
regional organizations. In 1897 a group of twenty-six clubs in
the New York area founded the Metropolitan Golf Association.
In 1899 eleven Chicago-area clubs formed the Western Golf
Association. The Southern Golf Association was chartered in
1902, and the Pennsylvania Golf Association appeared in 1909.
All four groups staged a number of events that provided competitive opportunities for their members and for outsiders.

These four groups represent merely a portion of the massive
organizational explosion that helped to define golf in America
prior to World War I. Today there are countless local golf associations that stage tournaments for players just beginning a competitive career. Success at this local level often tempts a player
to move up to state or regional competition. A player successful at this level moves up through the system to national and international events.

These golf associations, of course, did more than provide
competition. As the years passed they took on all sorts of functions: teaching the rules, raising money for charity and scholarships, honoring officials for "long service to the game," establishing "halls of fame," and publishing magazines and newsletters
that tied members to the group. Socially, these associations
provided gatherings of like-minded people with an interest in
the game, but also for people who simply enjoyed a good time
and who liked meeting golfers from other parts of the state or
the country. Perhaps nowhere else in golf is it clearer that the
game creates community. Local and state organizations became
precious assets in the lives of golfers. Annual local events and

annual local and state tournaments structure the years and the lives of golfers. Simple, prosaic newsletters circulate news not only of golf scores, but also of honors won and lost, of births and deaths, and of the general health of the community.

Francis Ouimet came to the U.S. Open in 1913 a product of this new organizational system. It is important to understand that he was also the product of another quite different institution: he learned about the game as a caddy. The door into the game for him and for countless great players was, in fact, a job.

If America in 1910 was democratic, egalitarian, individualistic, and antiaristocratic, then the job of caddying, serving a master of sorts, should have had no place in America. But, of course, it did. In the American golf community, the caddy was defined, almost exclusively, as a young boy. To caddy was virtually the perfect job for the young male, especially city boys. It was a summer job that allowed work in the fresh air when school was out. It brought young boys into contact with successful older men who could mentor and act as role models and help the caddies find jobs when they outgrew caddying.

To some extent this image was true, but it was much more complicated. Everyone quickly understood that the boys would often see the men (their boss for the duration of the round) in a less-than-flattering light. These potential role models cheated at golf and at business, when not cheating on their wives. This idea that caddying gave young lower-class boys a glimpse into upper-class hypocrisy and double-dealing was commonplace by 1910. It was also commonplace to assume that caddies would see community leaders blow their tops after a missed two-foot putt. By 1921 the sportswriter Grantland Rice could claim that caddying was a threat to baseball among young male Americans. He estimated that there were approximately 150,000 caddies in the United States and some of the larger clubs employed 300 young boys each summer.

There can be little doubt that the caddie introduced novel social tension into the golf community. Just having lower-class boys spend four hours carrying the clubs of middle- and upper-class men and women has no real parallel in American sport. These tensions (and the resulting humor) allow us to miss an important point: caddying served to introduce thousands of lower-class young males to golf and golf competition. The story is a common one. A young man starts to caddy and gets a chance to play. He shows some skill and while most at the golf club do not care, a few do. The young man gets some help. He receives free clubs; he plays in a caddie tournament and does well, and at many clubs caddies were allowed to play on Mondays when the club was closed.

By 1905 the founding of numerous golf associations and the evolution of caddying as a path into golf and golf competition had created an informal system that identified and advanced the most talented players. Brief portraits of three players—Francis Ouimet, Bobby Jones, and Walter Hagen—can serve to illustrate how this system worked.

Born on May 8, 1893, Francis Ouimet arrived just as golf was beginning its ascent in the United States. He grew up in a house across the street from The Country Club in Brookline, Massachusetts. We like to think that such places are effectively sealed off against nonmembers, but such was not the case for Francis. He often crossed the course on his way to school; he found lots of lost golf balls. Soon he followed his brother Wilfred into the caddie ranks at the club. Francis, more than his brother, was entranced by the game. In order to have a place to play they constructed a makeshift course in the cow pasture behind their house. It was there that Wilfred, with Francis's help, constructed a three-hole course. As Francis described it, "the first hole was about a hundred and fifty yards long, with a carry over a brook. . . . The second hole was very short, hardly more than fifty yards. The last was a combination of the first two and brought the player back to the starting point. We used tomato cans for the hole rims."

Once he had mastered his homemade course, Francis started

to play at Boston's Franklin Park, one of the country's earliest municipal courses. He and a friend, Frank Mahan, would walk more than a mile to the streetcar line. This began a long trip to the course. Once there they made the best of it, playing the nine-hole course as many as six times before the long journey home.

It was not clear how much Francis got to play on the famous course across the street. But he does recount one occasion when a member for whom he was caddying asked him to play along. The member's name was Mr. Hastings and he usually played alone. One day he asked Francis if he played. When Francis said that he did, Mr. Hastings suggested that they make it a twosome. Francis impressed Mr. Hastings with a 39 on the front nine. However, when they approached the fifteenth hole and Francis knew they would be within sight of the caddie master, Dan McNamara, Francis made a mess of the hole. At the end of the round, Mr. Hasting signed Francis's caddy card and told McNamara that he had enjoyed the round. McNamara, knowing that Ouimet had played, merely asked Francis what he had shot (84) and what had happened on the fifteenth.

Francis left no account of his decision to begin competing in tournaments. Apparently he just naturally gravitated toward competition. His first step in this direction was provided by the Greater Boston Golf Association. All male students in high school were eligible to play in its annual championship. In 1908 Francis played in the event, winning his first match against J. H. Sullivan, who later became his brother-in-law and business partner. Ouimet lost in the second round.

High school golf was important to Ouimet's evolution as a competitor. At sixteen he felt that "the greater Boston inter-scholastic championship was the most important golfing event in the world." At sixteen he won this "most important golfing event," defeating Ronald Waitt 10 and 9 in the thirty-six-hole final. As Francis recalled it, "a happier boy never lived. I figured that this was the ultimate in golf and there were no more

worlds to conquer. I soon changed my mind." Four years later
he would win the U.S. Open.

Francis had made up his mind to play golf as an amateur.
This imposed several restrictions upon him. According to the
United States Golf Association (USGA) rules at the time, in order to remain an amateur Francis had to give up caddying. The
USGA contended that anyone who caddied after age sixteen was
deemed a professional. Furthermore, in order to enter most
amateur events, Francis had to be a member of a club recognized by the USGA. Francis learned that dues for a junior member at the Woodland Golf Club were "only" twenty-five dollars.
He borrowed the money from his mother, even though she was,
as Francis remembered, "certain that golf would ruin me." Instead of caddying he worked all summer at a dry goods store in
order to pay his mother back. As Francis's case illustrated, the
USGA and its obsessive concern with amateurism was actually
inhibiting the rise of truly open amateur competition. Players
like Francis certainly had a harder road than others from more
advantaged backgrounds. And this would not be the last time
that Francis would confront the USGA and its rules on amateurism.

Having fulfilled all the requirements, Francis entered the
U.S. Amateur played at The Country Club. In the two qualifying
rounds, Francis fell one shot short of advancing to the match-
play portion of the championship. He remained to watch and remembered that "I gained many a fine lesson watching the stars."
Three weeks after the Amateur he entered The Country Club
Cup Tournament played across the street from home. This was
one of the literally thousands of events played each year at private clubs. The qualifying rounds went much better this time.
Francis tied for the medalist prize with one P. W. Whittlemore.
After losing in the match play, Francis won the playoff for the
medalist prize. Francis won easily; on the tenth hole Whittlemore was attacked by a swarm of bees and could barely finish
the round.

It was another club event that did the most to convince Francis that he could play on a very high level. In the spring of 1911 he played in a thirty-six-hole medal-play event at the Woodland Golf Club. He put together rounds of 70 and 71, and he later recalled that "playing two consecutive rounds such as these had more to do with steadying my game than any other thing and helped me win several minor events."

Apparently buoyed by those two rounds at the Woodland, Francis began to do well in statewide events. In 1912 he lost in the finals of the state amateur championship. In 1913, at Wollaston, he won. So while it was not widely reported, Francis entered the Open as the year's best amateur golfer in Massachusetts. It was easy to present Francis as a modest young man who "came out of nowhere" to defeat the foreign invaders, Vardon and Ray, at Brookline in 1913. The fact was that Francis was the beneficiary of a system of associations and private clubs that had constructed a ladder of competitions, of tests, that Francis passed. Golf in the United States had, institutionally, reached a critical mass that allowed a young man like Francis Ouimet to pursue his passion for the game.

While Ouimet became famous for his victory in 1913, he would not become the most prominent amateur golfer of his age. That honor fell to Robert Tyre Jones Jr., better known as Bobby. Jones, however, climbed a competitive ladder similar to one provided for Ouimet. There were, however, some important differences.

Born on March 17, 1902, Jones was a decade younger than Ouimet. Francis Ouimet faced the open hostility of his father when it came to golf. College was never a possibility for Francis. Caddying and summer jobs were a necessity that cut into practice time. Bobby Jones's life, as a youth, was in many respects the opposite of this picture.

We should see the young Bobby Jones as a somewhat heedless young man reveling in his freedom and privilege. As Jones himself put it, "Golf began for all of us — Mother and Dad and me—in the early summer of 1907 when we moved out of the city [Atlanta] to board with Mrs. Frank Meador in a big house about a mashie pitch from what was then the second fairway of the East Lake golf course." Golf was, at first, a very minor part of his summer life at East Lake. He played tennis, baseball (as did Ouimet), and fished in the ponds on the East Lake course. Jones also created his own little private course along a road near the main course. His childhood summers were, by his own admission, idyllic. He would never carry other people's clubs for money or see the game through the eyes of a caddie.

Jones began playing golf at age six. At nine, he won the East Lake Junior Championship, defeating a sixteen-year-old. *The American Golfer* published a picture of the young champion. However modest this victory was, Jones had clearly started down a path that made him an American athletic icon. He would succeed locally and, thus encouraged, he would move on to state and regional tournaments. Jones and his father had a deal. As long as he was making sufficient progress his father promised to let him enter the Southern Amateur when he was fifteen, but when the Southern Golf Association announced that the event would be held at East Lake in 1915, the elder Jones reconsidered. The thirteen-year-old shot 83 in the qualifying round, only one shot behind the medalist. He won his first match and lost his second. He dropped down to the second flight and after three wins in this flight, he reached the thirty-six-hole final. He lost 2 and 1.

His play in the Southern convinced the elder Jones that his son should play in a big invitational tournament held at the Roebuck Country Club in Birmingham. Young Bobby won the event and, as he recalled, this victory "started me off on a sort of orgy of invitational tournaments and club championships." In 1916 Bobby won three invitational tournaments and, most notable, the Georgia State Amateur. Played at the Capital City Club in Atlanta's oppressive heat, Jones won the state title by defeating his long-time friend from East Lake, Perry Adair, in the final.

The state amateur victory was important because as Jones later recalled, "This performance got me the chance to enter my first national Amateur Championship, played that year at the great course of the Merion Cricket Club, near Philadelphia." This marked a major move upward. It would be played in the North and on faster greens, not the slow Bermuda grass of the South. Jones also noted that "it was my first big trip away from home."

At Merion his youthfulness was fully on display in the qualifying rounds. His opening round of 74 on the West Course in the morning drew a large gallery for the afternoon round. People flocked to see the Dixie hotshot, who responded by turning in a dismal 89, but he still qualified for match play. His temper was a significant problem. In his match against Eben Byers, both acted badly and played poorly. Jones later claimed, "I think the main reason I beat him was because he ran out of clubs first. Somebody playing behind us said later that we looked like a juggling act."

Jones won his second match, and in the third round he lost to the defending champion, Robert A. Gardiner. The loss did nothing to obscure the fact that Jones had established himself at the highest level of American amateur golf. He was only fourteen but his performance at Merion actually came at the end of a long process that began at age six with informal junior tournaments at East Lake. The coming of the war would alter, but not derail, this process. In the 1920s, Bobby Jones would become one of the heroes of the decade. Perhaps only Babe Ruth rose to the same exalted level as Bobby Jones.

The process that both Jones and Ouimet went through was designed to identify the most talented amateur golfers. For professionals, the situation was quite different. It took some time for America to begin to produce its own professionals. Immigrants from Great Britain and, especially, Scotland, filled the increasing number of pro jobs at golf and country clubs. Getting and keeping one of these jobs was not generally the product of playing ability. The men who succeeded in these positions were good teachers of the game, knew how to care for the course, and were sober, industrious types who had the diplomatic skills necessary to deal with the membership.

A typical example of this kind of pro was Robert White, the head professional at Ravisloe in Chicago. White came to the United States from St. Andrews and carried with him the prestige that this conferred. He also possessed the skills that helped him please the members at Ravisloe. He attended classes at the University of Wisconsin and eventually became an expert on golf course soil and turf issues. White was clearly not a threat to win a major event. In 1900, at the U.S. Open at the Chicago Golf Club, White's total for the four rounds was 378, 65 shots more than Harry Vardon, the winner.

White was, without being even a good player, an important professional, however. His recommendation could secure a club job for a recent arrival from Scotland. When the Professional Golfers' Association (PGA) was formed in 1916, White was elected the group's first president.

Walter Hagen, on the other hand, was a very different sort of golf professional. He was not a Scot; his background was mostly German. Born on December 21, 1892, in Brighton, New York, a lower-class suburb of Rochester, Hagen began caddying at age seven at the Country Club of Rochester. He rose to the position of assistant head pro. His considerable skills were formed early on, just as with Jones and Ouimet, on a private little four-hole course he constructed in a cow pasture. His formal education stopped at the seventh grade. The idea of taking a college course on turf science, I am sure, never crossed his mind.

Unlike Ouimet and Jones, Hagen had few opportunities to establish his worth as a player. There were a few professional events besides the U.S. Open but work kept him from competing. By 1915 pros could play in open championships conducted by the bigger associations, notably the Western Open, and several hotels staged events that pros could enter. The Shawnee Inn in Pennsylvania put on the Shawnee Open, beginning in 1912. Pinehurst Resort in North Carolina first played the North and South Open in 1902. Hagen won this event in 1918 and again in 1923 and 1924.

But in 1912 he had never been out of Rochester and, odd as it may seem, he had no idea how good he was. This changed in a strange way. He attended, but did not play in, the 1912 U.S. Open held in nearby Buffalo. He played the course before the event began and compared his play with the scores of the actual competitors. He concluded, quite correctly, that he was a very good player. This experience convinced him to enter the Open in 1913. Lost in the great contest between Ouimet, Vardon, and Ray, Hagen tied for fourth. In 1914 he made the trip to Midlothian, near Chicago, to play in his second U.S. Open Championship. With much less fanfare than Ouimet received, Hagen won the event by a shot over Chick Evans. In its report on the 1914 Open, the *New York Times* noted that the winner was from Rochester "and had not made any record outside his native city until this present tournament." The paper missed his decent finish in 1913, perhaps because in the reports on that event, Hagen's name was often misspelled.

In the world of the *New York Times* Hagen had no record, but in the golf community he did. In *Golf Illustrated*, Max Behr's account of the 1914 Open notes that Hagen had finished fourth at Brookline a year earlier "and that any fair score in his last round at Brookline would have seen him the champion instead of Ouimet." So the U.S. Opens of 1913 and 1914 announce the arrival of two important competitive golfers: Ouimet and Hagen.

Hagen was by far the more important. Almost single handedly he invented the modern professional golfer who made his living from his playing skill and the opportunities that those skills can provide. While he held club jobs, his focus was always on producing a living from competitive play and from paid exhibitions. Unlike Jones and Ouimet, Hagen represented the move to make of play, work. Both Ouimet and Jones went on to make careers in other traditional fields. Hagen, in fits and starts, created a new category of golfer: this was the professional who made his reputation and his livelihood solely from his playing ability. Hagen also sought to escape the label "manual laborer." The professionals at the club pro shops still worked with their hands. They sanded shafts and connected them to the wood and iron club heads. They repaired broken clubs. They did manual labor for people who could afford to have someone else do it. When Hagen escaped the pro shop at Oakland Hills, he adopted a new identity that did not include manual labor and all that that implied.

By 1915, especially in baseball, Americans were growing familiar with the idea of professional athletes. In golf, contests between professionals had always had a unique educational value. In 1894 Joseph Lee, in commenting on the contest at Shinnecock Hills between Willie Dunn and Willie Campbell, could claim that "those who witnessed the match were enabled to see the game of golf as it should be played."

This educational function has proven to be a durable foundation for the growth of professional golf. As the number of golfers grew to substantial proportions, so too did the number willing to pay to see some of the very best demonstrate their talents. Hagen was a major factor in the development of exhibitions and open tournaments as moneymakers. By 1930 golf tournaments and exhibitions would draw large paying audiences. Often they would pay to see Walter Hagen who, in a sense, had become a teacher.

Hagen, in retrospect, presents us with a unique quandary. He came to public attention at a time when Victorian values were being challenged but were still strong. For the Victorians the core of a sound and virtuous life was work. Victorians were also devoted to the idea that only people of sound and sober character should be celebrated and put forth as models. If we assume that golf spectators came from that level of society

where Victorian values were still strong, why did they so readily embrace Hagen? He had clearly made his work play. He also
carefully nurtured an image as a big drinker, a womanizer, and
a lover of the late-night party.

This was the Hagen legend, and a good deal of it was exagger-
ated or simply fake. People did not really want to see a golfer of
great character play the game in a safe and cautious way. They
wanted color, personality, and a certain recklessness. And Hagen gave it to them. He was the master of disaster. He could get
himself into awful positions on the course and he could usually
pull off the seemingly impossible escape. As for the drinking and
the late nights before a match, most of it was vastly overblown.
Hagen was a truly superior player; you cannot play at the level
he did while hung over and short of sleep. Hagen knew that he
was creating a myth and he let it grow. Late in life he confessed
that he never denied any story written about him.

The rise of Walter Hagen from the caddie yard to international fame only came to fruition in the 1920s. Yet as the war approached, Hagen was clearly beginning to establish something
new in golf. He was at the very beginning of a long process that
would ultimately produce the PGA Tour and make playing professionals internationally famous athletic and cultural figures.

By looking briefly at the pre-1917 careers of Jones, Ouimet,
and Hagen, I have tried to show that most of the system was in
place to snatch up young boys with talent and put them through
a series of tests. As a boy continued to pass the tests, he moved
toward national and international competition and a genuine
measure of renown. This system worked best in the amateur
ranks. Ouimet and Jones became well known, as did a few others like Chick Evans. The caddie ranks produced the first generation of American-born pros. These caddies who aspired to
greatness as players did not have the well-organized system that
amateurs enjoyed. But its outlines were clearly present. Regional
associations had launched open events like the Western Open.
Hotels and resorts attracted guests and entertained them with

professional events like the North and South Open. Florida and California attracted professionals to a number of events that paid prize money to pros who held positions at northern clubs shut up for the winter.

In essence, the golf community was organizing itself. From clubs came the USGA, and from the USGA came any number of crucial actions. The period between 1900 and 1917 was full of contention and strife for the USGA. While it did not garner much attention, the rule that competitors in the U.S. Amateur be members of recognized clubs was very important. In order to compete, Ouimet had to make considerable sacrifices to make himself eligible. It was easy to argue that golf, or at least USGA golf, was exclusionary. The USGA, in an attempt to counter this charge, began to hold a national Public Links Championship in 1924.

Furthermore, this period was rife with debates over amateurism, other rules, and the nature of the rule-making process. In 1904 Walter Travis (born in Australia but claimed by Americans as one of their own) won the British Amateur using the Schenectady putter, a center-shafted implement. After considerable controversy, the Royal and Ancient Golf Club of St. Andrews (the R&A) banned the club. The USGA refused to go along with the ruling. This marked the first time the USGA and the R&A took conflicting positions on the rules.

Certainly the most newsworthy controversy involved amateurism and Francis Ouimet. In 1916 the USGA revoked Ouimet's amateur standing because he opened a sporting goods store with James Sullivan. The USGA had struggled mightily with the rules that governed amateurism. Much of the problem stemmed from the 1894 original rule:

> An amateur golfer shall be a golfer who has never made for sale golf clubs, balls, or any other article connected with the game; who has never carried clubs for hire after attaining the age of fifteen years, and who has not carried clubs for hire at any time

within six years of the date on which the competition begins; who has never received any consideration for playing in a match or for giving lessons in the game, and who for a period of five years prior to the 1st of September 1890, has never contended for a money prize in any open competition.

The problem with this definition and with the changes that followed was its essentially negative nature. It attempted to define all the things an amateur was not, thus leaving anyone who could not escape all the forbidden activities as a professional. It would have been much easier to define positively what made a player a professional. But this was not what they did.

The action against Ouimet enraged much of the golf community and particularly the editor of the *American Golfer*, Walter Travis. As a three-time winner of the USGA Amateur, Travis was in a position to understand the hypocrisy and inconsistency that characterized the situation. He was making his living writing about golf but this, oddly, was allowed. At one point he had been labeled a pro because he was also a golf course architect. The USGA then reversed itself and in January 1917 it reinstated the rule making architects professionals. Travis, in the pages of his magazine, constantly attacked the USGA and established two themes that would last to the present day. Regarding the USGA's stand on amateurism he argued that the USGA was attempting "to make golf so that only a man with plenty of money can afford to play it. This is snobbery." More generally, Travis hammered the USGA for being unrepresentative. Given that only the most established and wealthy clubs were given privileged active status, and that these clubs controlled the executive committee that made all the important rulings, Travis had a point.

The USGA also ran afoul of the Western Golf Association in the Ouimet affair. In January 1917, they declared Ouimet an amateur and invited him to play in the Western Amateur at Midlothian. Ouimet accepted and he cruised through the early rounds and won the title one up in an exciting match with Ken Edwards of Midlothian. The field was an excellent one; it even included a fifteen-year-old rising star from Atlanta named Bobby Jones.

The conflict would have continued to deteriorate further if the war had not intervened. Ouimet was drafted and this encouraged the USGA to end the controversy. Early in 1918, they reinstated the 1913 Open champion as an amateur. Nothing had really changed; Ouimet was still in the sporting goods business.

What exactly was at the bottom of this curious controversy? The USGA position was oddly unbalanced. They allowed Chick Evans, an amateur, to write a golf column and to receive a car as a "gift." They finally allowed course architects to retain their amateur status. In 1914, when Francis won the U.S. Amateur at Ekwanok, he was employed selling sporting goods at Wright and Ditson in Boston. Yet, given all this, they stuck to their decision that stripped Ouimet of his amateur status.

Why? The easy answer is that it was a class issue. The villains in the drama were "bluebloods," the upper crust, the wealthy, the privileged. They sought to keep their game free of commercialism and professionalism. They talked about purity and keeping the game "clean." To them, being a "pro" was merely a step above hustler and cheat. They wanted to keep the amateur realm free of such influence and to allow in only the right kind of people. The victims were hardworking decent sorts such as Francis Ouimet and Walter Travis.

There can be little doubt that class feeling had something to do with the USGA amateur policy. But why did they let Evans have his automobile? Why let amateurs earn money writing about golf? Why change the amateur rule so many times? The answer to these questions is two-fold. First, the USGA officials who made and carried out policy were incompetent. I do not mean this in a bad way. There was no training period for USGA officials. Presidents and other officials served short terms, and there was only a small permanent staff to handle a game that by 1917 was growing explosively. Frank Woodward came to the office of president determined to "do something" about creeping professionalism. There was, apparently, no one to stop him. The organization was not designed to temper "reform movements" like those pushed by men like Woodward. Once they had revoked Ouimet's amateur status and saw the firestorm of public criticism, they stiffened their position and wrapped themselves in lawyers who fought back every challenge. They even claimed that Ouimet, when reinstated, had severed his ties with the sporting goods enterprise when clearly he had not. The men who ran the USGA before the war were usually wealthy businessmen who had no idea how to run an organization that controlled a game played from coast-to-coast by more than a million players. No one did.

I have already alluded to the second cause of the Ouimet affair. The USGA in 1917 was by design an unrepresentative organization. The president and the executive committee were out of touch with much of the golf community for which they sought to write rules. Most of the thoughtful criticism of the Ouimet decision focused on this issue. The USGA did not understand that golf, as an evolving community, had spawned other agencies that cared about the game. Most notable in this regard were the golf magazines and the regional associations, especially the Western Golf Association. Because the USGA so jealously guarded its powers, it left itself open to angry critics who took the deeply American position that the USGA was an unrepresentative, unchecked power. W. W. Young, in *Golf* (April 1917), reflected the core of the outrage many felt: "The mere idea of a great game like Ouimet's being spoiled by an organization that represents only about five percent of the golf clubs of the United States, and not more than about four-and-three-quarters percent of the real golfers, is enough to make genuine sportsmen savage, and it has done so."

One can only estimate the long-term impact of the USGA's

actions against Ouimet. The golf community could hardly see the organization as working for the best interests of the game. The quest to purify the game, to cleanse it of professionalism and the taint of money, was relatively short-lived. By 1922 the USGA was charging admission to the Amateur Championship. The organization had taken on a number of expensive responsibilities, the USGA Green Section being only one. The money taken in was also used to pay the expenses of sending the amateur Walker Cup team to Great Britain and entertaining the British when they came to the United States. Up to this point the USGA had fought paying any expenses incurred by amateurs when they competed. Five years after voting against Ouimet, the same organization was selling tickets and providing trips to England for amateurs. The crusade by the USGA to control the influence of money on the game would return again in a different form in the 1950s.

The USGA has never totally recovered from its actions during this period. Too many American golfers came to see the organization as distant, unrepresentative, stubborn, and hypocritical. The 1920s would be a time of continued controversy, especially with the Western Golf Association. Increasingly it became apparent that among most American golfers, the USGA was not popular and, worst, not relevant.

Perhaps one reason for this unpopularity was the ugly rhetoric employed by the USGA to characterize professional golfers. Given this situation, it was important that just as professionalism was being condemned, the professionals were organizing an effort to improve their image and their position in the golf community.

The Professional Golfers' Association was born at a meeting of New York–area pros on January 16, 1916. Several factors led to this development. The British professionals had organized in 1901. There were local organizations of pros in Chicago, Boston, and New York for several years prior to 1916. The more immediate motive for organizing was the offer by department store owner Rodman Wanamaker to underwrite a tournament for pros only. He offered to put up an ample purse and a permanent trophy. It seemed that Wanamaker saw an opportunity to publicize his golf equipment department and become a force in professional golf. Up to 1916, the most important sponsor of professional golfers was clearly Spalding and Brothers. Since 1900, when Albert Spalding had induced Harry Vardon to come to America to promote the game and a ball that bore Vardon's name, Spalding had dominated the new business of selling golf balls and clubs by paying pros to endorse them.

Wanamaker had an entrée to the pro ranks through his employee Tom McNamara, a professional himself. McNamara sported a fine competitive record; he had just been the runner-up to Jerry Travers in the 1915 Open at Baltusrol. It was McNamara that did the legwork and called the pros together for the January 1916 meeting.

The inducements offered by Wanamaker were important, but the pros had several other reasons for forming an association. Because the USGA was apparently devoted to making the term "golf professional" a negative one, the American pros in 1916 needed an association to advance and "professionalize" their occupation. In this they no doubt followed their British colleagues who dedicated their organization to promoting the game in general, to advancing the "trade interests of its members," to holding championships, to creating a fund for the relief of members who needed it, and to creating an employment agency. The British group made it difficult to become a member. One had to have served "a bona fide Golf Club" for five years either as a pro or as an assistant. Since the majority of pros at American clubs were from Great Britain, it seems reasonable to assume they shared the goals of their home country's association.

All of these motives blended with Wanamaker's offer and the PGA was born. This was an important development because the club pro was a significant factor in the evolution of the golf community. He was the average player's connection to the game. It was from the club pro that an American player learned to play, learned the rules and the history of the game, and learned what was new in equipment. Conveniently, the new clubs and balls were for sale in the "pro shop." The pro shop to this day is perhaps the most important focal point in the golf community. The local PGA pro since 1916 has occupied a very central role in the game. He or she stands at the center of a small communication system dispensing gossip, real news, and tales of the game.

Before the war came, the PGA was able to stage only one championship and then decided to shut down all competition for the duration. But an important element of the golf community had taken root. It would never get entangled in the controversies that shaped the early history of the USGA. It was a very different kind of organization; it was essentially in the business of making golf professionals more respected and economically secure. Over the next ninety years it evolved into one of the nation's most successful sport organizations.

By 1918 the golf community had emerged on the American sport landscape. The private golf club had become an established part of American sporting and social life. America had begun to produce its own champions — Ouimet, Hagen, and Jones were representative of a much larger group. America had silently declared its independence from Scottish and English golf. Players with skill rose through a system of local and regional championships to compete finally on the national stage. The caddy yard proved to be an unusually rich source of great players, especially professionals like Walter Hagen and Gene Sarazen. In 1912 America welcomed quite silently into the world three boys who would dominate professional golf between 1935 and 1960. Ben Hogan, Byron Nelson, and Sam Snead (all born in 1912) would learn their golf as caddies and would replace Jones, Hagen, and Sarazen as the leading players in the game.

The golf community was, of course, part of the larger American community. Events that shaped the larger community also influenced golf. In 1918, history intervened.

Golf and World War I

The golf community thrived between 1890 and 1917 because it had a potent historical wind at its back. People had more time and money to spend on diversions. In general it was a prosperous quarter-century; golf was nourished by this prosperity. The speed of streetcar lines and the resulting suburbanization helped golf grow. Many Americans wanted out of the cities and into nature, even if it was the contrived nature of a country club. There were less obvious historical forces that benefited golf as well. The beginnings of women's liberation potentially doubled the number of players who would take up the game. Both genders responded to expert advice that called for less sitting, less work, and more exercise.

After the turn of the century, golf got another mighty boost from historical change. In the early days, golf and the country club movement were clearly constrained by the necessity to build courses where urban railroads and horse-drawn transport (coaches) could move people from home to the course. After 1900 all this was forgotten as the automobile arrived on the American scene. Probably no technological advance has had a more profound impact on American habits. It spurred and transformed suburbanization by detaching people and housing from the rail lines. Suburban developments moved farther from the city center, and where suburbs went golf courses soon followed. People were liberated; the automobile opened up life, especially leisure-time life.

This intrusion of the auto into American life began in the years just after the turn of the century. It would reach some measure of fruition in the 1920s, but by 1916 the die was cast. In 1900 there were eight thousand motor vehicle registrations, in 1920 there were eight million. Detroit was manufacturing approximately a million automobiles in 1916. This number would jump to 3.6 million in 1923. By 1929 Americans owned twenty-three million private autos. The American with a car had to wait while the nation went on a road-building binge. In 1921 there were 290,000 miles of roads; by 1929 there were 660,000 miles of roads for the American driver.

The automobile quickly defeated the electric trolley as the preferred mode of urban travel. The trolley companies made it easy. Essentially public utilities, the companies were often corrupt and they charged high prices for poor, erratic service. There were many grisly accidents.

But the auto won out mostly because of the liberation it seemed to offer. In 1903 James P. Holland, in *Munsey's Magazine,* argued that the automobile offered freedom from "the bondage of the iron roadway." He talked about the car as if it were a person. It was "free to come and go by highway and byway." It was as "trustworthy as a faithful hound. Time tables and beaten paths are not for it." Holland asked, "Why should men be compelled to live within a stone's throw of a rail road or street car?" He claimed that "within sixty miles of every large city may be found the most delightful locations for small dwellings, which are at present inaccessible on account of the lack of transportation facilities." The low-priced auto, he suggested, would change all this. The automobile would push suburbanization in ways the trolley never could.

The coming of the auto had at least two direct impacts on golf. For one thing, it made the local golf club seem like an even better idea. Unhooked from the trolley, a family could go to the club when they pleased and return home when they wished. Clubs no longer had to provide shelter and care for horses and coaches. Down came the stables and in went the parking lots. Americans loved what they called "automobile parties." They would drive into the countryside and end the day with dinner at the country club. More importantly clubs could now be built on almost any piece of land. The auto unhooked the golf club from the rail lines.

The golf resort was also a major beneficiary of the automobile revolution. They had always been largely dependent on railroads and steamships to get the customers to their hotels and golf courses. Leonard Tufts, the owner of Pinehurst, knew that the automobile was the key to the growth of golf tourism. In 1904 the first automobile completed the trip from Massachusetts to Pinehurst. After that, rail travel declined and Pinehurst guests increasingly arrived in their personal cars. Tufts was a tireless advocate for good roads, especially roads that began in New England and ended in North Carolina.

By the early 1920s, the vacation by auto had been linked with golf to create the golf road trip. As early as 1917, Henry MacNair was publishing detailed articles that guided golfing car owners on carefully crafted trips in which he took the driver from golf course to golf course, from hotel to hotel. These articles usually came with elegant maps produced by MacNair himself. MacNair had simply linked golf and the automobile-based vacation. As he put it, "With respect to the annual vacation motor trip, there should be no argument necessary to insure its perpetuation. As a restorer of energy, both physical and mental, the automobile is second only to the Royal Game, and when the two are combined, the union is invincible. The proof of this particular pudding lies in the fact that new golf courses are springing up wherever the passenger automobile has penetrated."

The automobile changed American life profoundly. Oddly, I think, we have underestimated its impact on everyday life. Certainly we live in an era that dwells on the massive impact of car culture on the city and the environment. This makes it easy to forget that the car transformed the everyday existence of millions of Americans. The automobile in 1916 allowed Americans to fundamentally rethink their daily existence. The auto offered escape from the city, the home, and the restrictions imposed by limited mobility. One of the places they escaped to was the golf club and golf resort. The automobile allowed affluent Americans to make their golf country club an extension of their home, a second home of a sort. This reality would come to pass in the 1920s and we shall discuss it fully in the next chapter.

The coming of World War I tended to mask the impact of the evolving car culture. When America entered the fray in the spring of 1917, golf responded like a community. Editors of golf magazines asked, "What will golf do?" As golf answered this question it was clear that they had divided the game in half. One half constituted "golfing competition among the ranking players," and everyone argued that this half "must surely be no more until peace returns." The Western Golf Association did conduct its open in 1917. The WGA was criticized, but when the group donated most of proceeds to the war effort the criticism stopped.

The other half of golf was made up of everyday play at the private golf clubs and public courses. The editor of *Golf Illustrated* stated bluntly that "the old will carry on at the club while the young will fight." The government, in fact, encouraged recreation as one way to keep workers healthy and the war effort humming. So golf below the championship level continued, even as players watched the conflict in Europe turn into a massive human catastrophe.

Golfers who stayed home responded with a remarkable outburst of exhibitions and events, all designed to aid the war effort. Led by the game's national and regional organizations, golfers and golf fans turned out for tournaments and exhibitions designed to get into the public's pockets and pass the money along to groups like the Red Cross. These organizations led the drive to raise money. The Professional Golfers' Association

(PGA), the United States Golf Association (USGA), and the Western Golf Association (WGA), all in their own way, sought to use golf as a way to raise money.

The PGA purchased a Ford ambulance and donated it, along with a thousand dollars, to the war effort. They also sponsored the largest charity golf event of 1917. Played in late July, this event featured four teams playing over four days on four New York–area courses (Englewood, Baltusrol, Siwanoy, and Garden City). There were three teams of professionals: "homebreds," or Americans; the English; and the Scots. The fourth team was made up of amateurs. The most famous of the amateurs was probably Bobby Jones, known during this period as "Little Bob," as if he were some sort of circus attraction. Also on the amateur team was Grantland Rice, a friend of the Jones family. Young Bob stayed at Rice's Riverside apartment during the matches. It was the start of a lifelong friendship between Rice and Jones.

Over the four days, the teams competed in a variety of formats. On the first day at Englewood, the professionals teamed up with some female players from the area. This was the beginning of a theme of sorts: the public seemed to like watching the genders play together. Some of the more successful Red Cross matches were mixed-foursome contests.

Overall the matches used a scoring system based on total holes won. In this system a match was not over when a player was, for example, three down with two holes to go. The match would go the full eighteen and the winner received a score equal to the total holes won. This allowed for team scoring that was similar to football. Over the four days, it was Homebreds 152, Scots 87, English 72, and the amateurs 28.

The USGA could not contribute to the war effort in the same way as the PGA and WGA. It had no personnel like the PGA that they could deploy for charity matches. It had "member clubs," but not in the same way the WGA did. Regional organizations such as the WGA and others were actively using area courses as the venue for charity matches. The USGA did, however, promote what was probably the first attempt to get golfers nationwide to do the same thing on the same day.

Early in 1917, the USGA issued an appeal asking every golfer to participate in a nationwide event on July 4, 1917. Called the "Liberty Tournament," it had no stipulated format. Each club was free to stage whatever type of competition it wished. The USGA issued to each course that took part an engraved certificate, and the Red Cross gave each winner a medal. Each golfer was expected to donate at least one dollar as an entrance fee, but no one discouraged larger contributions.

While the PGA and the USGA did their part, in retrospect, it seems that the Western Golf Association and Chick Evans did more than could be reasonably expected. In January 1918 the WGA voted to hold "patriotic tournaments" and donate the proceeds "to war charity purposes." Eventually the group designated the Red Cross as the beneficiary of their efforts.

At the heart of the WGA effort was Chick Evans. Charles E. Evans Jr., always known as Chick, was certainly a prominent person in the history of American golf. A lifelong amateur, he compiled a fine competitive record. He won both the U.S. Open and Amateur in 1916. He was the first to win both titles in the same year. He won the Amateur again in 1920. He won the Western Amateur nine times, which included a streak of four wins in a row between 1920 and 1923. Evans would certainly have been the best amateur of his day if it were not for the existence of Bobby Jones.

As a contributor to the golf community, Evans had few peers. Evans was introduced to the game as a caddy at the Edgewater Golf Club in Chicago. When he could no longer caddy without being labeled a pro, the club gave him a pro shop job and let him use the course to develop his game. That he evaded the USGA rules by this method suggests the many loopholes in those rules. After his double win in 1916, Evans produced a set of golf lessons on phonograph records. He could not accept the money that came from the sale of the records and remain an amateur.

It was his mother who suggested that he put the proceeds into a fund to provide scholarships for caddies. After a slow start, the program eventually grew into one of the largest privately funded charities in the United States. Since 1930 more than nine thousand Evans Scholars have received college degrees.

The coming of the war seemed to profoundly stimulate Evans's patriotism and his desire to use golf for good causes. He was an advocate of the simple idea that golf matches could attract audiences that would, one way or another, pay to attend. Evans claimed that he played in the very first of the "war matches." In 1916, before America had entered the war, Evans played George Lyon, one of Canada's best players, in a match staged at the Guelph Golf Club in Canada. There was no entrance fee; money was raised from the sale of pins, each representing a Canadian soldier.

Evans attempted to join the Army Air Corps but was rejected. So he began, at his own expense, to play matches in the Midwest and the East, the money raised going to the Red Cross or the Navy League. Evans claimed that these matches raised fifty thousand dollars in 1916 and 1917. He was convinced that better planned and publicized matches could do even better in 1918.

Evans asked the USGA to organize these matches. The executive committee tabled his request. After this rebuff, Evans approached WGA president Charles F. Thompson and received a much more positive response. It was agreed that the WGA and the clubs would do the organizing; the players would just play. The plan worked.

There is no way to count the number of WGA matches. But clearly, everyone, pro and amateur, stepped up. A number of matches pitted co-ed teams against each other. In one much publicized event, Bobby Jones and Elaine Rosenthal were matched against Perry Adair and Alexa Stirling. Evans himself was by far the most active player in the WGA-sponsored events. He played in forty-eight of the WGA organized matches and another four planned separately. At war's end, in November 1918, the president of the WGA announced that the golf matches sponsored by the WGA had netted $302,713.50 after expenses of only $1,016.50.

The charity matches had two effects on the golf community. The first was to suggest that golf could be a money-producing spectator sport. As noted earlier, the USGA began charging admission to some of its championships in 1922 as a way of defraying the cost of their expanding program. The wartime matches also helped bolster Walter Hagen's notion that he could make a living playing matches and exhibitions. He felt that gate receipts would be so good that he could do without a regular club job. In some limited sense, the war matches announced the coming of the "touring pro."

Secondly, the wartime matches established a charitable tradition as part of the golf community. These matches did more than merely charge admission. They auctioned off balls and clubs used by the players. They sold the right to caddy for the golfers. It was clear that the combination of a good cause and golf was an excellent fit. And so it has been to this day. When planning a charity event, nothing seems to go so well as a golf outing. Today's planners use many of the same tactics invented during the World War I matches.

Golf's reputation was certainly enhanced by its response to the war. Perhaps more important was the fact that the war years produced a number of changes that shaped golf profoundly. For one thing, the war made hickory hard to come by and this led to a gradual turn to steel shafts. Wood shafts did not go quietly; they hung on through the 1920s. But the direction of change was clear—metal would replace wood.

Much more important were a number of actions by the federal government that had a marked impact on golf. The introduction of Daylight Saving Time in 1918 was motivated by the need to save fuel. It did, however, have a clear impact on golf. By creating one additional hour of daylight after work, the program created one more hour for golf. Federally mandated DST was repealed in 1919. However, the adoption of the program became a local option. Massachusetts and Rhode Island took this option as did a number of large cities like New York, Philadelphia, and Chicago. It was not until 1966 and the Uniform Time Act that almost all of the United States accepted DST. The point, however, is that the war brought the idea that produced one more hour per day of daylight leisure for Americans.

Some wartime measures influenced leisure and golf in another important way. The National War Labor Board arbitrated conflicts between labor and management. One of their decisions was to order the eight-hour day and to mandate time-and-a-half pay for overtime. These rules applied only to war workers but they marked a significant step in reducing the workweek and increasing leisure time.

The same labor board endorsed equal pay for women workers. And there were a lot of them. Women flowed into jobs normally held by the men who were in the military. It was a small step toward gender equality. After the war it became harder to argue that a woman who had worked installing axles in trucks could not play sports. The golf community became a bit more open to women.

The federal measures mentioned so far had the tendency to increase leisure and alter the nature of work. They influenced golf only indirectly. However there were two measures rooted in the war years that had a large and direct impact on the game. The first was Prohibition. While not a war act, its passage was clearly aided by the wartime atmosphere. German-Americans were, after all, big players in the brewing industry. Introduced in 1913, the Eighteenth Amendment was ratified by the states and took effect on January 20, 1920. It was not repealed until 1933.

It is easy to forget what a massive social experiment Prohibition was. While it did cut alcohol consumption, perhaps its most profound effect was to produce a national outbreak of law breaking. In retrospect, it seems clear that the law was virtually unenforceable. People gathered together and sought ways to collectively flout the law. The New York Yale Club, just before Prohibition went into effect, purchased a fourteen-year supply of wine and hard liquor.

It is reasonable to assume that country clubs played a significant role in evading the law. As private, often isolated, social gathering spots, it was easy to avoid detection by law enforcement. Also, since club memberships included prominent, influential people, the local police often made it a policy to leave country clubs alone. There is very little evidence in the record to support the idea that Prohibition made country clubs more popular. But it just makes sense. A country club membership for the decade of the 1920s meant you could play golf and other sports and have a safe place to drink.

The last wartime measure to influence golf did so directly—as directly as taxation. The government had to fund the war and it did it in a number of ways. Most central, perhaps, was the imposition of new taxes and higher rates for older taxes. One of the new taxes was placed on golf and country clubs. Section 701 of the Revenue Act of 1917 included a 10 percent tax on dues or membership fees (including initiation fees) paid to any social, athletic, or sporting club where the fees or dues were twelve dollars or more. In the Revenue Act of 1918 this figure was reduced to ten dollars.

These seemingly simple provisions set off a long conflict between the clubs and the Internal Revenue Service. For example, were special assessments taxable? No. Were green fees, locker fees, and club storage fees taxable? Yes, then no. Were shares of stock or membership certificates that had to be purchased to become a member taxable? Yes, but many clubs did not collect the tax on stock sales and ended up with big penalties for this oversight. In 1927 the government reversed itself on this point—stock sales and the like were not taxable. The IRS set up a bewildering system whereby the clubs could obtain refunds. The tax stayed on the books until 1966, when it quietly disappeared.

The impact and meaning of this tax is hard to figure. In simple terms, the government increased the cost of belonging to a club by 10 percent. Looking back, it seems that the tax did not slow golf down. By almost any measure golf grew rapidly in the twenties. The tax does suggest that the government saw golf at a private club as a luxury and ripe for taxation. This seemed to be the point of the ten-dollar limit. Fraternal lodges with much lower fees were exempt.

When clubs complained about the tax, they argued that the government should not be taxing a nonprofit organization that provided healthful recreation. They had a point. The government taxing a nonprofit enterprise is rare. This suggested that the government, especially Congress, saw private sporting clubs as special. While no one openly admitted it, the tax seemed just another way to tax affluent people who could easily afford to pay.

The United States emerged from the war years a much more powerful nation. The country had rapidly put a formidable military force on the ground in Europe, and it had loaned the Allies vast sums of money. But the fact remains that the forces of modernization were even more powerful than the war. Technology (the automobile) was transforming everyone's life. Beyond the automobile there was the telephone, the radio, and the growth of mass production. People continued to move from rural areas to urban centers; and from urban centers they moved to the suburbs. More people finished high school and more people went to college. The move for gender equality grew stronger. In this complex and confusing context, the golf community thrived. Golf, and the private golf club particularly, seemed to answer the collective emotional needs of generally affluent white Americans. While the golf community had a number of historical forces on its side, it would also flourish because there was something irrationally intoxicating about being on a golf course and hitting a golf ball.

At least some individuals were deeply intoxicated by the game before the war. Mr. W. H. Evans of Philadelphia wrote to *Golf Illustrated* in April of 1917 to detail his golf obsession. Evans claimed that in the three years from 1914 to 1916, he played 657 days at a private club in his home town. He had kept detailed records. His total cost for three years of golf was $1,274.82 or $1.44 per round. One hundred and eight golf balls had been expended to play 16,069 holes during which he had walked 3,805 miles. Evans had averaged between 85 and 87 for each eighteen. He had worn out eight sets of shoe strings.

As the twenties dawned and prosperity spread, the slightly insane intoxication illustrated by Mr. Evans would find its historical moment and golf would boom.

Golf's Golden Age?

The question mark in the title of this chapter is meant to challenge the belief that the 1920s was a glorious era of growth for the golf community. By most measures, the game, fueled by the decade's prosperity, did grow spectacularly. Percentage increases in the number of players, clubs, and courses were huge. The growth took golf to every corner of the nation, ending the dominance of the pioneer clubs in the Northeast. Golf's growth was so rapid that some commentators began to suggest that it could replace baseball as the national pastime.

A second hallmark of this era was the evolution of golf into a spectator sport. The glorious but short career of Bobby Jones was one factor. The United States Golf Association (USGA) discovered that Jones drew thousands of admission-paying fans to the U.S. Open and Amateur Championships. The quite different careers of pros like Walter Hagen was another important factor. While there were many doubters, golf, by the late 1920s, had begun to establish itself as part of the boom in spectator sports that highlighted the decade. Golf loomed large in the public consciousness. Bobby Jones stood on the same level as Babe Ruth and all the other sport heroes of the decade. Towns across the country saw it as progress when the parks department opened a municipal course or the local elite established a country club.

However, if we remember for a moment that we are tracing

the rise of a community, then we are forced to see that what happened to golf in the 1920s was much more complicated than mere growth. As the game grew, it was shaped by powerful forces in American culture. By the end of the decade, the identity of the game and the structure of the community that grew up with it had solidified, and it became clear that a hierarchy of sorts had evolved. While golfers still evoked the egalitarian, democratic, Scottish golfing tradition, plainly American golf had moved away from that tradition. Golf in the United States, as it grew, was defined by gender and racial attitudes and by other less obvious but deeply held cultural beliefs.

The growth of golf, between World War I and the Depression, was truly spectacular. By many measures it grew more rapidly than the other popular sports. By 1930 Americans had become much more knowledgeable about what was happening in their lives. The first three decades of the twentieth century had spawned an army of sociologists, statisticians, and "society watchers." This army fired off opinions at a steady rate, but they also sought to keep accurate counts of what was growing and declining in American life. By 1930 Americans could read any number of accounts that detailed the luxurious growth of golf in America.

One of the best was *Americans at Play* (1932) by George Steiner. Drawing his numbers from several sources, Steiner confidently stated that "the spectacular growth of golf during the recent years is unparalleled in the history of American outdoor sports." He had the numbers to back this up. He estimated the number of courses before the war (1917) at approximately 800. By 1923 this number had grown to 1,903. The dramatic increase came between 1923 and 1930. At decade's end, Steiner claims, there were 5,826 golf courses of one kind or another in the United States. This was a 207 percent increase over the 1923 figure.

The majority of these courses were private. After noting the difficulty of separating municipal from private daily-fee courses, Steiner sets down what he believes to be solid approximations.

In 1930 there were 543 public, 700 private daily-fee, and 4,613 private courses. This amounted to an inventory of courses; Steiner suggests that the value of this inventory was $830 million. Some of the private courses built during the twenties have taken up places on today's lists of truly great courses. Most critics would agree that Cypress Point (1929), Seminole (1929), the East and West Courses at Winged Foot (1923), Riviera (1926), Baltusrol (1922), Oak Hill (1923), and the No. 3 Course at Medinah (1928) belong on any list of America's best courses.

Counting golfers was more difficult. Resorting to a set of reasonable assumptions, Steiner puts the number of private club members at approximately 1.1 million and the number of regular players at public courses at 900,000, for a tidy total of 2 million players. These players spent more money on equipment than the participants in other sports. The federal census for 1930 calculated the annual wholesale value of golf equipment at just a bit over $21 million, which was 37.4 percent of the total spent on all athletic equipment. Steiner concluded that "no other single sport approaches golf in the amount of money annually invested in equipment."

Steiner is also able to show that the dominance of the Northeast was undermined by the growth in courses between 1917 and 1930. Only the sections labeled "New England" (96.4 percent) and "Middle Atlantic" (129.6 percent) had growth rates under 200 percent. He divides the country into nine sections and provides a growth rate for each. The "West South Central" led all sections with a 530 percent growth rate. The "Pacific" section was second at 295 percent. New York State still had the most courses, with Illinois in second place. If, however, we look at the number of courses per one hundred thousand of urban population, New York and Illinois were clearly "undercoursed." New York possessed only five courses per one hundred thousand in urban population and Illinois only seven. Iowa with twenty-one and Kansas with thirty led this category.

These statistics allow us to make some educated guesses about the nature of the growth in courses between 1917 and 1930. Clearly the expansion was more rapid outside the Northeast. Middle-sized towns in the Midwest and other sections adopted golf and built courses with a passion. This reflected not only the acceptance of golf but also the fact that land for courses was more readily available in these areas. It also reflected the fact that municipal and daily-fee courses were more commonly found outside the Northeast. It is my guess that many if not most of the daily-fee courses were hotel or resort courses. The rapid development of Florida and other Southeastern states as resort areas during the 1920s had no doubt produced a boom in the construction of daily-fee public courses.

Clearly the center of gravity of American golf was moving away from the Northeast. Steiner concludes, for example, that the most rapid growth in municipal course construction was in the "East North Central" section, which we may know better as the upper Midwest (Illinois, Ohio, Wisconsin, Minnesota, and Michigan). This trend was evident as early as 1924. In a survey taken that year and published in the magazine *American City,* Rebecca Rankin attempted to count the municipal courses in the United States—she found one hundred forty in one hundred cities. Of this total forty-seven, or 34 percent, were in the five upper Midwest states. Illinois and Ohio had twenty-nine, or 21 percent, of the total. Only New York State came close to these totals with twelve (six in the Greater New York City area).

Rankin, in her 1924 survey, found more than just raw numbers. The average course took up ninety acres, but the courses varied greatly in size. The cost of golf on these city courses also varied. A few courses had different rates for men and women. Some charged by the game or day, some for the season. Of the 140 courses listed, only ten provided free golf.

Rankin also notes that "in a good many cities it has been found advantageous to have clubs even on public courses." A player may join or not, but such clubs "in connection with a municipal golf course increases its popularity and is to the advantage of all who use the course." These clubs "keep the morale of the players to a high standard and help enforce the rules, and they are also a means of securing for players reciprocal privileges with private clubs."

Cities embraced the installation of public golf courses for a number of reasons. Roy Lambert, the commissioner of parks in San Antonio, Texas, gave a clear list of reasons his city had built the Brackenridge Park Course. He allowed that many had fought the appropriation of forty thousand dollars for the course. Many saw golf as a gentleman's game, but after three years of operation the critics were silenced. The course, Lambert stated, "has added to the wealth of the city." It had become clear that the course drew tourists to the area, and San Antonio also discovered that golf, unlike other public recreational facilities, was self-funding. The Brackenridge Park Course produced a profit of about two thousand dollars in each of the two years it had been open. This profit was reinvested in the course. The city had raised the daily fee from twenty-five to thirty-five cents.

San Antonio also benefited from public golf by staging the Texas Open at Brackenridge Park. Lambert claimed that the event was beneficial for the city; the tournament lured five thousand golf fans to San Antonio and Lambert claimed that "the publicity gained in this way costs nothing and it is of the best sort." San Antonio reflected the odd conjunction of boosterism and progressive attitudes. By the mid-1920s it seemed that every alert and up-to-date city needed golf as proof that it cared about the health of its citizens and the town's economy. As a use for empty public land, municipal courses just made sense.

While the growth of municipal and private daily-fee courses was dramatic, the growth in private country club courses was explosive. In 1930 there were approximately 1,200 public courses of all kinds and approximately 4,600 private courses. The 1920s was the great age of country club construction. Some of these clubs were almost absurdly large and complex. Especially after 1925 it seemed that some sort of competition had commenced to see who could build the club with the most amenities and the largest clubhouse. The motives that fueled this competition were complex, but clearly the desire to play golf on a modern, well-designed course was a central motivation. While the golf course was vital, as time passed, clubs added tennis courts, swimming pools, and areas for other sports. Most importantly they built huge complex clubhouses and expanded older clubhouses.

I have tried to count the number of large expansive and expensive clubs in order to put this explosion of country-club building into context. Of the clubs built in the 1920s, how many were of the huge, expensive variety and how many were modest affairs? My conclusion is this: the number of small modest clubs far outnumbered the big ones. However, the press emphasized and lavishly publicized the big projects. Clearly the country-club movement split into two very different wings. The first built big complex affairs while the second, larger wing built relatively modest, often small-town clubs.

A good example of a big splashy club was Olympia Fields, twenty-seven miles south of Chicago. The plan for the club was hatched in 1914; the four golf courses opened between 1916 and 1923. The whole project was finally finished in 1925 when the million-dollar clubhouse opened. The press found Olympia Fields to be a fascinating subject. By 1925 it clearly had begun to serve as a model for other groups starting a club. In the East, the lavish Westchester Country Club served much the same function.

The idea to build Olympia Fields originated with Charles Beach and a small group of prominent Chicagoans. Their first step was to attract five hundred charter members. Amos Alonzo Stagg, the University of Chicago athletic director, was president of the club between 1916 and 1921 and nurtured the project through the war years. Before 1919 the initiation fee was $60 and the annual dues $25. During the 1920s these figures rose; in 1927 an equity membership was valued at $1,100. By 1929 the club boasted a thousand regular members and three hundred members of other types.

The founders, from the beginning, envisioned a four-course club with the courses radiating out from a huge clubhouse for a large membership. The project began with a $500,000 bond sale for the first members. In 1927 the club carried an appraised value of $3.5 million.

It was the clubhouse that made Olympia Fields famous. Designed by George C. Nimmons, it was heralded as the largest and most complete clubhouse in the world. Generally Gothic in style, it was designed to imitate, as the architect claimed, "the large country houses of England during the Tudor period." Certainly the idea was to make people who saw the building think of England's aristocratic country houses and English churches. Inside there was "a great hall" built to mimic "the principal room in an old baronial hall." The giant timber trusses, oak-paneled walls, and fireplace created, in an instant, a sense that the room had been there for centuries. There was also a dining room for six hundred and a "café" for three hundred. The five-hundred-foot veranda evolved into the center of the club's social life. Locker rooms for men and women were separated by a large swimming pool. The men's locker room contained twelve hundred lockers. Members could bring their clothes to a club laundry; they could also have clothing repaired at a tailoring and valet service.

The defining features of Olympia Fields were its size and completeness. It contained a small hospital, an ice-making plant, a huge playground for children, a dancing pavilion, and a dormitory for three hundred employees. There were fourteen hundred registered caddies housed in a building that could never have been called the "caddie shack." Beyond all this, there was a hotel with eighty rooms to rent and a number of cottages also for rent.

Olympia Fields was not the product of robber-baron money spent lavishly and foolishly. The idea was to provide an upper-class experience on a budget. The club gladly allowed play on its courses by nonmembers and used these fees to defray the $250,000 annual budget. The restaurant was profitable and this profit also reduced the budget. Most significantly, the club retained eighty of the original seven hundred acres purchased. When the club was complete this land had risen dramatically in value. It was sold after 1925 and the proceeds were used to pay down the club's bonded indebtedness.

Olympia Fields symbolized a significant development in golf history. Across the country, but predominately in affluent areas near large urban centers, golf took up a place in the complex phenomenon we call country clubs. The relationship between these lavish clubs and golf became so close that many Americans still find the two indistinguishable.

This poses a significant problem for anyone interested in the history of golf in the United States. Is golf just a tool in the quest to create exclusive enclaves where the nation's economic elite can play far from the unwashed masses? The answer is no. While urban elites were constructing their lavish clubs, other Americans were following a more austere path. During the 1920s the founding of simple clubs and courses may well have outstripped the number of large, urban, exclusive courses and clubs.

Early in the 1920s, a few commentators noted that golf was no longer solely a rich man's game. One important aspect of this view was the debatable notion that in England and Scotland the game had always been democratic and open to all. In golf magazines and in newspapers like the *New York Times* writers noted that the popularity of golf had spread widely through the economic classes. A number of the writers seized on the victory of England's William Hunter, "a telegraph operator," in England's amateur championship as a sign of the times. They also noted the victory of Charles Hodgson, "a tobacconist," over Francis Ouimet in the same event. In America the spread of golf down the class structure was most evident outside the Northeast. An unsigned article in *Golfer's Magazine* stated, "If any proof were needed that golf is likely to become the diversion of the multitude it could be found in Indiana, Illinois, and the Iowa corn belt."

The example of this development most often cited was the construction by George Ade of a course near his home in Indiana. By some accounts most of the players at Ade's course were simple farmers gone nuts over the game. In a *Golfer's Magazine* editorial the writer emphasized the "democratic" atmosphere at Ade's course. It claimed that on the course "it is difficult to tell J. Brown, farmer, from Jasper Brown, banker, and J. Brown often is the better golfer."

In 1923 the *American Golfer* sent Earl Chapin May to investigate the growth of golf in Iowa. He discovered the Oak Hill Country Club, a symbol of the "strictly rural country clubs" that were "sprouting like mushrooms." Located in Red Oak, Iowa, the club was clearly designed to serve families. A ladies' auxiliary arranged the social calendar. The club featured a large well-used playground for children. Children also played the course but they were banned after 5:00 p.m. on weekdays and all day Sunday. May concluded that the club was simple and democratic, largely basing his assertion on the absence of caddies. Members of both genders carried their own clubs.

In 1921 *Golf Illustrated* published a piece entitled "The Country Club in the Small Town." In it the author, Ralph Kingwalt, makes some interesting claims. He asserts that in small towns the businessmen and professional people work harder and longer than in the big city. Businesses are open all day Saturday and "the country doctor is never beyond the demands of his telephone, nor the country lawyer far from his office." These habits have led to poor health and the general prescription that more exercise is the answer. This prescription and a love of golf have been the twin motives behind the creation of small-town country clubs. In general, Kingwalt believed that small-town clubs have a tendency to break down the social barriers that exist in the town's elite because there is only enough wealth to create one club and the various factions are thrown together in a common social experience.

The article described a typical small-town club, an incredibly modest affair in Mount Vernon, Ohio. Founded in 1916, the club sold shares of stock for one hundred dollars. It purchased a one-hundred-acre tract and hired a course architect for one day for a fee of one hundred dollars. The members built the course themselves, advised by local Scots who had some idea what a course should look like. Total cost for the course: three thousand dollars. For eleven thousand dollars the members constructed a clubhouse containing a living room, dining room, "a ladies room," and a kitchen. In short, a home without bedrooms. Of course, the structure was surrounded on three sides by a huge porch where one had a view of the entire course. The food service was in the hands of a "steward" who was paid seventy-five dollars per month and any profit he might make. The social schedule of teas and card parties was under the direction of a committee headed by a woman.

The Country Club of Mount Vernon was clearly a financial success. There were 150 members who paid annual dues of thirty-five dollars. The size of the club was tied, in the by-laws, to the population of the town. Every year the club made small improvements and paid down the mortgage. Perhaps more important, it achieved its objectives. Kingwalt claimed that the club was the social center of the town. He stated that "no one thinks of entertaining elsewhere. Most Sunday automobile parties end at the club. It is the favorite picnic ground. . . . To many it has repaid in health ten times what it has cost."

As we examine the growth in the number of golf courses in the 1920s, we are driven to a paradoxical conclusion: the game was becoming, all at the same time, more exclusive and expensive, and more inclusive and inexpensive. Simply put, golf was evolving quickly on both fronts; big private urban clubs grew expansively while at the same time municipal and inclusive private clubs, usually in smaller towns, were also rapidly growing.

The upshot of this was to convince many that golf was soon to be, in some poorly defined way, the nation's number-one sport. As early as 1921 *Golfer's Magazine* could claim that "golf as the great American game is the first real rival of baseball since it began to be generally played in the seventies. It is an antidote for Prohibition, a sure cure for the blues, and promises to become the principal recreation of the multitude who have to work for a living."

In 1922 Grantland Rice, America's premier sportswriter, gave credence to the idea that golf was a challenge to baseball. He noted that Connie Mack, the manager of the Philadelphia Athletics, was worried about all the young men who were rejecting baseball for golf. Rice suggested that golf had a built-in advantage. It was caddying that made golf attractive. Young boys could earn money while learning the game. Rice thought that the example set by ex-caddies such as Walter Hagen, Gene Sarazen, Jack McDermott, and Chick Evans deeply influenced young boys from lower-class backgrounds. Walter Hagen was a particularly potent role model. Rice claimed that Hagen made between twenty and forty thousand dollars annually.

Whatever its relationship to baseball, golf was clearly growing as an avocation. People came to understand that one could play it from childhood to old age. Furthermore, golf was becoming essential equipment for go-getters in business, which baseball could never be. Golf, indeed, became profoundly associated with business and businessmen. This was a connection that would, in the long run, be problematic, but in the twenties, a decade that celebrated "the go-getter," it was a plus.

Many of those who thought golf would overtake baseball believed that golf would never become a spectator sport. Baseball was easy to commercialize but most observers thought this would never happen to golf; it would always remain a player's game.

They were wrong. As the twenties wore on, golf grew significantly as a spectator sport. Key elements within the golf community came to understand that golf matches were a saleable commodity. This was a complex development in which a number of agencies (towns, the USGA, and the PGA) found creative ways to use golf as a means to make money. The wartime exhibitions that had raised so much money were clear evidence that golf had money-making potential.

By the end of the 1920s a remarkable number of competitive events had become something like fixtures on the spectator's calendar. The summer was dominated by the big four events: the Open and Amateur in Britain and in the United States. Just beneath these were the regional opens and amateur championships such as the Western, Metropolitan (New York), and Southern. As the cold descended on the North, fans could escape to warmer climes and watch golf. The November 1926 issue of *Golf Illustrated* listed seventeen open events to be played between November and March. Most were in Florida or California but there were also significant events in Texas, North Carolina, Mexico, and Bermuda. The list began with the Hawaiian Open in November and ended with the North and South Open at Pinehurst in March.

Of course we see the faint outline of today's PGA Tour in the advent of these warm-weather tournaments. In the twenties they reflected a significant change in the life of America's golf professionals. Only a very few could make a living playing for prize money. Most held club jobs in the North, and when those clubs were shut by snow and ice, many went south to another club or merely to escape and work on one's game. More than a few sold real estate. In this they were just following their more affluent members — people with the means to divide their year between the North and the South (and for some, the West).

The rise of these winter tournaments had several causes. Certainly, the general prosperity of the decade was important. Many Americans had increased discretionary time and money and this changed habits. For the generally affluent, a two-week break or longer from winter became an annual ritual. Places like Pinehurst in North Carolina and the Florida hotels developed a regular calendar of events to entertain their guests. Indeed, resort owners like Leonard and Richard Tufts, who put on the North and South Open from 1904 into the early 1950s, looked upon the players as temporary employees. Pinehurst Resort passed out free room and board and modest prize money in order to ensure an exciting attraction for their guests in late March — the busiest period at Pinehurst.

The tournaments were also occasionally the product of a town's desire to promote itself. Thus we have open or pro-am events in Pasadena, San Gabriel, and San Diego, California, and in Texas tournaments in El Paso and San Antonio. The business class in these towns, often acting through the Chamber of Commerce, was unusually important in getting these events off the ground.

The development of "spectating" as a significant element of the golf community was also the product of the unique nature of golf and the venue in which it was played. The golf spectator, in many respects, was unlike those in other sports. Watching a golf event in the 1920s was clearly different from attending a baseball, football, or basketball game. In watching a golf event, the spectator was not confined to an assigned seat. The golf spectator often can be mere feet from a player. Such a spectator can hear the exchanges between caddies and players, and often members of the galleries (as they are called in golf; no other sport uses this term) can affect play in numerous important ways, including, but not limited to, getting hit by the ball.

The inability of officials to control stampeding galleries became a serious problem. The 1928 U.S. Open provided an example of how an uncontrolled gallery could influence the outcome of an event. Bobby Jones and Johnny Farrell had finished the tournament in a tie at 294. Out on the course a young professional named Roland Hancock came to the seventeenth tee, needing just a par and a bogey to win the event. It took thirty minutes for tournament officials to clear the seventeenth fairway. In today's sport jargon Hancock was "iced" not by an opponent but by the fans. A double-bogey on seventeen and a bogey on eighteen put poor Hancock one shot out of the playoff that Jones eventually won. Examples like this were disturbingly common in the twenties; over the years since then, golf galleries have been disciplined by the use of ropes, better-trained marshals, the use of small grandstands, and the invention of the "stadium course," designed expressly to control the habits of spectators.

If we look at sport spectating as an extension of theater, it is clear that the nature of the venue is crucial. In all the major sport venues, except golf, the spectator's vantage point is fixed. A stadium or an arena is simply very different from a golf course. The site of the action is clearly fixed to a prescribed area and, in contrast to a golf course, the area is relatively small. The typical golf fan may wander for miles as he or she watches the action, or they may simply take up a position and watch the event pass before them. Finally, a golf fan may be at the event to see a course and a club that is ordinarily closed to the public. In the twenties, and even today, a golf tournament's attraction may include the chance to wander the grounds and see the famous holes at Augusta, Merion, Oakmont, Baltusrol, Winged Foot, or Pebble Beach.

Beyond all this, golf spectating offered Americans a chance to see heroes. Much has been written about the 1920s as the golden age of sport heroes. No matter how much politicians and commentators babbled on about individualism as the core of the American spirit, the rise of large corporations, the growth of the cities into heartless megalopolises, and the coming of mass production and consumption had produced a deadening conformity and sameness. Sport heroes like Babe Ruth, Red Grange, Bill Tilden, and Jack Dempsey seemed to prove that there was still room in American life for dashing and daring individuals.

The athletic heroes of the 1920s were not a homogeneous group. Football and baseball heroes were the products of a corporate effort. Their deeds were individual, but clearly part of a collective endeavor—the team. While spectators came to see Babe Ruth or Red Grange, in a larger sense they came to see the New York Yankees or the Chicago Bears. Indeed, one might convincingly argue that the highest form of spectator passion in the 1920s was reserved for college football.

On the other side of the ledger stood the stars of individual sports. Tilden in tennis, Jones in golf, or Gertrude Ederle swimming the English Channel. The dominant individual sport of the twenties, however, was boxing. Fights that grossed more than $100,000 were commonplace in the decade. In September 1927, more than one hundred thousand fans saw the second Dempsey-Tunney fight and the controversial "long count" at Soldier's Field in Chicago. It was reported that for his efforts that night Tunney earned $990,000. Boxing, particularly, generated interest by creating heroes and villains and supposed personal feuds between fighters.

The emphasis on sport generically, and on heroes as the product of a public need for talented athletes to replace the pioneers and frontiersmen of the previous century, has obscured an important fact. In the 1920s each sport was establishing its own community with different sorts of heroes and heroic narratives. This led to clear differences between sports and something like a generalized value clash. Golf fans thought boxing too violent and corrupt. Boxing fans thought golf too effeminate and team upper crust. There was also a deep conflict between corporate sports like football and individual sports like golf. As the century evolved, these communities would become more deeply rooted and more central to the ways an American would establish an identity. Out of "fandom" would arise surrogate "nations," complete with "tribal" customs and costumes, and the almost continuous construction of heroes as objects of veneration and emulation.

For golf in the twenties, the two dominant heroes were Robert Tyre Jones Jr. and Walter Hagen, two very different men. Hagen was twice married and twice divorced and was often a poor father to his children. Hagen dropped out of school in the fourth grade and found in golf his life's work. In many ways he invented the job of touring professional, who made his living solely from his playing skill and his ability to entertain. Whatever may have lurked in his soul, on the surface he saw life and golf as a lark. He was dashing and freewheeling on and off the course. It was Hagen who said, "I never wanted to be a millionaire. I just wanted to live like one." And he succeeded. Hagen was often found in the vicinity of expensive cars, beautiful women, and big bets. Near the end of his life he said, "You're only here for a short visit. Don't hurry. Don't worry. And be sure to smell the flowers along the way."

Bob Jones was a very different sort. A devoted husband and father, he was a son of the South, bringing genteel Georgia manners to the nation. Jones was the best-educated premier athlete in American history. He held degrees in engineering from Georgia Tech and English Literature from Harvard. He studied law at Emory and was admitted to the Georgia and federal bars. Jones grew up at the country club and never thought about being a professional like his older friend Hagen. Jones did not simply live up to the amateur ideal, he defined and personified it. Competing at the highest level of the golfing world was, too often, agony for Jones. In 1930, after he won the national amateur and open titles in the United States and Great Britain, he quit competition and never looked back. Through it all, miraculously, he had been only a part-time golfer.

For the American golf fan there was no time between 1922 and 1930 when Hagen and Jones did not seem to be at the top of the game. In those years Jones was the winner or the runner-up in the U.S. Open every year except 1927. He won five U.S. Amateur titles during the same period. In 1926, 1927, and 1930 Jones won the British Open. Hagen won in Britain in 1922, 1924,

1928, and 1929. Only Arthur Haven, in 1923, and Jim Barnes, in 1925, broke the Jones-Hagen control of what was virtually the world's medal-play championship. Hagen's record was different; he played many more events than Jones. Hagen won the PGA Championship a remarkable four straight times between 1924 and 1927. He won the Western Open five times, the last in 1932. Beneath his name we might also list a great number of lesser open titles; he was, after all, trying to make a living winning golf tournaments.

It was this intention to make a living from purse money and exhibitions that sets Hagen apart. After his two U.S. Open wins, in 1914 and 1919, he took a job at the newly created Oakland Hills in Detroit. Exactly why he gave up this job will never be fully known. Clearly, he wanted to make more money. Briefly, in addition to his club job, he tried the brokerage business, an occupation for which he was astonishingly ill-suited. In 1919 Hagen remembered that

> I decided to give up my job and become a full-time "businessman-golfer." I figured I couldn't do justice to a club and follow golf as a business, too. I could concentrate on playing if I left the club. I felt the revenue from exhibitions would be sufficient to compensate for the pro job. This decision of mine caused considerable discussion among both the press and my fellow pros. Most of them were against it, believing I could never make it pay. I suppose my idea originated during the Red Cross exhibitions, when I discovered a great demand for my appearance. Never again did I take on a steady pro job at any club.

In essence, Hagen decided that between purse money and exhibition fees he could make a good living. Very quickly a pattern evolved. Hagen would tour the country following the decent weather from California to Texas to Florida and then north through the Carolinas and the summer season of major events in the North. In order for this to work, Hagen needed to add two elements: a manager and a playing partner.

The manager came first. Hagen had, at first, employed H. B. "Dickie" Martin in this role, but in 1921 Martin decided against throwing in with Hagen full time. Martin's replacement was Robert Harlow, a graduate of the University of Pennsylvania and a journalist with the Associated Press. He abandoned his newspaper career and became Hagen's business agent. Actually a more accurate title would be manager-promoter. Harlow took to the job of selling Walter Hagen, or better yet of selling a concocted image of Hagen. Thus were born the nicknames "Sir Walter" and "the Haig." Thus was born the image of the hard-drinking, fast-living, gambling, golf pro who could stay up all night and still beat almost anybody the next day. Beneath the image-making was the much less glamorous job of making travel arrangements, writing contracts, settling the terms for exhibitions, and handling the many details that arose in what was, in reality, a prosperous small business.

The partner came second. His name was Joe Kirkwood. Born and raised in Australia, he learned the game at an isolated ranch where he had come to work as a drover. He came to dominate golf in the region. After winning the Australian and New Zealand Opens in 1920, he left Australia to test his game against the pros in Britain and the United States. Kirkwood was a fine player but never really came close to winning a major title. In 1922 he won the North and South Open at Pinehurst. Kirkwood brought a second talent to the United States, though. He had learned a number of trick shots when given the job of entertaining war veterans in Australia. This began when he tried to envision how a veteran who had lost an arm or leg might learn to play golf. Over time, Kirkwood developed an act that including hitting shots on one leg, hitting a ball off a watch crystal or a man's foot, and hitting two balls with two clubs swinging simultaneously.

Hagen and Kirkwood met at Pinehurst where both were playing in the 1921 North and South Open. Oddly, they played all four rounds together and shot exactly the same score. On Sunday,

Kirkwood put on a trick-shot demonstration for the hotel guests and many of the other competitors, including Hagen. Halfway through the show Kirkwood claims that a man whom he thought was Jimmy Walker, the mayor of New York, asked the crowd to express their appreciation for this wonderful show. The hat was passed and Kirkwood was handed $770, a staggering amount. The person most staggered by Kirkwood's success was his new friend, Walter Hagen, who suggested that they team up for "some exhibition golf." In a few months, a pattern was set. Kirkwood and Hagen would contract to play a thirty-six-hole exhibition against local pros or amateurs, and Kirkwood would put on an hour-long trick-shot exhibition after the match.

There was a substantial market for this product. An ad for the Hagen-Kirkwood tour that appeared in the *American Golfer* claimed that between July 1922 and April 1923 the duo had played 115 exhibitions with a record of ninety-seven wins, fourteen losses, and four ties. The base fee for the team's services was five hundred dollars. In addition, Hagen played a number of benefit matches for which he received no fee. On top of this, both Kirkwood and Hagen played a full schedule of open tournaments. In the 1922–1923 season, Walter Hagen probably played three hundred rounds of golf. By the middle of 1923, Hagen had proven that you could make a good living as a "touring" professional. All you had to do was play an insane amount of golf and travel wherever there was a club or organization willing to pay your fee.

This idea of a golfing tour by famous players was not invented by Hagen and Kirkwood. As Hagen noted, he and other pros had learned a lot about their potential audiences during the wartime exhibitions. The tours of Vardon and Ray earlier in the century were also instructive. But Hagen and Kirkwood perfected the idea. For them there was no golf season; they toured year-round, going wherever the weather was good and wherever there was an open tournament with a decent purse. In later years, Kirkwood would take up with Sarazen for a tour of

South America and Australia, sponsored by Pan American Airlines. The idea was to show that air travel into these areas went together with golf. Later in the thirties, Kirkwood and Hagen reunited for a world tour. At the end of his life, Joe Kirkwood claimed that he had played 6,500 golf courses.

In the course of the 1920s, Hagen discovered, with Harlow's help, other sources of income. People would pay to have clubs and balls with certain names on them. At first Hagen tried making the clubs himself, but this venture failed. He sold the company and the rights to his name to L. A. Young from Detroit. In addition to an upfront cash payment, Young agreed to pay annual royalties on the sale of any equipment bearing his name. Over time Young established "Haig Ultra" as an iconic name in golf equipment that, to this day, has a place in golf shops and sporting-goods stores.

When one looks at all of the Haig's activities during the 1920s, it is clear that he was a seminal figure. While he did not invent the idea of a touring professional, making a living solely from his playing skill, what he did was to prove that it was possible. And he did it in grand style. Always finely dressed, always keen for the contest, always eager to add to the myth of "the Haig," of "Sir Walter," the drinker, the womanizer, the dashing escape artist, Walter was at bottom a very good golfer, one of the two or three best players of the twenties.

Certainly one might contend that Bob Jones was better. It would be a fruitless debate. The important thing is that Jones was different; he occupied a completely different place in the golf community. Jones was *The Amateur*, a man who did not play for money, a man who played part-time as an adjunct to his real life as a lawyer, businessman, a husband, and a father. We can only wonder how good he would have become if he had played full time. Jones, every year, put his clubs away for long periods as he pursued more education and established himself as an Atlanta lawyer. While Hagen was saturating the market with hundreds of exhibition rounds each year, Jones was making himself scarce. When he did appear for the summer season of national opens and amateurs, the public turned out in huge numbers to see him. The financial benefit flowed not to Jones but to the USGA.

Jones, as a player, was a marked contrast to Hagen. Hagen's swing was never one to emulate; he seemed to sway off the ball and his swing action finished with what looked like a lunge. His magical putting made up for what was not a very good swing technically. Jones, on the other hand, was a golf genius. His swing had a natural fluidity and grace that Hagen's lacked. For Jones there were fewer heroic recoveries; he ground out pars and rounds of amazing consistency. When he putted well he was unbeatable.

Jones made a choice about what to do with his golfing genius. Jones made it clear that he had chosen not to commercialize his talent. He admitted that some thought him a "jackass" for remaining an amateur. But the endless travel and long absences from home held no attraction for him. He made his living as a lawyer and he chose to compete as an amateur. It was also clear that Jones, at some level, did not like performing before huge crowds (he had little patience for rowdy galleries), and he found the intense competition agonizing. Bob Jones was at bottom a modest, private man who sought victory at the highest level of golf while never really embracing the experience.

This was why, as the 1920s ended, he decided to make his 1930 campaign an attempt to win both the national amateurs in Britain and the United States and both the national opens. It was clear that 1930 was going to be a special year. Jones began the season by playing more golf. He actually began to "work out," as we would say today. He played a game called "Doug," a cross between badminton and tennis, supposedly invented by Douglas Fairbanks Sr., the actor. Jones's weight dropped from a winter high of nearly 190, to a trim 165. He played in a winter event for the first time since 1927. In fact, he played in two—the Savannah Open and Southeastern Open, both in Augusta. Players who watched him destroy the field in the Southeastern by thirteen shots thought that Bobby was unbeatable. Bobby Cruickshank predicted that no one could stop Jones from winning the four great titles. Late in April, Jones, with his wife and friends, left for England.

The first order of business was to win the Walker Cup, the biennial contest between teams of American and British amateurs, played in 1930 at Royal St. George in Sandwich. The Americans won seven of the eight singles matches on the way to a 10–2 victory.

The British Amateur began on May 26 at St. Andrews. It was only the third time Jones had entered the British Amateur, with the other two in 1921 and 1926. He had never won this terrifically difficult event. To win, one had to win nine matches, only the final was thirty-six holes, the first eight were eighteen holes. The winner very often was the player who never confronted an opponent who produced a round far over his normal level of play. Some said luck was crucial in determining the winner of the British Amateur and they were right. In the early rounds, Jones experienced great good fortune. In the fourth round he defeated Cyril Tolley, one of Britain's best, in nineteen holes. In the fifth round, Jones holed an eight-footer on the last hole to defeat Harrison Johnston, the American Amateur champion. In the semifinal he defeated George Voigt one up, after being down two after thirteen.

Jones faced Roger Wethered in the thirty-six-hole final. Wethered was one of Britain's finest players, but on this day he did not play well and his putting was particularly unsteady. Jones won 7 and 6, winning the only "major" title that had eluded him. He was the first player to win all four national titles (designated golf's Grand Slam) in a career. Press reports throughout the world had noted how anxious and tired Jones looked. He said that he was happy to win, but admitted that "I never worked so hard, nor suffered so much." Bobby and his wife took a trip to France where Jones did little but rest and recharge.

The British Open in 1930 was played at Hoylake in mid-June. While this was a four-round medal event, luck was still a factor. On day one, Jones completed his round, recording a 70 in good weather in the morning, avoiding the thunderstorms that arrived in the afternoon. After a 72 on the second day, Jones led by one. In the thirty-six-hole final day, Bobby struggled to post a 74 and 75, but it was good enough to win. His challengers, particularly the Englishman Archie Compston, faded badly in the afternoon final round. He had electrified the massive crowd with a 68 in the morning, but could only muster a more than disappointing 82 in the afternoon. British journalists admitted that Jones had won but clearly they also thought that Compston had lost. Again, many witnesses described Jones as an exhausted golfer who seemingly was beating himself to death as his quest for the titles rolled on. Jones was so tired that when he sailed home on the *Europa*, he forgot his clubs, which made the trip later on the *Aquitania*.

When Jones arrived in New York he was greeted by a country that wanted to express its affection. For Jones it was embarrassing. After a ticker tape parade down Broadway, the mayor of New York spent ninety minutes praising Jones and his many virtues; all of it broadcast over NBC Radio. The night of his arrival there was a banquet honoring Bob at the Vanderbilt Hotel. More speeches, more praise.

The next challenge began soon enough. The U.S. Open was played at the Interlachen Golf Club in Minnesota. Here he would be joined by at least one new challenger. Walter Hagen had skipped the British Open to tour the Pacific islands and Asia with Joe Kirkwood. While Jones was collecting trophies in Britain, Hagen was bringing golf to Fiji and discussing the game with the emperor of Japan. Kirkwood and Hagen returned to the United States on June 21, in time to get ready for the Open that began on July 10.

The Open at Interlachen was a punishing physical test. Played in record heat, both players and spectators suffered. A Red

Cross doctor treated a number of cases of heat prostration on the first day alone. But the heat could not keep the fans away; more than ten thousand brave souls showed up on the first day. They saw Jones shoot a 70 that put him in the lead. He benefited from one stroke of good fortune that would become part of Jones lore. On the par-five ninth, Jones was attempting to hit the green in two when he was distracted in the backswing by a young girl moving just in his vision. His shot struck the surface of the pond near the green and skipped across, ending up just in front of the green. He chipped close and made four. Some witnesses claimed that lily pads kept the ball from a watery grave and thus was born the legend of the "lily pad shot."

The Open ended with the traditional thirty-six-hole final day, played on a Saturday to avoid offending local laws and attitudes that frowned on Sunday play. Jones probably won the Open with a morning 68 that gave him a five-shot lead. He eventually won by two over Macdonald South. The wait for the fourth challenge, the U.S. Amateur, would be long; it did not begin until mid-September. It was an uneasy nation that waited with him. As Jones made his way to Merion in Philadelphia, Americans were beginning to suspect that the country's economy was entering something greater than a temporary downturn.

By the time the qualifying rounds were over, and Jones had won the qualifying medal for the fifth time, every American sports fan was hanging on the news from Philadelphia. The weather was glorious and huge throngs turned out to watch Jones. The money they paid did not, of course, go to Jones; it went to the USGA. This was one of the first examples of a situation that has come to plague amateur sport. While the players cannot cash in on their skill, the organizations that run the events can. Finally, the crowds were so large and eager to see Bobby that Jones was assigned a Marine guard to keep fans at bay.

The first two matches were contested over eighteen holes and Jones won both easily. Jones won the next two thirty-six-hole

matches easily; he defeated Jess Sweetser 9 and 8 in the semifinal. On Saturday eighteen thousand fans turned out for the final between Jones and Gene Homans. It was something of an
anticlimax; Jones was seven up after the first eighteen, eventually winning 8 and 7. Only later would the term Grand Slam
arise as the label for what Jones had done.

In the wake of the Slam, Jones made several statements about
his future. It is clear in retrospect that he desperately wanted
to retire from competitive golf. In the locker room at Merion,
just after receiving the trophy, Jones told a fellow player that
tournament golf was "wrecking my health, stunting my business ambitions; and I am sick of it all." It was this feeling that
won out—on November 17, Jones officially retired from competitive golf. At age twenty-eight he simply walked off the stage
he had just come to dominate.

This dramatic exit by the game's most popular player provides a clear end to golf in the twenties—the so-called golden
age. Golf, after 1930, faced a solid decade and a half of decline
and transformation. If we look back on golf in the 1920s, on Hagen, Jones, and the dramatic rise in the number of courses and
players, we can easily conclude that the golf community had its
best decade. On the competitive side, two great lasting models
had been established—Jones, the pure amateur, and Hagen,
the "touring" professional. On the participant side, the private
club was the dominant sort of course, but there were growing
numbers of municipal and daily-fee courses.

However, if we are trying to create a full picture of the golf
community, this summary obscures more than it reveals. First,
the Jones model had very little influence on the future, particularly at the national level. Jones was the best and last of his kind.
After 1930 the national opens of the United States and Britain
would be dominated by professionals. The national amateurs
would sharply decline in importance. The followers of the Jones
model would, in the future, be found at the state and local level.
Men, almost always businessmen, would have Jones-like careers

winning state and regional amateur titles multiple times and become "famous" on the more limited stage. The Hagen model had a much brighter future. By the late 1930s a new generation of professionals was stepping forward, moving along the path created by Hagen and Sarazen. Nelson, Hogan, and Snead would give way to Palmer, Nicklaus, and Player. All owe a debt to Walter Hagen. He was their patron saint.

Second, and most important, something subtle but crucial happened to the way Americans thought about golf. This was the culmination of a long, complicated process that began in the early 1890s. Golf, as a leisure time activity and sport, was linked, in a special way, to white male businessmen and real estate speculation. These linkages would have a significant impact on the evolution of the golf community up to the present.

In order to explain what I have in mind here, it is helpful to paint a picture of the average 1920s member of the American golf community. First of all, everything we know about golf suggests that this person will be a white male and a businessman. Statistics quoted earlier in the chapter make our average Joe a member of a private club. Let us also assume that Joe holds a set of attitudes that have slowly been constructed since 1890. He is a member of the second full generation in American golf. His father took up the game in 1895, the same year Joe was born. In 1925, Joe would be thirty.

Joe would believe at a superficial level that golf was for everyone. He would have read magazine articles that linked golf with equality. His wife goes to the club and enjoys the game as do his children. But at a deeper level his views are more complex. Golf in the fullest sense was not for everyone.

By 1910 two things would happen that Joe, as he grew to adulthood, would absorb at this deeper level. The first was the idea that golf in America had special qualities that made it uniquely valuable to business and professional men. There were varying arguments, but they all came down to the idea that modern business was producing a generation of nervous and anxious men who saw success and profits as all-consuming goals. They worked fewer hours, but those hours were more intense and exhausting. Golf was the antidote. As Walter Travis put it in a 1910 *American Golfer* editorial, golf was "eminently suitable and especially adapted for the great mass of professional and businessmen of all ages." Because of its special link to businessmen, Travis was convinced that "in the next decade it [golf] will become an impressive national institution."

In the same 1910 editorial, Travis noted that the attitude toward the land upon which private golf clubs rested was beginning to change. Early in golf's development clubs rented land and, in general, avoided making big investments in a game that might have turned out to be a passing fad. By 1910, as Travis claimed, the land devoted to golf was increasingly seen as an investment and the private club was becoming less a low-cost lark and more a potentially profitable business. Travis testified that clubs were making every effort to own the land upon which their courses lay and that they were trying to acquire adjacent land because "the history of all golf clubs shows a substantial enhancement in the value of adjacent property."

By the middle of the 1920s these two elements—the dominance of businessmen and role of real estate speculation—had become central tenets of the golf community. Joe, our average American golfer, found himself in an unusual, ironic situation. He joined a private club because he needed an escape from business, but he soon realized that the club he had joined was a business itself. He served on committees that considered club expansion, that debated moving the club to a better (and perhaps more profitable) site, or he spent hours examining the club's budget, which became larger and more complex every year. The quest for restorative leisure had led to what looked a lot like work. It should be noted, however, that Joe was producing the leisure venue that he and his family were consuming. In the evolving consumer culture, this connection between consumption and production would become exceedingly rare.

The placement of businessmen at the top of golf's hierarchy led, inevitably, to the placement of other groups below them. Reflecting an intensely racist era, golf found only a small place for black Americans. Blacks no doubt played, but for our average Joe, they did so out of his sight. There is no way to measure play by African Americans prior to 1930. There were several black-only clubs, most notably the Shady Rest Golf Club in New Jersey. The barriers to competition for blacks were impenetrable; black golfers simply never appeared in regional or national championships. Shunned, they created their own organizations and staged their own tournaments.

There was at least one exception to this bleak picture. His name was Dewey Brown. Born in North Carolina, in 1898, Brown took a job at the exclusive Morris County Golf Club where he learned to make clubs under the eye of Tom Hucknell, the club's professional. Over time his game developed to a high level, and he earned a reputation as an excellent teacher. He made sets of clubs for many notable people such as Warren Harding and Calvin Coolidge. In 1928 the PGA took him in as a member; the organization was apparently unaware of his race. In 1934, without explanation, they revoked his membership, beginning the white-only era of the PGA that would last until the early 1960s. Dewey Brown was still in the golf business by then and was re-admitted to the PGA.

African Americans were allowed one role in golf, and that was the job of caddie, especially in the South. As winter golf in the South became popular in the 1920s, the black caddie became something like an institution at the resorts that sprang up from Pinehurst to Key West. At Pinehurst, in the twenties, there were 550 caddies, all African Americans. They made up to three dollars a day, which in the Sandhills was a good wage.

Something like the myth of the "happy caddie" grew up in these resort areas. Whites came to believe that black men were ideally suited to carry the clubs of visiting white people. They had the "temperament" of servants and took to the subservient position naturally. This myth was in sharp contrast to the preferred image of caddies in the North. There the ideal caddy was a white teenage male who learned the habits and skills that would serve him well as he moved on to a career in business or the professions. Francis Ouimet and Chick Evans were the models. The job was temporary for white youngsters in the North; it was permanent for black men in the South. Courses in the South turned to African American adult males as caddies for one very practical reason—teen-aged whites were in school during the fall and winter seasons.

As Southern blacks took up caddying, they also took up playing the game. At a number of resorts black caddies found ways to get on a course and play. At Pinehurst, the caddies had a rough course of their own and from their ranks a number of good players emerged.

While African Americans were bluntly excluded from golf, women were admitted, but only under confusing and complex rules. Certainly golf had been presented as a game for both genders. Between 1890 and 1930, women played an important role in the growth of golf. But there was always a complex tension between the women and the men who dominated the game. There were a few men-only clubs that made excluding women a virtue. There were several attempts to create women-only clubs. However, the real issue was played out at the typical country club, which was decidedly a family affair.

At these clubs women had ample, but not complete, access to the game. Certainly the best female player of the 1920s was Glenna Collette. The foundation of her career was laid at the Metacomet Country Club in Rhode Island. At age fourteen, she watched her father tee off and asked to play. As Collette described it in her autobiography, her first attempts were amazingly good and her father and his friends were quite open in their "lavish praise and warm encouragement." Glenna also drew inspiration from watching a Red Cross match that featured Alexa Stirling and Elaine Rosenthal teamed up with Bobby Jones and

Perry Adair. The next day, properly motivated, Collette broke 50 over nine holes for the first time. By the mid-1920s she was the dominant American woman player. In 1924 Collette won fifty-nine out of sixty matches. She did it in fine style; she was a truly long hitter and fierce competitor.

Because a player like Collette could emerge from the country club environment does not mean that all women were treated equally. At most clubs, tee times were structured to accommodate businessmen. Women were often excluded on weekend mornings and commonly on certain weekday afternoons. Notions of what constituted a proper female did not simply evaporate. The idea that a woman could be a competitive athlete won some ground in the 1920s but it was nothing like a total victory.

The best evidence of this comes from Glenna Collette herself. Her 1928 autobiography was full of hope and encouragement for women. She argued that golf, in all respects, was good for women. The game was "singularly fitted to meet the needs of women desirous for keeping slim and healthy" and it could prevent "monotonous hours in beauty-parlours." She believed that only the ability to drive the ball comparable distances kept women from level competition with men.

By 1930 Collette seems to have experienced a change of heart. In a magazine article, in the *Outlook and Independent,* she stated that very few women could or would follow her example. She claimed that golf required that a woman "harden those arm muscles, toughen those wrists, flatten that chest, and soften those curves," but few women were willing to do this. She also believed that if a woman took up the game seriously she would confront huge obstacles, the most important being male dominance at American golf courses. Collette married Edwin H. Vare Jr. in 1931. She continued to compete, but she seemed sure that few American women would follow her example.

The presence of Jews on American golf courses and at golf resorts profoundly complicated the picture of the 1920s golf community. Anti-Semitism among gentile elites led to the exclusion of Jews from clubs, neighborhoods, and resorts. At Pinehurst the resort made strenuous efforts to exclude Jews from the hotels and expressly banned them from buying property in the village. Many golf clubs invented either outright bans on Jewish membership or found less overt methods to keep their membership free of Jews. In the towns that could support three or more clubs, segregation by religion in golf was the general rule.

Jewish groups fought their exclusion by building their own notable clubs and courses. In 1926 *American Hebrew* magazine claimed that there were fifty-eight Jewish country clubs, seventeen in the Greater New York area. Several of these were among the earliest founded: Inwood Country Club was established in 1902 and the Century Club in 1898. As suburbanization changed the nature of every major city, Jews and Gentiles created rigidly exclusive enclaves. As these enclaves grew, residents created golf and country clubs as the social center of the suburb. Lake Shore Country Club (Chicago) in Glencoe, and Westwood Country Club, still within the city limits of St. Louis, were examples of this process. This suggests yet another way in which real estate issues shaped the American golf community

While Jews were barred from gentile clubs, they exhibited a considerable amount of gender and ethnic exclusivity themselves. The *American Hebrew* estimated that of the 17,500 members at Jewish clubs only 4,164 were women. Twenty-two of the clubs had all-male memberships. The clubs were founded by German Jews who had had a much longer history in the United States. One of their motives in founding new clubs and suburbs was to seal themselves off from the more recent Jewish immigrants who came from eastern Europe and Russia.

Golf, because it was the most important country club sport, became implicated in this social drama starring gentile and Jewish clubs. Because so many clubs were closed to Jews and African Americans, and because they often limited participation by women, golf was convicted by some critics of being inherently sexist, racist, and anti-Semitic. The game was found guilty by association.

In fact, though, golf helped to weaken barriers between groups. The game created a place where both Jews and Gentiles could play and compete and where the rules called for absolute equality. Gene Sarazen, who as an Italian understood ethnic bias all too well, was the pro at Fresh Meadow Golf Club, a Jewish club on Long Island. He thought that golf was "one of the most potent forces" bringing Jews and Gentiles together. Jewish clubs joined local, state, and regional golf associations. Inevitably golfers of all backgrounds were thrown together in tournaments and charity events. Jewish clubs also hosted notable national championships. The U.S. Open was played at Inwood in 1923 and at Fresh Meadow in 1932 (Sarazen won). The 1921 PGA was contested at Inwood and the 1930 edition at Fresh Meadow. Country clubs helped people express their fears and biases; they were associations created to a give a group, usually white Protestants, an enclave safe from contact with groups deemed alien and threatening. Golf helped, if only in a small way, to undercut this purpose. The game's traditions called for equality and equal access.

In essence, golf by 1930 was shaped by the same struggles that defined American culture. The reality of exclusionary racial and gender attitudes warped the evolving golf community. But this warping was subtle and complex. The golf community was a hierarchy with white businessmen at the top. African Americans were the most rigorously excluded, but they seeped into the game in small numbers. Their role as caddies, especially in the South, gave them a tiny door into the community of golfers. Women were pushed into a subordinate position, but certainly golf was easier on them than most other sports. Golf seemed more allowable, more appropriate than other more violent, personally competitive games. It is also just a brute fact that some significant portion of women could play the game better than the vast majority of men. Glenna Collette could play better than 99 percent of the American male players. Given this, what excuse could be offered for excluding women from the game?

Was there any excuse for excluding children, especially males, from the golf community? Again, by the 1920s, the attitude toward children and golf was subtle and complex. Everyone agreed that taking up the game early in life helped one become a better player. Yet there was a view that limited participation by young males. A 1925 *Outlook* article by Charles K. Taylor expressed many of the typical attitudes. He claimed that one no longer needed "to make any apology or defense of golf." Golf, "for the mature man — the office man in particular — has come as a very real godsend, because its fascination will get him out into the open air as few other interests can."

However, "when the growing boy comes into the picture, other considerations arise." Taylor believes that golf will be physically harmful to young boys. He thinks that golf is "a body-twisting exertion — all in one direction." Because of this, too much golf "seems likely to produce a kind of lopsided development." Plainly, this is just ill-informed. There is no evidence that golf distorts bodily development.

Taylor is in fact more interested in "the social side" of the issue. He worries about the boy who learns to play well and plays often with grown men. The praise and flattery of old men will have a bad effect; it will "encourage the boy away from the normal sports of boyhood — the fine cooperative combat sports, which mean so much — to a noncombative game, an individualistic game, played in the society of men rather than boys." One can only guess at the fears that underlay this view.

Taylor argues that boys need combative, cooperative, team sports as the key to developing a good character. He wants boys playing a sport "in which the boy acts as a member of a team, each member sinking his own individual impulses and desires for the benefit of the team as a whole." In the end, Taylor advises boys to play golf with moderation and to play "in the society of his boy friends, and not in the adult environment of the usual golf club."

Certainly, attitudes like these were contested. Schools adopted golf as a regular sport. Young males found in golf and caddying a healthy way to spend a summer and to make a bit of money. No theme in golf literature seems more durable than narratives that trace the passing of the game and its values from father to son (and rarely to a daughter). Over the years, however, golf has lagged behind team sports as they became increasingly important in high schools, colleges, and universities.

"Golf ideology" was itself stirred by the issue of character building in sport. On one side were advocates of golf as the best builder of character. The game taught self-reliance within a stout contest of civility, honesty, and rule-bound behavior. At the same time, there were those, like Taylor, who thought that team sports that taught cooperation and submerging of the self were superior to golf. By 1930, a vague but important pattern had begun to emerge. One played team sports as a youth, learning cooperation and teamwork, and turned to individual sports later in life as stress-reducing, healthful diversions. As for team sports, youthful participation prepared you for a lifetime of spectating, of watching the very best play your childhood game. Ironies abound: major league baseball players, especially when released from their paid jobs, turned, of course, to golf.

As we know, the 1920s came to an end with a crash and a slow slide into the Great Depression. It seemed to bring so many things to an end—the end of Republican Party dominance, the end of talk about permanent prosperity, the end of play, and the end, for a time, of a business-dominated American culture.

In golf, too, there was a profound sense that something had come to an end. This had much to do with Bob Jones. His retirement marked the end of an era. The dominance of amateur golf ended with Jones. Since then a few figures have arisen in the amateur ranks to challenge the pros, but these are single, lonely figures. After 1930 the best players were the pros, and the PGA would rise with the talent of its members. Somehow this was all symbolized by the fact that Jones was the last premier player to use only hickory shafts.

The crash and Depression ended a fabulous era of growth for golf. From 1890 to 1930 (stemmed only by the war) golf grew luxuriously. From zero to almost six thousand courses. From no players to more than two million. Hundreds of millions were spent for equipment, clothes, and gimmicks. Its temple was the country club, its priest was the professional, and its patron saint was the businessman.

So this must have been the golden age of golf? In some respects this was clearly true. Who can doubt that Bob Jones was truly a remarkable athlete? Who would not wish to see his like again? Who can deny that the 1920s was a great era for course construction?

But all golden ages come with excesses and flaws. Golf during the twenties lost its simplicity and, in predictable ways, moved away from its democratic, egalitarian traditions. Watching others play eroded the commitment to play the game. Too many accepted the vicarious thrill of watching a hero play as a substitute for playing the game itself. But most important was the onrush of money. There had been warnings that golf was a simple, austere game and that there was no room for huge clubhouses and expensive trappings. In the 1920s these warnings were brushed aside and courses found themselves overshadowed by clubhouses modeled on the homes of European aristocrats. Along with a golf course, affluent Americans grasped for something they could not really have — aristocratic distinction in a democratic mass society. So it was not all golden. After 1930, the golf community went through a long period of reappraisal, self-criticism, and rebuilding.

CHAPTER SEVEN

Golf in the 1930s

I have a friend who claims to know the iron rule of golf history. Its short form goes like this: golf, in all of its manifestations, thrives when the stock market goes up and shrinks when the market goes down. Simple as that.

Certainly there is some truth to this view. Golf is dependent on discretionary dollars, and when the market is up, people have more of these dollars. They play more, buy more equipment, build more expensive courses, travel to see more tournaments, and join more country clubs. During the bull market of the 1920s, affluent Americans poured a fortune into golf. At the time, going into debt seemed like a good idea; everything was going up, so why not expand the country club, buy new clubs (steel shafts!), or travel south for a winter golf vacation? Everything, one assumed, would cost more next year. Luxury crept into every aspect of the game: more cashmere, more leather, more fancy country clubs, more expensive travel to Europe, South America, and the American South and West. Golf was no different than many other aspects of American life; wretched excess and debt crept in, unnoticed, and became the norm.

As the Depression settled in, Americans looked back and saw the foolishness of the previous decade's extravagance. For the golf community, the early thirties was a time of reflection and self-criticism. The collapsing stock market did not merely shrink golf; it made golfers and country clubs reconsider what they had done since the war. Out of this reconsideration, a conflict emerged between two traditions that structured the game. One tradition called for a simple, inexpensive game, while the other tradition called for luxury and complexity (it should be noted, however, that both of these visions of golf called for the exclusion of "undesirable elements"). This conflict between "cheap-simple" and "expensive-complex" is one of the defining elements of the golf community to this day. Also, if we focus solely on the economy of the 1930s and its impact on golf, we will surely overlook the fact that many elements of the game stabilized and became more deeply rooted during the decade. All the basic structural elements of the golf community survived the thirties, and by the early fifties it had emerged from two decades of economic strife and war ready to get big again.

There can be little doubt, however, that the golf community got smaller in the 1930s. The massive growth in courses and players that occurred in the twenties slammed to a halt. Despite these setbacks, it is crucial to note that, ultimately, golf never actually went into reverse. The most important golf organizations suffered but survived. A 1936 *Business Week* survey found that membership at social, professional, yacht, and country clubs was down 14 percent between 1929 and 1936. The United States Golf Association struggled throughout the decade. Approximately 1,100 clubs belonged to the organization in 1930, but this number had dropped to 763 in 1936. *Business Week* estimated that the total number of country-club members had shrunk by one million between 1925 and 1936. On the other hand, daily-fee and municipal courses actually increased. Municipal courses tripled their numbers between 1925 and 1936 (184 to 576). Daily-fee courses grew to slightly more than a thousand in 1935.

Certainly, there was a relationship between all of these numbers. It was especially common for a private club to go under and emerge as a municipal or private daily-fee enterprise. Geoffrey Cornish and Ron Whitten, in their very useful history *The Golf Course*, estimate that between 1932 and 1952, six hundred courses closed permanently (ultimately becoming lots or parks), and approximately one thousand new courses opened. Some of these new courses were important in the evolution of golf. Too often the emphasis is on the lost courses of the thirties, rather than on those gained.

In the public realm, one project clearly stands out: the four-course complex installed in Bethpage State Park, located near Farmingdale on Long Island. In 1934 the Bethpage Park Authority acquired almost 1,400 acres that had once been a private estate. The parcel contained a private golf course designed by Devereux Emmet, and plans were drawn to renovate the existing course and construct three additional courses. A. W. Tillinghast was hired as a consultant and designer. The federal government, through the Civilian Works Administration, provided the funds for the labor and material. The most notable of the courses, the Black, opened in 1936 and has hosted many important events, including the 2002 and 2009 U.S. Opens. When completed in the thirties, Bethpage was undoubtedly the largest public golf facility in the world.

Also noteworthy was the construction of the George Wright Municipal Course in the Hyde Park section of Boston. The course was named after the Cincinnati Reds and Boston Red Sox baseball player whose sporting goods store in Boston had become a fixture. Wright was a promoter of public golf; he had laid out the city's first course at Franklin Park in 1890.

The George Wright Course was built on the failed plans for a private course. A group had acquired the Henry Grew estate and was going to establish a club with a course designed by Donald Ross, but these plans were abandoned in 1929. They were revived in 1931 when the city, by eminent domain, took over the site. The land turned out to be an enormous problem: it was mostly rock and swamp. In a newspaper story, Donald Ross remarked that to build a course on the site, you would need one of two things: "a million dollars or an earthquake."

There was a third possibility: the federal government could

decide to fund projects that provided work for the unemployed and produced something worthwhile. By 1938, when the course opened, the project had cost more than a million dollars. At times there were over one thousand workers laboring on the project, which included the construction of a $200,000 club-house of indeterminate style designed by Walter Greymont, a Works Progress Administration architect. It had some Norman and Tudor elements; the whole pile reminded one of an English manor house. Over seventy-two thousand cubic yards of soil were spread, thirty tons of dynamite was used to dislodge the rock ledge, and more than eight thousand feet of drainage pipe were used to dry up the wet areas. The best student of Ross's work, Bradley Klein, believes that Ross never had to do more work to make a course "fit the land."

The course opened with great fanfare. Boston's mayor Maurice Tobin hit the first shot wide right and out-of-bounds. This was quickly deemed a "practice shot"; his second attempt was straight and long. Newspaper accounts describe the mayor as surrounded by 250 of the 350 "members" who had paid thirty-five dollars in annual dues. The daily fee was two dollars. Klein suggests that George Wright Municipal was "nominally public, but the clientele was disproportionately upscale." The clubhouse became a favorite site for parties, proms, and weddings. For a public course, the city made great efforts to keep people out, and it was one of the first in the nation to be surrounded by a security perimeter of rock walls and fences.

Both Bethpage and George Wright Municipal suggest that growth in municipal courses during the thirties was not a complete turn toward simple, inexpensive courses for the masses. There were members who had considerable sway over what happened at the course. This led to efforts to keep "rougher" elements out. The model was substantially based on the private clubs and courses built earlier in the century. Bethpage Black was clearly modeled after Pine Valley. A 1934 *Golf Illustrated* article on Bethpage suggests that the courses at Bethpage will allow players "to enjoy a round under conditions parallel to a first-rate private club." The article also notes that "polo matches will be conducted every Sunday afternoon."

The long-term future of the municipal courses built in the thirties was not often good. A steady commitment to facilities built with federal help and deflated Depression-era dollars was frequently not forthcoming. In addition, upscale golfers who took to municipal courses in the thirties often returned to private clubs when the economy improved after the war. Golf and golf courses were hard to defend during downturns. The history of George Wright Municipal serves as an example. By the middle of the 1970s, Boston's city golf courses had deteriorated considerably. In 1976 the Franklin Park Course was closed, and George Wright was on life support. City officials struck notes that were familiar in city after city. Staffer Barry Brooks, from the mayor's office, explained that closing (and not funding) golf courses was a matter of priorities. He claimed: "You must maintain vital services. A recreational program serving so few, and mostly adults, does not compare in need with some of the city's other programs." In 1975 Boston's city courses recorded a deficit of $146,637. These courses had 315 full-time members and 13,155 paid single rounds. These numbers were the product of a decline in the conditions at the city's courses. Indeed, Franklin Park had been in an "almost unplayable condition" for years, the *Boston Globe* claimed. The paper also noted that Franklin Park was close to a "deteriorating area." There had been robberies and muggings on the back nine. The course had given up putting pins and flags in the cups; they were stolen as quickly as they were replaced. In 1975 the Franklin Park clubhouse burned to the ground.

The George Wright Course was in a better condition than Franklin Park. The *Globe* reported, however, that vandalism was much worse, because there was more to damage. There was more play at George Wright, but the operating deficit was much larger than at Franklin Park. The culprit was a decline in daily-fee players, coupled with the low daily charge of only three dollars on weekends. There were accusations that members were routinely given special privileges by those running the course, referred to as the "inner club." One city official charged that the course was run "like a private club." Members dominated weekend-morning tee times and actively discouraged walk-ons. The *Globe* also claimed that many city workers paid no fee at all. This was especially true of policemen and firemen.

George Wright lives on in good shape. There is considerable irony to this situation: a course and a clubhouse built as a social and economic experiment, built by men paid by the federal government, was saved by the intervention of a private, voluntary association. In 1983 the Massachusetts Golf Association leased the course from the city. The MGA turned to Bill Flynn, a professional who had won the New England Professional Golfers' Association (PGA) Championship and had considerable experience running golf courses. His plan was simple: "We want to turn this [George Wright] into a public country club with a good course and a good restaurant." Faced with a tax-cutting ballot initiative (Proposition 2½), the city had no choice; they could either close the course or lease it to the MGA. In 2004 the city regained control of the course, and it is widely considered one of the best public courses in New England.

Public municipal courses, since the thirties, have often gone the way of George Wright. Bethpage slowly deteriorated until a huge infusion of cash from the USGA saved it and made it into the poster child for public courses. Other cities have done better, but clearly cities in general have often proven to be poor stewards of good golf courses. Taxpayers generally do not like to subsidize golf. Courses often fail as the section of the city in which they reside slides downhill. Finally, private daily-fee courses and the companies that operated them complained that tax-supported courses constituted unfair competition. In the end, the golf community has often found public ownership of courses to be problematic and unreliable.

Among the private courses that the golf community produced and maintained in the thirties, there are two that serve as pertinent examples. Both took root outside the Northeast homeland of golf (one in California, and one in Georgia). Both were connected back to Scotland, since both were—for the most part—designed by the transplanted Scot, Alistair MacKenzie. The two courses—Pasatiempo, in California, and Augusta National, in Georgia—were three thousand miles apart, but deeply connected in a number of other ways. They both illustrated some of the fundamental realities that confronted golf during the Depression.

Pasatiempo was the production of Marion Hollins, certainly one of the most important women in golf history. Hollins grew up on Long Island in an atmosphere shaped by affluence. Her father, Harry B. Hollins, was wealthy enough to provide Marion with whatever she wished on the family's Long Island estate, Meadow Farm. At first it was horses, then Marion took up golf at the Westbrook Golf Club (1894), where her father had been one of the founders. Marion traveled extensively in Europe and Great Britain, where she saw all the famous courses and picked up the habits of the English upper class.

After 1913, when her father went bankrupt, Marion was on her own. She continued to play golf and became one of America's best players. She won the USGA Women's Amateur in 1921 and routinely did well in most of the better women's events. Perhaps more importantly, she was drawn to the creation of clubs and courses. She was the prime mover in the creation of the Women's National Golf and Country Club on Long Island near Glen Head. Hollins was a genius at raising money for such projects. The Women's National was financed by women, most of them recruited by Hollins, and only women could become members. Hollins was adept at getting to the wives of the ultra rich. Money came in from ladies with notable last names: Mellon, Pratt, Whitney, and Frick. The club, which opened in 1923, survived for eighteen years, and is today part of the Glen Head Country Club.

By the midtwenties, Hollins had fallen in love with California. She had met Samuel F. B. Morse III while on vacation in the West, and he offered Marion a position that would place her in the middle of Morse's attempt to develop the Monterey Peninsula as the golf capital of the West. In this position, she did many things, but most notably, she was the key figure in the founding of Cypress Point Golf Club. This club and its course have, over the years, become iconic.

Hollins was not satisfied to be just an agent of someone else's success. In 1928 she purchased a piece of land near Santa Cruz, and after raising money in the East, she built Pasatiempo Country Club and Estates. It opened on September 8, 1929, just before the crash. The club had everything: an expensive course designed by MacKenzie, a polo field, a steeplechase course, a swimming pool, a huge clubhouse, and housing lots for sale along the fairways. Hollins thought, with good reason, that she could ignore the deepening Depression. Just as she was opening Pasatiempo, Hollins entered into an oil venture with Franklyn R. Kenney. Marion, once again, was able to raise money from back East, and the first hole they punched into Kettleman Hills produced a gusher. In May 1930, Hollins sold out for $2.5 million.

Even this fortune did not insulate Hollins and Pasatiempo from the challenge of the Depression. In the thirties, the club had been a center of elite social life in California. Movie stars like Mary Pickford and Brian Aherne were frequent visitors, where they mingled with the Vanderbilts and the Crockers. By 1937, however, Hollins was hopelessly in debt. The cost of water to keep her course alive was a major factor. Never had the phrase "sucked dry" been more appropriate. That same year, she was seriously injured in an automobile accident. In 1940 she sold her interest in Pasatiempo and returned to work for Del Monte Properties. She had lost all of her oil money, plus $650,000 in an attempt to save her club. In 1937 her childhood club, the Westbrook Golf Club, where she had learned to play golf and love the life, folded for financial reasons.

After Hollins gave up on Pasatiempo, it went through a long period of strife and litigation. It emerged as a hybrid; there were private owners, but the public played the course for a daily fee. Today, it ranks as one of the nation's very best courses open to the public.

At about the same time that Hollins was beginning to pour her oil money into Pasatiempo, two men in Georgia were planning a club that would become more than iconic (if that is possible) in the golf community. Augusta National Golf Club was the product of Bob Jones and Clifford Roberts. Not only did they create a club and a course, they created a tournament to promote the club. This tournament, of course, has become one of the four most important golf events in the world, and the only one played on the same course each year.

Jones had often expressed a desire to build a championship course in the South. After the Grand Slam and his retirement, Jones returned to Atlanta and his legal career. He also produced a series of instructional films that may have netted him more than a quarter of a million dollars. He signed a lucrative deal with Spalding, and by 1932 golfers were the target of a glossy ad urging them to buy a set of clubs that included a replica of Jones's famous putter, Calamity Jane. As a celebrity, he found certain aspects of his life difficult. He discovered that a weekday round with friends at East Lake could easily turn into something like an exhibition with sizable gallery. Jones wanted a place to play that would protect his privacy.

In 1926 Jones had met Roberts and the two had become friends. Roberts knew that Bob wanted to build a course as a private preserve. In 1930 it was Roberts who suggested that such a club could be built in Augusta, Georgia.

Clifford Roberts was to become a very important person in the history of American golf. Born Charles DeClifford Roberts Jr., in 1894, on a farm near Morning Sun, Iowa, he was not from a background that one would associate with the world of exclusive golf clubs. David Owen, whose *Making of the Masters* is the most well-researched and careful picture of Roberts, the club, and the Masters, has painted Roberts's early life as grim and strange. Basing his conclusions on the diary of Roberts's mother, Rebecca, Owen suggests that "the underlying themes are of dislocation and despair." His father was something more than restless. He would purchase a business and quickly trade it for a store or some other kind of business. The family moved often, and their financial status and security would wax and wane dramatically. Clifford's father was often absent pursuing some deal in another state, and his mother was often ill with one of a number of ailments. She was clearly depressed. In 1909, at age sixteen, through a careless act with a match, Clifford burned down the family home. In 1913 his mother gave up the fight; she went out early one morning and shot herself in the chest with a shotgun.

By 1915 Clifford was on his own, selling men's clothing wholesale in a huge territory that included most of the Midwest. Roberts, at this point in his life, reflected the values we associate with the young men in the Horatio Alger stories. His goal was to rise in the world, and like many Alger heroes, the rise began with a move to New York City. He purchased new clothes, he studied the lives of men who had become wealthy, and he learned whatever he could about colleges and universities that had produced the Eastern elite. School for Clifford Roberts had stopped with the eighth grade.

After one failed attempt to establish himself in New York, Roberts tried again in 1918. This time he put down some roots. He was drafted into the army, where he trained at Camp Hancock in Augusta, Georgia; Roberts spent much of the decade after the war struggling to make it as an investment adviser and broker. It is important to note that Roberts never became wealthy in the twenties. When he met Jones, Roberts was, at best, a minor figure in the New York financial world.

Why exactly did Bob Jones and Clifford Roberts become partners of a sort in the making of Augusta National? I have never read a satisfactory answer to this question. Certainly, Roberts proved to have a knack for assisting heroes; he proved this with both Bob Jones and Dwight Eisenhower. In any event, for almost fifty years, Clifford Roberts contributed in countless ways to the construction and evolution of golf's most iconic and controversial club and course. He was the most important influence in shaping the Masters Tournament.

The first step in the building of Bob Jones's course was to determine a place to set the club. Augusta, Georgia, made a lot of sense for a number of reasons. It was convenient to Atlanta and familiar to both Jones and Roberts. There was already a resort hotel and the Augusta Country Club in place. Perhaps most crucial was the existence of a virtually perfect piece of land. Jones and Roberts saw a 365-acre parcel that, since 1858, had been the Fruitland Nurseries, owned by Prosper Berckmans. By 1918 the nursery had gone under, and in the twenties it had been the site of a failed attempt to construct a golf course and hotel. In January 1931, they took an option to buy the property.

This set in motion the creation of the business side of the endeavor. Roberts assembled a group of underwriters, which included Bob Jones and his father. A real estate company was created — the Fruitland Manor Corporation — which purchased the land for fifteen thousand dollars in cash and the assumption of sixty thousand dollars in debt.

The plan for the club was modeled after the megaclubs of the 1920s. There would be 1,800 members, two golf courses (a championship course and one for the "ladies"), tennis and squash courts, and a new, expensive clubhouse. When this plan was drawn, Roberts and Jones no doubt thought the economic downturn was temporary and that raising money for a club connected to Bob Jones would be easy. The incorporated club would lease the land for the courses and, over time, eventually buy it. The real estate company would retain a sizable chunk to sell as house lots. Almost none of this came to pass. As the economic darkness spread, Roberts slowly and steadily pared back the original plan.

Roberts began his membership drive in the spring of 1931. Armed with massive mailing lists and an aggressive pitch that emphasized the uniqueness of the club and the connection to Jones, Roberts had high hopes. A year into the drive, the club had attracted thirty-six members. The search for a membership whose fees would fund operations never really worked until after World War II. The club was able to limp along only because the costs were born by a small group of underwriters who loaned the club money that was never repaid.

The irony is that economic reality forced Augusta to greatly simplify the original plan and, in the long run, this is what made the club successful. The plan for a grand multipurpose country club was abandoned, and the focus was put on building the course. There would be no tennis courts, no house lots, no new grand clubhouse, and no women. Instead, there would be just the one course, and they would remodel and enlarge the existing manor house into one of the most familiar buildings in golf.

The course grew directly out of the desire of Bob Jones to duplicate in Georgia the golf design he had seen in California and Scotland. In 1929 Jones lost in the first round of the U.S. Amateur played at Pebble Beach. After the loss, he and others, including Francis Ouimet, played a round at Cypress Point. The next day, he was a part of an opening-day exhibition match at Pasatiempo in Santa Cruz. This was his introduction to the work of Alister MacKenzie. Jones already knew Marion Hollins. Cypress Point and Pasatiempo convinced Jones that when he built a course he wanted MacKenzie as its architect.

MacKenzie first visited Augusta and appraised the site in July 1931. Construction had, at that point, not been approved. This did not come until February 1932. Once started, the course was built with astonishing speed. MacKenzie returned to oversee the final contouring of the greens. Workers were mowing the course early in June. By one account, the course was completed in seventy-six days. The total cost: approximately $115,000. The club paid the workers who labored on the course, but MacKenzie was not so lucky. When he died in January 1934, the club still owed him most of his fee and related expenses.

The resulting course was clearly the product of Jones and MacKenzie, but there was also input from Marion Hollins. At MacKenzie's request, she visited the course just before construction and passed her observations on to MacKenzie. Since the club famously became a male bastion, it is ironic that a woman played some part in the design.

Some have assumed that the invention of what was to become the Masters helped the club get on its feet in the 1930s. Gene Sarazen's legendary double eagle on fifteen, in 1935, made great newspaper copy but it did little to help the tournament or the club. Actually, the tournament, by one measure, shrank during the thirties. In 1934 seventy-two players accepted an invitation to play, but that number had sunk to fifty-six in 1939. Pros found it difficult to add the Masters to their schedule when they had to get back to their northern club jobs. Many simply gave up playing the so-called winter tour altogether.

The most interesting aspect of Augusta's early history is that it did by necessity what many in golf thought the whole sport needed to do. Augusta National survived because it simplified its original plans. Instead of building a multicourse, multipurpose family country club with lots for sale, the club, led by Roberts, focused on the single golf course, and on being "just golf."

As Augusta was taking its first steps in this direction, several commentators were calling for all of golf to embrace a return to simplicity. In the end, the demand for simplicity turned out to be not so simple. As the Depression set in, there was a tendency to examine the excesses of the twenties. Golf clubs were deemed to be one such excess. A *New York Times* survey of Westchester clubs found that the average budget was $101,000, but that the cost of course maintenance was only $38,000. The *Times* suggested that many golf clubs had evolved to serve as high-class social gathering spots, with "liveried flunkeys everywhere and a

general air of expensiveness." Another *Times* survey found that
at a number of clubs, the high cost of golf was often caused by
expensive nongolf amenities like pools, club houses, and tennis courts.

In 1933, in the *American Mercury*, Kenneth P. Kempton portrayed the situation in a mildly fictionalized essay. He laid out
the history of an imaginary club founded in 1899. The early
history of the club was simplicity itself. The "fathers" of the club
built a simple course on a few acres of pasture. Golf took root
and the membership grew. Women began to play along with
the men. Kempton believes Americans tend to take everything
to excess. Every aspect of "White Brook," the imaginary club,
grew and became more expensive. Kempton notes that in the old
days, members played in "rough and comfortable clothes," but
by the end of the twenties, players needed "plus fours," match-
ing sweaters and hose, chamois gloves, leather windbreakers,
rubber cape coats, and every new device to improve your swing.
Manufacturers saw the simple game of 1900 as a place to sell
things to an affluent clientele.

At White Brook, the members grew disenchanted with the
early clubhouse. They decided to buy more land for the clubhouse, and they began to sell lots on the edge of the club property to pay for it. Soon they were adding onto the clubhouse.
By the end of the 1920s, White Brook, once a simple male golf
club, had women members, a skating rink, house lots for sale,
a toboggan run, tennis courts, and a new caddie house. Many
of the additions had one goal: to expand the use of the club by
the whole family.

The costs were enormous, but Kempton claims that in the
twenties, the members were "as happy as larks." But then, late in
1929, the curtain began to gently fall on the happy 1920s. Res-
ignations from the club increased, membership drives failed,
and the club began to offer bargain memberships. By the end
of 1932, White Brook was in profound financial trouble.

The essay ends with Kempton's account, again fictionalized,

of the 1933 annual meeting. Barely 10 percent of the membership attends. Those in attendance hear some sound advice from an old gentleman who joined the club in 1900. He claims that golf is not a rich man's game, but that it had become one at White Brook. His program calls for a return to the simple days of 1900. Shut the clubhouse and fire all but ten of the caddies, who will only work for players over seventy. Members should do much of the course maintenance themselves. The members can no longer have a country estate, but they can have a Spartan, austere golf club. Kempton vaguely suggests that the mindless expansion of his club had something to do with the arrival of women. The old club of 1900 was a simple male place; the club of 1927 was a family affair, aristocratic and feminized.

In a 1934 *Golf Illustrated* essay, the New York newspaperman George Trevor was not so subtle. He begins with a question: "How do you like your golf? Simple, homespun, unadorned, with emphasis on the game and its good fellowship, or dolled up in sybarite luxury, embellished with such extravagant and exotic side-shows such as swimming pools, billiard rooms, banquet halls, a solarium, Turkish baths, formal drawing rooms, dance pavilions, and all the other flamboyant accessories which have distorted the original purpose of a golf club."

Trevor favors simplicity. For him, simple golf clubs were done in by "the opulent boom era." This process had a lot to do with women. Trevor sees the old austere clubs as "emasculated" after the war. They lost their "virile qualities" and were "sickled over with feminine fripperies." For women have been "chiefly responsible for the sumptuous excrescences which have transformed golf clubs from plain, unvarnished hang-outs for the devotees of Scotland's game into palatial country clubs." In the new, transformed clubs, men are afraid to "sit in the Louis XV chairs"; they crave a "a soft yet substantial Morris chair." Perhaps most important, a man wishes to be able to "swear like a boatswain if he chooses." The presence of women inhibited this desire. The Depression will tend to create more male-oriented places and peel back the excesses of the roaring twenties. Trevor believes that "the pendulum is swinging back to the bread and butter of recreation after an orgy of pink-iced angel cake."

Thus it was clear that the thirties did more than merely shrink the golf community. As American culture took stock of itself, there was a sense that, during the twenties, things had gotten out of control. There had been too much money, and too much of that money had been spent foolishly. In golf this theme had played itself out in a number of forms. Equipment and clothes had become too expensive — too much cashmere and leather. The most crucial issue was the venue upon which the game was played. From the beginning, there had been two tendencies when it came to courses. One was the simple golf club where the clubhouse was merely functional, and the emphasis was on the course and the game. The second was reflected in the evolution of the American country club. These clubs were significant business enterprises, where land sales and future appreciation of club property was too often uppermost in a member's mind. At the American country club, the game was linked with the social aspirations of affluent American families. The golf course became just one of a number of amenities. The country clubs of the twenties became a way for affluent Americans to have, collectively, a country estate and to take on aristocratic pretensions.

During the 1930s the basic rules under which the game was played were fundamentally stabilized and simplified. Two decisions by the USGA, concerning the ball and the number of clubs allowed, created a stable platform that, to a great extent, has lasted to the present. Late in the 1920s, the USGA grew concerned about the great distances the best players could drive the ball. From 1921 to 1931, the dimensions of the official ball were set at 1.62 inches in diameter and 1.62 ounces in weight. In 1930 the USGA tried an experiment with a lighter ball, and the results were not good. Ordinary players disliked the ball because they believed it reduced the distance on full shots. While the better players seemed to lose no distance at all, people began to call it the "balloon ball." In November 1931, the USGA announced that starting on January 1, 1932, the official ball should not be less than 1.68 inches in diameter and weigh no more than 1.62 ounces. This left ball makers with considerable latitude to make a ball either larger or lighter than the official standard. As any contemporary player knows, this hardly ended the debate about the ball, perhaps the most important piece of a golfer's equipment.

In January 1937 the USGA made another even more basic ruling. Starting a year hence, on January 1, 1938, players would have to make do with a maximum of fourteen clubs. Up to this point, players were allowed any number of clubs; the only limitation was the ability of the player or caddie to lug the clubs around the course. Some very good players, Chick Evans, for example, played and won major events with seven or eight clubs. The ruling came as players and club manufacturers began to experiment with an ever-increasing number of clubs. The USGA thought that "shot making" skill was being taken out of the game by the growing number of clubs. Some players carried as many as thirty clubs. The limit on clubs applied, of course, only to championships; the weekend golfer was still free to employ as many clubs as he or she could get the caddy to carry.

Over time, however, the fourteen-club limit has become virtually universal. Players at all levels accept it as a basic condition of play. I have seen few players, in any context, carry more than fourteen clubs. Fourteen has become, like nine, eighteen, and seventy-two, one of golf's basic numbers. This does not mean that within the fourteen-club limit anything like a standard set was created by the USGA edict. Certainly, a player would find in the 1930s pro shop something like a standard set. It would include four woods, eight irons, and a putter. Over the years, the number of woods has decreased; the two-wood, or brassie, has virtually disappeared. The iron set has come to include as many as four specialized wedges for short shots. This proliferation of wedges also began in the thirties, when Gene Sarazen invented the sand wedge. In doing so, Sarazen took some of the terror out of bunker play and clearly made the game easier. Today one of the little joys of golf is manipulating your frame of mind by subtracting a club (a one-iron, a two-iron) and adding a new, useful implement (a five-wood, a utility club, a lob wedge), all within the fourteen-club limit.

High-level competition during the early thirties entered what might be politely referred to as a lull. The number of lesser events contracted, and in the major events, no compelling figures appeared. Attendance went down as hard-pressed spectators found cheaper alternatives, or simply gave up being fans until the economy improved. Golf missed Bob Jones, and it missed Hagen, who faded rapidly after 1930.

There were some high points. Gene Sarazen had a spectacular year in 1932. He won the British Open at Prince's, a course next to Royal St. George's in Sandwich. This victory came with one of the great caddy stories in golf history. In 1928 Sarazen had purchased from Hagen, for two hundred dollars, the right to employ Old Daniels, a legendary caddy at Royal St. George's. Sarazen played superior golf, except on one hole: the fourteenth at Royal St. George's. In the second round, Sarazen hit his drive far left, avoiding the out-of-bounds to the right. Old Dan suggested an iron to get the ball back in play. Sarazen took a wood instead, and barely advanced the ball. He was lucky to take a seven. He lost the tournament to Hagen by two shots.

When Sarazen arrived at Prince's in 1932, he was advised not to employ Daniels. Near seventy, the once great caddy was nearly blind. During the practice rounds Sarazen did not get on well with his new caddy. As the first round approached, the American was mired in a siege of poor form that he blamed on his caddy. He fired the replacement and returned Old Dan to his rightful place. The old caddy acted like a magic spell on his employer; Sarazen's play improved. Sarazen won by five shots. Old Dan died a few months later.

Sarazen returned to the United States and began to tune up for the U.S. Open, to be played at Fresh Meadow Country Club. Since Sarazen had once been the pro at the club, he was quickly installed as one of the favorites. He played cautiously in the first two rounds and it did not work; he was trailing badly. In the middle of the third round, he changed his approach and began to aim for the pins and go for broke. A third-round 70 got him back in the tournament. His 66 in the last round gave him the title. He would come close again, but Sarazen would never win another national title.

In both the wins in 1932, Gene carried his new creation, the sand wedge, in his bag. It was a simple invention; he had merely added a heavy flange to the bottom edge of a standard nine-iron. Sarazen said that the new club took away his fear of bunkers and made it easier to shoot at pins. Golfers everywhere noted Gene's success in 1932 and began demanding sand wedges for themselves. The manufacturers were happy to oblige.

A final word about Sarazen: he first attracted notice with his Open win in 1922. From that point until his death, in 1999, Sarazen was a significant and positive figure in the golf community. A man with little formal education, Sarazen came literally to personify class, civility, and personal charm. Golf has had no better ambassador. Coming from a humble Italian background, Sarazen, together with Hagen, proved that a golf professional could be more than a humble employee of a golf club. Sarazen represented the game that made him famous with class and humility for over *seventy* years.

Sarazen's fellow pros in the 1930s were, for the most part, fine fellows, but they lacked the qualities of Hagen, Sarazen, and Jones. In describing the pros of the thirties, Herbert Warren Wind (who saw them all) wrote, in *The Story of American Golf,* "There was no denying the skill of the young men who had become leaders in professional golf, but when it came to color and the ignition of personal ardor, the new stars couldn't hold a candle to the old boys." Of Ralph Guldahl, who won two U.S. Opens in a row, Wind thought he "was sensationally dull to watch, but steady as rock." There were "comers" sure enough, but they would blossom later. The age of Jones and Hagen would be followed, after more than a decade-long lull, by the age of Nelson, Hogan, and Snead. Herb Wind did make several interesting and important points about the infant PGA Tour in the thirties. He presented the earnings, in dollars, of the top twelve money winners for the calendar year 1936:

Horton Smith	7,884
Ralph Guldahl	7,682
Henry Picard	7,681
Harry Cooper	7,443
Ray Mangrum	5,995
Jimmy Thomson	5,927
Jimmy Hines	5,599
Gene Sarazen	5,480
Byron Nelson	5,429
Johnny Revolta	4,317
Tony Manero	3,929
Ky Laffoon	3,592

Wind then offered an objective, eye-witness-based account of how they played and what factors were shaping the game at the very top. First of all, he noted that no player made enough money to distinguish himself. Wind also noted that, almost without exception, the best pros of the midthirties were long hitters. They benefited from new high-compression golf balls and improved steel shafts. The generally lower scores were also the product, until 1937, of the fact that while pros often carried as many as thirty clubs, the sand wedge was clearly the most important. Wind also contended that golf courses were made easier in the thirties: roughs were shorter, fairways improved, and dangerous bunkers removed.

Wind points out correctly that the money list was the product of fewer tournaments, but he also argues that they were "well-paid for their services." In the full context of the time, he is certainly right. Most of the twelve men on the 1936 money list also had club jobs that paid them a salary. They also made money from endorsements and the publication of instructional articles and books. We can put the yearly take of the touring pro into context if we remember that the men who built the Augusta National Golf Course received a dollar a day for their labors.

Wind notes that the fortunes of the touring pro were enhanced after 1936 by the arrival of Fred Corcoran. Born in Boston, Corcoran had been connected to golf most of his life. He caddied at the Belmont Country Club and became the caddie master. He worked for the Massachusetts Golf Association, where he learned to manage tournaments. In 1936 he was hired by Pinehurst to run the press relations at the PGA Championship being held at the resort. This led to a job with the PGA as its tournament director.

Corcoran was very good at his job. He possessed both the ability to work hard and something that might be called marketing genius. Taking advantage of improved economic conditions and the arrival on the scene of new, compelling figures like Nelson and Snead, Corcoran grew the PGA Tour dramatically. In 1936 the tour consisted of twenty-two events; a decade later there were approximately forty-six money events. Total money available in these events had increased six fold. When World War II ended, the American public was actually more aware of the PGA Tour than it had been in 1932.

It's easy to skip over the 1930s as a hard time for the golf community. It was a decade in which many Americans turned against the rich and, to some extent, all businessmen. For some, it was the reckless business class that had caused the Depression and who fought Roosevelt's attempts to help the little guy. And golf was, for many, still the rich man's game, the businessman's game.

Beneath this black-and-white view of things, however, there was another reality. It involved the relationship between work and leisure. The Depression seemed to call for a return to the solid values of the Protestant work ethic. For others, the Depression called for a different attitude, one that put an emphasis on the acceptance of leisure and a reformed attitude toward work.

Many commentators noted that the Depression had not been caused by laziness or a lack of work. In fact, the problem was overproduction. Work in the half-century after 1880 had been transformed by technological and social advances. Humankind had become more productive than anyone prior to the Civil War could have ever dreamed. At Pinehurst, where Leonard and Richard Tufts watched American attitudes toward leisure like hawks surveying a rabbit patch, their newspaper, *The Outlook*, consistently took a radical attitude toward leisure and work. Speaking through the editor, Arthur S. Newcomb, the Tufts articulated attitudes that would have shocked their Protestant ancestors. The paper argued that mankind did not need to work so hard. Science and technology had overcome the problem of production. For centuries the issue had been whether humankind could produce enough. Now the issue was overproduction. Why else were we plowing under cotton and pouring milk down the sewer? Newcomb concluded that the time had come "for men and women to give more hours and thought to leisure and diversion." Of course, when this came about, places like Pinehurst would "take on a new and added importance and responsibilities."

In an *Atlantic Monthly* article, in April 1933, the advertising executive Ernest E. Calkin took a less self-interested view: "It is obvious that the necessary work of the world can now be done in comparatively few working hours." Calkin noted that his first job in 1885 took up sixty-five hours of his week. Since then, the coming of the Saturday half-holiday and the move to the eight-hour day and Daylight Saving Time had dramatically cut into that sixty-five-hour week. But now the rise of leisure had become "a problem." What would men and women do with this time? Calkin believed that Americans, unfortunately, had not turned to authentic play, but instead "[their] playing [was], for the most part, by proxy." In his article, Calkin advocates a childlike sense of play in the citizen who is healthy and active. He praises walking, reading, community work, study, learning, and gardening. Americans, he fears, are becoming addicted to activities that are passive and "destitute of the spirit of play." The movies, radio, and sport spectacles are really not play; they are "distractions" and "amusements." He concludes with a prediction: the future of American civilization will in some sense depend on how we solve the problem of leisure. Will we play ourselves, or will we merely watch and become addicted to "vicarious amusements"? Will we have "paid entertainers" to solve the problem of leisure for all of us?

This debate about leisure had profound relevance for golf. When good economic times returned, would Americans play golf, or would they watch golf? Would they turn increasingly to vicarious experiences, or would they seek to play themselves? There were many developments in the future that would influence this decision, most notably the advent of television. But before we could get to the age of television, all Americans would have to endure another experience as daunting as the Depression—a half-decade of war.

Golf and World War II

A s 1938 drew to a close, Clifford Roberts began to believe that his reason for being, Augusta National, would survive the Depression. The club, he thought, had passed through the darkness and would soon emerge into the light. The membership had finally reached one hundred, and there was cash enough for Roberts to pay down the mortgage a bit. The attendance at the 1939 Masters finally surpassed that of the 1934, the high-water mark to that point. A new generation of players was slowly taking over from the solid, but stolid, players of the thirties. Byron Nelson, Sam Snead, and Ben Hogan would become the uncontested leaders of this new generation. Roberts had every reason to think that his club and golf in general had survived its most severe challenge.

It was not to be. The promised land turned out to be a good seven years in the future. America and the golf community would have to face perhaps its most difficult years. If we focus on golf alone, it is clear that, between 1941 and 1946, the game in all its aspects confronted a complex set of circumstances that threatened to drive it out of the national culture. The spring of 1944 may well have been the low point for American golf in the twentieth century.

Unlike the Depression, which hit most leisure activities equally, the war was especially hard on golf. As with most all-encompassing national emergencies, activities deemed frivolous or marginal were seen negatively. However, during World War II, this disapproving attitude toward play was clearly secondary to yet another set of factors that hit golf directly. The war drew off into the service the young men and women who made up the "core" of club members and regular players on public courses. Wartime rationing of key materials was also devastating. Steel for shafts and rubber for balls were diverted to war production. Gas rationing was probably the most harmful. People would simply not use their weekly allotment for a trip to the club when they barely had enough to get to work. When the war cut the supply of gas to consumers, it showed exactly how much golf was tied to the automobile. At the course, maintenance declined because of gas rationing and the inability to replace workers gone off to war.

There was more. To pay for the war the federal government raised personal income taxes to unheard of levels. Indeed, it was during the war that the income tax became the federal government's primary revenue source. The income tax passed from being a tax on a limited class of earners (only 5 percent of the public filed returns during the 1930s) into a mass tax that was deducted from paychecks beginning in 1943. High earners (who were likely golfers) saw their discretionary income cut by taxes. At the golf and country clubs, taxes took another bite. The Revenue Act of 1943 raised the tax on club dues and initiation fees from 10 to 20 per cent. This increase came with a wave of excise taxes and taxes on many forms of amusement. However, on top of gas rationing, the inability to find balls to play with and the decline in the courses made the increased taxes seem to some like the last straw.

The years 1944 and 1945 were probably the worst for private courses in all of the twentieth century. This was a complicated phenomenon and certainly the war was only part of the problem. A number of clubs had wobbled during the thirties but had survived. The war was a blow from which a club in a weak position could not recover. The *New York Times* reported the sale of

seven clubs in the New York area in 1945. There were undoubtedly more that did not make the papers. Some of these clubs
were marginal, but even Shinnecock Hills Golf Club went up for
sale. All across the country private clubs, in debt and unable to
pay their taxes, were auctioned off to the highest bidder. Many
of the earliest clubs faced other problems that had become apparent during the 1930s. They found themselves the victims of
relentless urban expansion. As cities grew, the need to extend
streets and sewer lines often put golf clubs at risk. A number of
fine courses lost battles with the ever-expanding urban grid.

Of course many clubs survived. Those that did illustrate the
heroic measures necessary to keep a club afloat. The Morris
County Golf Club (New Jersey) was one of the earliest and most
interesting of the 1890s ventures into golf. Founded by women, it
was eventually taken over by men (not without considerable ran-
cor). It became one of the most exclusive of the early golf clubs.
The Depression hit it hard. In the four years between 1932 and
1936, revenue from dues plummeted from fifty-eight thousand
dollars to forty-one thousand. The club cut expenses and services, but it was weakened by the general decline in the thirties.
The war was almost too much. Seventy-seven members were away
in the service, and when gas rationing was announced, the club
thought about closing. For three years the members made do
with limited use of their club—only ten holes were kept open.
Dues were cut in half and the club's financial health deteriorated. When the war ended, members returned, but not enough of
them. By 1953 the vast majority of stockholders were not members. It looked as if the old club would fall into the hands of
nonmembers, trusts, and estates that held the stock. The situation was made worse by the fact that the club was $125,000 in
debt. Many clubs in this type of situation folded. Morris County survived only because they were willing to endure a nervous
period of dramatic restructuring.

One old club, the Essex County Club (1893), just north of
Boston, offered another example of how some survived. The

Depression pushed the club's annual budget into the red almost every year of the decade. Use of the club declined. Members were given "season privilege cards" that could be passed on to a friend; the cards allowed the friend to use the club's golf course and other facilities at member rates. In 1939 holders of the bonds issued by Essex County were asked to waive their interest payments.

The war pushed the club to the brink. By 1944, 61 of the 282 paying members were off to war. Annual events, in both tennis and golf, attracted very small fields. The back nine of the golf course was abandoned and quickly became overgrown. Also in 1944 the club faced a severe financial crisis. The club had issued bonds to build a new club house and twenty-five thousand dollars of these bonds were coming due on February 1, 1944. The bonds were secured by a mortgage on the club's property. There was no money to pay State Street Trust Company that held the bonds. Members could not be asked to provide a rescue. Salvation came in the form of a former club official, Nathaniel T. Winthrop. He established a $20,500 trust for a local hospital; the trustees were empowered to use the funds to buy Essex County Club bonds. When foreclosure proceedings began, the trustees of the hospital, using leverage created by their bond holdings, were able to buy the club for a bargain price—about half the estimated price. They paid off the other bond holders at twelve cents on the dollar and the trustees became the owner of the Essex County Club. They conveyed ownership of the club to a new corporation, also called Essex County Club, taking in payment a note for thirty thousand dollars from the new corporation. Any number of golf clubs went through similar transactions to keep their ventures alive. Those that could not find such a device usually disappeared.

The war hurt other clubs in other ways. At Augusta National, Roberts and Bob Jones gradually came to the conclusion that the club would have to close for the duration of the war. The problem was transportation; members simply could not get to

Augusta, especially after 1942. When Roberts announced the closing of the club in October 1942, more than a few members assumed that it would never reopen. Dues were suspended, but members were asked to make voluntary contributions and many did.

Bob Jones suggested that the club raise cattle on the empty fairways. This would control the Bermuda grass, help the war effort, and maybe turn a profit. In the end, the club raised both cattle and turkeys. The cattle operation did not go well. The animals ate grass to be sure, but they also ate the valuable azaleas and camellias. They sold the cattle into a glutted market and lost five thousand dollars. The turkeys worked better. They produced a profit and Roberts was able to send each member a Christmas turkey raised at the club.

Augusta reopened in December 1944. The course was not restored to playing condition until the spring of 1945. Much of the restoration work was done by German prisoners who had been engineers in the German army. Men who once had built bridges for Rommel's tanks, built a bridge for golfers over Rae's Creek near the thirteenth tee.

Other courses did not fare so well during the war. Near Pinehurst, in North Carolina, Mid Pines Country Club, with its beautiful Donald Ross course, was taken over by the Army Air Forces. The military took less than ownership care of the property. The course became overgrown with vines and underbrush—it virtually disappeared. The clubhouse and hotel was retrofitted for military use by simply punching holes in walls to run wires and cables. The entire interior was painted army beige.

People close to the top of the golf community responded to the intense pressure on golf by ensuring that the public saw the game as contributing to the war effort. The U.S. Open was suspended in 1942 and wasn't held again until 1946. The men's and women's Amateur were also suspended in the same fashion. Many in the golf community fell back on the notion that golf helped workers stay fit for work. Herb Graffis, in the March

1942 issue of *Golfing*, summarized the prevailing attitude: "Golfers and their club officials recognize that the sole justification for golf in these times lies in its demonstrated capacity to restore mental and physical zip to workers. And today it's work or fight."

The Professional Golfers' Association confronted a different situation. The PGA president, Ed Dudley, formally asked the government what the organization should do during the war. Washington told the golfers to give exhibitions and when the pros played for money they should be paid in U.S. War Bonds. During the heart of the war (1942 and 1943), the PGA did its best but, essentially, the tour as it existed then collapsed. Players couldn't get enough gas to get from tournament to tournament. Most of the big-name players entered the service. Sam Snead and Jimmy Demaret served in the navy; Lloyd Mangrum, Horton Smith, Dutch Harrison, and Ben Hogan were in the army. Most of these players saw little combat. Lloyd Mangrum was an exception; he was wounded twice in the Battle of the Bulge.

The war caught the PGA just as it was emerging from the Depression-era doldrums. The all-but-formal suspension of tour events stalled the careers of the three men who had begun to dominate before the war and who would literally define pro golf after 1945—Ben Hogan, Byron Nelson, and Sam Snead. Only Byron Nelson did not serve in the military; he suffered from a blood condition that prevented his blood from coagulating normally. He failed his physical twice and, as he put it, "So I was out of it. . . . It was an uncomfortable feeling, believe me."

According to Nelson, in his autobiography, Ed Dudley, the president of the PGA, asked if Byron would do exhibitions and visit hospitals and rehab centers. The PGA "wanted golf to do its part." Along with Jug McSpaden, who had also been rejected by the military, Nelson began a long series of exhibitions and visits to military installations. They were not paid for their services, but their equipment companies (MacGregor and Wilson) helped with expenses. By one count, Nelson and McSpaden put on 110 exhibitions during the war years.

Nelson also put on exhibitions with Bing Crosby and Bob Hope. They would play nine holes at a club and hold an auction. People would pay to hear Crosby sing "White Christmas," to hear Hope tell a joke, or see Nelson hit a shot. The money would go to the Red Cross or it would pay for war bonds.

Nelson openly admits that he was able to keep his game in good shape during the war years while touring the country. Many of the other pros would have to admit the same thing. Both Hogan and Snead found spots in the military that allowed them to play plenty of golf. There were a limited number of events held during the war. The United States Golf Association held a substitute for the U.S. Open in 1942, called the Hale America Open, which Hogan won. In 1943 there were few events, but as the war wound down in 1944, the tour came back quickly.

Looking back at the period between 1930 and 1944, we can only marvel at how durable the idea of golf as a spectator sport turned out to be. In a time of economic emergency, followed by world war, one might think that watching men play golf would fall by the wayside. Indeed, throughout this period the spectator sports generally remained strong. Therefore, it was no surprise that when the economy turned up and the war ended, America entered a period in which spectator sport of all kinds would grow luxuriously.

On the other side of the ledger, the participation side, the durability of golf was also surprising. Golf, compared to other sports and activities, was expensive. The thirties reduced the number of people with time and money to play. The war years, as we have shown, hurt golf in countless ways. But, as we all know, the game survived and entered a period of growth after 1950.

What lasting impact did the Depression and the war have? As a spectator sport between 1930 and 1945, golf was given over to the professionals. Everyone honored the tradition of Bobby Jones, but they also began to care more about the Open champion and few even knew who won the USGA Amateur. When the Open was resumed in 1946, golf fans knew this was now a tournament that a professional would win. There would be no "Second Coming" of Bobby Jones. Slowly the typical year for golf fans would take shape around the Masters, the Open, the PGA, and the British Open. Professional golfers were becoming uncontested sport heroes, sharing the stage with stars from football, baseball, and basketball. In the next chapter we examine the careers of three men who did more than anyone to solidify the position of the golf professional in American culture.

The Depression and the war also did grave damage to the private country club as the dominant venue for the playing of the game. The private voluntary association had been a dynamic vehicle for the creation of golf courses and golf clubs. Up to 1930 it had literally altered the American physical and social landscape. Often controlling several hundred acres of land, these clubs became landmarks in cities, large and small, in every section of the nation. They remain landmarks, but very few private clubs built after 1950 have been granted this status.

The private golf club too often was saddled with debt that had been taken on in the twenties. As we saw in the last chapter, critics came forth to condemn the luxury and complexity that had crept into the early clubs. During the war there were similar critics. For example, in 1943 the drama critic, Walter Prichard Eaton, Yale professor and lifelong golfer, looked back on his life in golf and saw a betrayal of the simple clubs of the past. Eaton claimed, "I have seen the demand for luxury in clubhouse appointments and facilities steadily increase beyond all reasonable requirements of the game. And I have seen the cost of course maintenance increase to what we in the '90s [1890s] would have considered astronomical figures."

Eaton assigns blame for this state of affairs to a number of factors. He blames "the modern ball and club" because they required courses to get longer and longer—and more expensive. The golf architect gets it for designing courses that require expensive watering systems and small armies of men to maintain them. The combination of behemoth clubhouses and expensive courses has put American golf in a situation where the club with both "can only be supported in periods of plentiful labor and financial prosperity." Eaton's essay appeared in the *Atlantic Monthly* in June 1943—a time when neither labor nor money was especially plentiful.

This call for simplicity that was heard in both the thirties and the forties suggests that the private clubs were hurt most fatally by their own ambitions. After the war, Americans would form clubs again but it would not be the same. Golf courses and golfing would take place more and more in new kinds of places—gated communities, daily-fee courses, and hybrid public-private clubs.

Hogan, Snead, and Nelson and the Rise of the Modern Touring Pro

The modern touring golf professional is a unique product of American cultural and economic evolution. The idea that professional golfers could make a living traveling from tournament to tournament (job to job?), getting paid based on how skillfully they performed, confronted a number of obstacles. By the mid-1950s it was clear that these obstacles had indeed been overcome. This triumph was largely the product of three men—Byron Nelson, Ben Hogan, and Sam Snead.

It is hard for us who tend to take the PGA Tour for granted to understand that it had to surmount significant roadblocks. For example, in 1898 the magazine *Outing* clearly reflected the distaste that some Americans had toward playing golf for money. In its popular "Golf" column, the magazine noted "the generally satisfactory condition of the game." The column warned, however, that "there is danger ahead if the spirit that breezes beneath the following notice is allowed to grow." The notice in question was from a professional at the "—— golf club" [*Outing* blanked out the name.] This professional announced that "he would gladly meet any professional on the links in a match on terms to suit." It was also suggested that the professional could get "backing up to $250 or more." The unknown writer for *Outing* stated that "the language, the form of the contest, and all that it suggests are in the worst golfing taste." This was the sort of thing you might expect from prize fighting. The writer concluded that "too stern a reception of such professionalism . . . cannot be meted out."

These sort of statements reflected the profound aversion to gambling among the middle and upper classes in America. This aversion was rooted in Christian doctrine: betting was wagering on God's will, on the intentions of the Almighty. The negative view of gambling was also profoundly class based. Many upper-class Americans believed that gambling was second only to excessive drink as a cause of destitution and want among the lower classes. Better to get a wage by hard work than to rely on chance. It took a while, but golf tournaments for money eventually overcame this deeply entrenched aversion to gambling. So successfully was golf able to do this that most do not even see the modern PGA Tour events as gambling at all.

The modern touring golf professional also had to overcome a second obstacle. We get a hint of this obstacle in a small piece by A. W. Tillinghast in the August 1933 issue of *Golf Illustrated*. Tillinghast's title was "Golf Pros not Servants." He noted that in the early days of golf in America, pros were not allowed in the clubhouse. The golfers wore red coats and generally fancy duds while pros did not. The pros, he cryptically suggested, "had not smoothed off the rough edges." They were, in short, manual laborers and they usually dressed like it.

By 1933 things had changed. Tillinghast explained that "today our professional *players* [my emphasis] do not smell of pitch and they wash their hands before sitting at table." In clubhouses all across the land it had become "hard to just distinguish them from the gentlemen about them — why, God bless my soul, they are gentlemen!" Tillinghast announced that "old barriers had been set aside" and that it was common to grant honorary membership to the club pro. Tillinghast admitted that it was Walter Hagen who had in some ways inspired his thinking on this subject. Recently, while in England, Hagan had shared a drink with the Prince of Wales, at the prince's invitation. Surely Hagen had enjoyed "his beaker" in the same way "that is his wont when performing in similar fashion with a gentleman of his own country and we are positive that he did not wipe his mouth with his coat sleeve."

So it is my sense that the modern touring pros pulled off a neat trick. They overcame the bias against gambling and they were able to convince Americans in large numbers that what a touring pro did was not manual labor—that, indeed, it was gentleman's work. Three men building on the work of Hagen, Sarazen, and the other pros of their era, were crucial to this process. Byron Nelson, Sam Snead, and Ben Hogan were, together, the most responsible for propelling the touring professional to the very top of America's athletic hierarchy.

All three men were born in 1912, making it easy for us to follow them through the decades. However, it is clear that each established himself as an enduring figure on the tour at different points in their lives. Hogan had the hardest, longest road; Snead was second; and Byron Nelson was the first to make it.

John Byron Nelson Jr. was born on February 4, 1912, on a 160-acre cotton farm in Long Branch, Texas. His parents were working-class people who struggled to survive during the 1930s. His father worked at a number of jobs, most notably as a truck driver and a part-time worker in a mohair wool warehouse. Earlier in Byron's life his parents either owned or rented small cotton farms. Early memories of those farms may have planted in Nelson the desire to own his own land, a desire that eventually shaped his life. Young Byron had several notable health problems. At age eleven he contracted typhoid fever. In a matter of weeks Byron lost half his body weight and, as he put it, "The doctors had pretty much given up on me." He survived, but the episode had important repercussions. Nelson claims in his autobiography, *How I Played the Game*, that the fever caused severe memory loss—he remembered little of his childhood before the illness struck. Later when he discovered that he was unable to father children, it was blamed on the high fevers that came with the typhoid.

His mother was a deeply religious woman; Byron called her "a wonderful Bible scholar." This influenced Byron's behavior profoundly; he was a lifelong member of the Church of Christ and, following the church's teachings, he never swore, smoked, or drank. On the pro tour there were few players as overtly Christian as Nelson.

At age twelve, Byron heard from school friends that you could pick up decent spending money caddying at Glen Garden Country Club. Byron's family had moved to a small town near Fort Worth called Stop Six (the sixth stop on the train to Dallas). Glen Garden was not that far away, but when Byron investigated, he found that the club had more than enough caddies. Byron would appear on weekends and holidays looking for a bag to carry. He came up empty six times before getting a job. Slowly he became an established caddie and the game began to tighten its hold on him. He used some of his caddie money to buy a used mashie (five-iron). Somehow he got his hands on an instructional book by Harry Vardon. Soon he had several Glen Garden players for whom he worked regularly.

In 1927 Byron began working in the shop for the pro, Ted Longworth. He did the manual labor required in a pro shop at the time. He installed new shafts into club heads, cleaned clubs, and buffed the rust off of irons. Soon he was constructing whole sets of new clubs.

The membership at Glen Garden provided some interesting perks for its shop assistants and caddies. There was a Christmastime tournament for the caddies in which the members carried the bags. In one of these events, as every student of golf history knows, Nelson ended up tied with another caddie, Ben Hogan. In the playoff, Nelson won by a single shot. Each was given a golf club as a prize. Byron soon began playing in local amateur events in which he won medals and golf equipment. He would sell these prizes to Hattie Greene, a good woman player at Glen Garden. In this way she financed young Byron's early golf career. After the momentous tie between Hogan and Nelson, the club gave both boys "junior privileges." It's fair to say that if Glen Garden Country Club had not existed, the lives of Byron Nelson and Ben Hogan would have been very different.

By the time Byron got to high school he was firmly in the grip of the game. Homework and school did not appeal to him and he quit halfway through the tenth grade. A Glen Garden member named Nottingham got him a job as a file clerk at the Fort Worth-Denver Railroad. He began work in the fall of 1928, but when the economy faltered in 1929, he was let go.

He hung on at Glen Garden, working in the shop and mowing greens. There were a number of opportunities to test his game. In 1930 he played in a pro-am as the partner to the Scottish pro Bobby Cruickshank. They finished second, but Cruickshank was unimpressed with his young partner. He told Byron that he had to change his grip—his right hand was "too strong"(too far to the right on the handle). At Glen Garden, Ted Longworth also worked with Nelson, changing his long caddie swing into a more controlled, tighter action. When Longworth left the club he was replaced by Dick Grout, who brought his brother Jack along as an assistant. Byron and Jack Grout became lifelong friends and often played pro-ams together. Jack Grout would, much later, tutor another world-class player, Jack Nicklaus.

Inevitably, Byron faced the question of turning pro. In his autobiography, he makes it seem like not much of a choice at all. He could not find a regular job. In 1932 Byron got a letter from Ted Longworth inviting him to come to his new club in Texarkana and play in a prize-money tournament—assuming that young Nelson would play as an amateur. On the bus ride to Texarkana, Byron began thinking about the prize money: "There was pretty good money going at these tournaments, and I felt I was good enough to have a chance at some of it." As Byron remembers it, "It was on that bus that I decided to turn pro."

At the event, Nelson asked what becoming a pro entailed. He was told, "Pay five dollars and say you're playing for the money." He finished third and won seventy-five dollars, which he thought "was all the money in the world." For a young man and a devoted Christian, turning pro was a radical act. His parents did not approve of their son playing so much golf. Byron admitted that "golf pros then didn't have as good a reputation as they do now." His parents surely did not understand exactly what kind of occupation that their son had taken up. But seventy-five dollars was still seventy-five dollars.

The obvious next step was "to go on the tour in California." For this Byron needed backing, and he got it from friends in Fort Worth who won money on Nelson in Calcutta pools. The "Calcutta" was a common feature of golf events at the time. By the mid-1950s, the Calcutta as a common form of golf gambling would become very controversial. Before an event began, there would be an auction of players or teams in best-ball events. The owners of the winning player or team would collect the money in the auction pool. Armed with five hundred dollars and a conviction that he was good enough to win, Byron found a ride to California. He was wrong; he was not good enough. He went broke and was lucky to find a free ride home to Fort Worth.

Back home in the late winter of 1933 and at loose ends, Nelson came into contact with the second element of a touring pro's existence: the club job. In April 1933 Byron replaced Ted Longworth at Texarkana when Longworth took a new position in Oregon. It was not a great job; Byron received no salary, only the money from lessons and whatever profit he could wring out of running the pro shop, selling balls and clubs to the members. In June of 1933, in a Bible study class at his new church, he met his future wife, Louise Shofner. Of course, his wife came with a father-in-law who financed, with a loan, his son-in-law's second try at the professional tour.

Again Byron took his game to California, and again he played poorly. However, when the tour returned to Texas in early 1934, our hero had something akin to a breakthrough. The Texas Open was one of the oldest events on what was still a very young tour. As Byron teed off in the first round (he hit his first tee shot fifty yards), he was nearly broke and owed his future father-in-law $660. But after the horrible start he turned in a 66 on the Brackenridge Park Course. This led to a second-place finish and $450. The next week, in Galveston, he played well and won three hundred dollars. Back in Texarkana, he went to Shofner's grocery and paid off his loan to his future father-in-law. His next stop was Arnold's Jewelry Store, where he paid the rest of his winnings for an engagement ring. He and Louise were married soon after. (For a summary view of what "The Tour" was like in the mid-1930s, see Appendix C.)

Getting married at that point was an audacious act. As Nelson put it, the PGA and its tour was "really struggling." He knew, as all his colleagues on the tour knew, that "back then to be successful in the golf business in any way, you had to get a club job in the East. You needed that type of experience." Nelson's job in the East came at the Ridgewood Country Club in New Jersey. The position was as an assistant to head pro George Jacobus. He worked from April 1 to Labor Day for four hundred dollars and half of what he could make giving lessons. The outlines of a tenuous existence became clear. He and Louise would spend the spring and summer in New Jersey, saving every penny possible. When Labor Day arrived, Louise would return to her parents in Texarkana and Byron would take what savings they had and what money he could borrow and head for California to try his luck on the tour.

Byron learned a great deal from George Jacobus. He learned to "always look neat, which meant wearing a shirt and tie every day." Nelson also learned to run a retail business that catered to a small, affluent clientele. The pro shop sold clubs, balls, and, increasingly, clothing designed especially for golfers. Byron was impressed by the way members dressed and clearly set out to mimic their style. One member, Chet O'Brien, was particularly important. O'Brien always wore custom-made clothes and, once he and Byron had become friends, he took the young pro to his tailor. There Nelson purchased his first pair of custom-made slacks; they were made using an "Arco and McNaughton pattern" and cost sixty dollars a pair. Nice pants for a young man making a bit less than four hundred dollars per month. Wearing such fine clothing was one way of stating that he was not a manual laborer and of establishing a link with the members who wore the same sort of duds.

By the mid-1930s Byron's career path was set. He would work the summers as a golf teacher and small businessman, and in the winter he would play the tour in the West and South. His "club job" improved steadily. In 1937 he became head pro at Reading Country Club, in Pennsylvania, and would move on to Inverness, in Toledo, in 1939. Each move came with better pay and more responsibility and authority. These moves upward were clearly related to his play on tour and his reputation as an honest, hard-working young man. Most important was his victory in the 1937 Masters. This win was set up by an opening round 66, which stood as the lowest first-round score at the Masters until Raymond Floyd shot 65 in 1976. In that round Nelson illustrated his incredible ball-striking ability; he almost never assembled a great round based on red-hot putting. In the 66, he hit every par five in two, and every par four and par three in regulation figures. He hit only thirty-two shots and thirty-four putts for a total of 66. He always said that the 1937 Masters was "the turning point, the most important victory of my career."

It was the 1937 Masters win that earned Nelson his nickname, "Lord Byron." O. B. Keeler, the man who had chronicled the career of Bobby Jones, was still in the business as a writer for the *Atlanta Journal* and the Associated Press. Watching Nelson win the Masters on the last day, Keeler was reminded of a bit of poetry by Lord Byron. The following day, Nelson opened the paper and saw the headline for Keeler's Associated Press story, which read, "Lord Byron wins Masters." Now Nelson had most of the necessary elements for a lasting career as a golf pro: a great swing, a good club job, really nice pants, and, lastly, a memorable nickname.

He parlayed all these elements into a number of important wins and good yearly earnings between 1937 and the war. There was his victory in the U. S. Open in 1939, which was only obtained after two eighteen-hole playoff rounds. Nelson defeated Snead in the final of the PGA in 1940 at Hershey Country Club. His job at Inverness had kept him so busy that he had not played tournament golf for two and half months before the PGA championship. In the final against Snead, Nelson came to the sixteenth hole of the afternoon round one down with three to go. Byron birdied the last three holes to win one up.

Byron's income during this period grew increasingly complex. His job at Inverness produced income from lessons, retail sales in the shop, the care and repair of clubs, and money he won playing with members. His income from the tour included money won in tournaments, an annual amount paid by his club manufacturer, plus bonuses for wins (Nelson switched from Spalding to MacGregor in 1939.) Nelson also made money in other ways. At Inverness, Nelson had met Lloyd Haas of the Hass-Jordan Shoe Company. Byron advised the company on the construction of golf shoes and golf umbrellas. He became a vice president for marketing. Nelson would visit the large department stores that sold Haas-Jordan products. Byron claimed he did no selling: "It was more of a public relations thing." The company paid him twenty-five dollars for each visit he made and a bonus check annually. Finally, Byron benefited in a small way from the Calcutta pools that were often part of tournaments. If he did well, and the person who purchased Byron in the auction won money, some of it would end up in Lord Byron's pocket.

This period, from the midthirties until the war, came to a brilliant climax when Nelson defeated Hogan in a playoff to win the 1942 Masters. His status as the top player, and Hogan's growing prominence, was illustrated when 125 of the pros who had played the event stayed over to watch the Monday playoff. Nelson, after dropping behind early, staged a comeback and won by a shot. Many thought that the 1942 version of the Masters would finally put the tournament and the club on solid footing, but it was not to be. The war intervened. Exempt from the service, Nelson and Jug McSpaden toured the country putting on exhibitions. Clearly Byron did what he could to serve the war effort.

As the war ground to an end, golf in all its forms began to return to normal. The PGA had worked diligently to keep the tour alive and, in 1945, Byron Nelson went on a tear that could not have done more to reinvigorate professional golf. The details of what has come to be called the "Streak" have been exhaustively presented in a number of works. The bare outline of Byron's greatest year is stunning enough. Actually, the streak, in its entirety, began in 1944 and continued into 1946. The PGA put on twenty-two tour events in 1944 and Byron was first, second, or third in seventeen of these tournaments, winning eight. He began 1945 playing well. In March he and McSpaden won the Miami International Four-Ball. In the next event, the Charlotte Open, Byron defeated Snead in a playoff. In all, he won eleven straight events, playing five months without losing a tournament. In August he finished fourth at Memphis. At the end of the year, he won the last two events and began the 1946 campaign with two more victories, for four in a row. There would be six victories that year and a tie for the U.S. Open title; he lost in a playoff to Lloyd Mangrum. By one count, in the period 1944 through 1946, Byron entered seventy-two events and won thirty-two. He was first, second, or third in fifty-seven of the seventy-two.

The streak has elicited much debate. The fields were weak. The courses were easy. Nothing, however can diminish what was, and still is, the most amazing three years of golf in the history of the game. Even more amazing is what Nelson said about his play during this hot streak. In his autobiography, he stated that in 1944, 1945, and 1946, "My game had gotten so good and so dependable that there were times when I actually would get bored playing. I hit it in the fairway, on the green, make a birdie or par and go to the next hole." The press began to complain that he was monotonous to watch. The journalists began to use the adjective "mechanical" and replaced "Lord Byron" with the "Mechanical Man." In the history of golf I cannot remember a player stating that he was going so good that it became boring.

Of course, there was a great back story to the streak; Lord Byron had decided to retire before it began. How many Americans have said to themselves: I'll work until I have *x* dollars and then I will buy a farm and escape the rat race. Or the more modern version: I'll save my money and retire early and just play golf the rest of my life. Thus we can sense the irony in Nelson's retirement. He gave up competitive golf for the "real work" of running a ranch. Byron had gambled on golf and his ability to play it, and he had won. The winnings from this gamble were invested, very profitably, in a 650-acre spread in Roanoke, Texas.

Byron Nelson made a huge contribution to the golf community in 1944 and 1945. As the nation emerged from fifteen years of economic hard times and war, golf's future, like that of all sport, was questionable. If the tour had started back up with humdrum results, with four or five players sharing the wins and the purses, golf's postwar spurt in popularity would not have been possible. As testimony to Byron's position in the minds of Americans, he was elected Athlete of the Year in both 1944 and 1945 by the Associated Press.

Nelson's retirement was far from complete. He moved his parents into a home on the land and commenced a study of ranching. There were failures. An investment in hogs turned sour. It soon became clear that Lord Byron's retirement from golf was not total. There was income from an instructional book, *Winning Golf*, and a series of articles on technique in *Popular Mechanics*. Nelson helped coach the North Texas State University golf team. He competed occasionally, especially in the Masters; going off to Augusta in the spring would be part of his yearly routine for decades. At some point, he admits, his appearances at Augusta, the U.S. Open, and the Colonial became "purely ceremonial."

In fact, he was slowly becoming a Golf Oracle. As the years wore on, Lord Byron advised young players on their games and, one presumes, on how to live one's life. Harvey Ward, Ken Venturi, and Tom Watson all have testified to Nelson's role as friend and adviser. Of course, the big new thing in the 1950s was television, and Nelson quickly became involved. He did commentary for CBS at the Masters in 1957. He was paired with Chris Schenkel, and the combination worked well. The two eventually became a long-lasting team at ABC. Byron's job was to dispense down-home golf wisdom, a job for which he possessed considerable genius. In 1961 Byron played Gene Littler at Pine Valley in what was the first match in the long-running television series *Shell's Wonderful World of Golf*. The PGA appointed Byron captain of the 1965 Ryder Cup team that played at Royal Birkdale, where the Americans won decisively.

In 1962 Byron helped architect Ralph Plummer (also an ex–Glen Garden caddie) build the Preston Trail Golf Course in North Dallas. Eventually the always shaky Dallas Open would move to Preston Trail and become the Byron Nelson Golf Classic.

Most importantly, in his later years Lord Byron would be accorded deference and respect second only to that given to Bobby Jones. Lord Byron died in 2006; he had been a professional golfer since 1932 — seventy-two years. In their appraisals, commentators belabor words like "nice," "gentleman," "modest," and "pleasant." Herbert Warren Wind called him "calm and efficient, rather than colorful." He was in large part a country innocent. His favorite movie was *The Sound of Music*. He could say, "Not everybody thinks chickens are special, but I put them right behind horses as my favorite animal." After meeting President

Eisenhower, Byron described him as "friendly like." It was this innocence and simplicity that defined Nelson's public personality. Remember, however, that in a short fourteen-year career, this apparently simple man beat everyone in sight.

One of those players regularly beaten by Nelson was Ben Hogan. Until his retirement in 1946, Nelson's record was much better than Hogan's. In several head-to-head contests, such as the playoff at the 1942 Masters, Nelson won. After 1946 Hogan, along with Snead, would dominate the world of professional golf. Ben Hogan, however, somehow transcends his record, which was extraordinary. He fascinated the golf community, and the larger community, in a way that Nelson or Snead never would.

Hogan's early life was profoundly unhappy. His father, Chester, was a blacksmith in Dublin, Texas. It was a bad time for blacksmithing; the world of horses and horse shoes was evaporating as the automobile took over. The Hogans moved from Dublin to Fort Worth and Chester attempted to become an auto mechanic. It did not work out. In retrospect, it seems clear that Chester Hogan was, in some sense, mentally ill. He was, after the fashion of the time, treated for depression. As his craft (blacksmithing) was consigned to the past, the life seemed to go out of him. His wife, Clara, took him to a Fort Worth hospital that specialized in mental disorders. The investigations by Hogan's best biographer, James Dodson, suggest that Chester suffered from a bipolar disorder, black periods of depression alternating with periods of optimism bordering on euphoria.

Chester Hogan had lost his trade. Occupationally, he had simply been cast off. So it is significant that he returned to Dublin and attempted to reopen his blacksmithing business. Once settled in Dublin, he traveled to Fort Worth, where his family had remained, to convince them to return to Dublin. The husband and his wife argued bitterly. Clara Hogan would not return to Dublin. Chester Hogan retreated to another room and shot himself in the chest with a .38 caliber revolver.

There remains to this day great controversy about the details of what actually happened. Most crucial is the question, Was Ben Hogan a witness to his father's act? The evidence suggests that he was, and that this experience, at age nine, helps explain Hogan's adult personality and his relentless search for golfing perfection. It is beyond debate, however, that if you are the son of a man who commits suicide in Texas in 1922, you will carry a burden, a stigma, for a very long time.

Chester's death obviously changed the economic prospects for the Hogan family. Ben's mother, Clara, made money as a seamstress; his brother, Royal, dropped out of school and took a job delivering office supplies. Young Ben sold the *Fort Worth Star-Telegram* at the railroad depot. He often had to fight to defend his spot. A little more than two years after his father's death, Ben heard about Glen Garden Country Club and the job called caddying. As Nelson had discovered, there were plenty of caddies and Ben had to fight his way in. But he stuck it out and he thrived.

Ben became the regular caddie for a man sent to Glenn Garden by his doctors. The man was Marvin Leonard, and he owned a huge department store in downtown Fort Worth. He was the victim of too much work and too little exercise. He began going to Glen Garden at dawn to get in nine holes before work. Ben Hogan became his regular caddie; Ben would often sleep in a bunker in order to be at the course when his patron arrived. On countless mornings they would spend two happy hours together. One wonders if they ever discussed their differing grips on the game. The older man ordered to the course for his health, to put down the burdens of work for a moment. The younger man slowly coming to see the game as his work, as his craft, as the vehicle to take him upward. When young Ben was forced to choose between his job as newspaper salesman and golf, he chose golf.

Ben evolved at Glen Garden much as Byron had. Both exhibited talent, both moved from caddying into the shop, both probably learned some of their golf from Jack Grout. Ben, particularly, liked working on and building clubs. During an interview with *Sports Illustrated,* in the late 1950s, Ben was asked why, during this period, he had chosen golf. His reply was vintage Hogan: "I don't know. I just loved it."

As with Nelson, Hogan got his first job outside Glen Garden through Ted Longworth. After dropping out of school at age fourteen, Ben took a job at Oakhurst (Longworth was part owner of the crude nine-hole course) running the shop and giving lessons. It was a starter job, a foot-in-the-door job. To boost his income, Ben also took a job dealing cards in a regular game at the Blackstone Hotel. Later he moved on to work at a gambling roadhouse between Fort Worth and Dallas. For most of his life Ben would deny he ever held these jobs. The prohibition against gambling was strong.

On February 30, 1930, Ben went to San Antonio, paid his five-dollar entry fee, and started his career as a golf professional. He shot 78-76, made the cut, and withdrew. The fact was, he could not play. He knew that he could not hit the ball well enough and that his nerves were not up to the competition. Later he put it simply, "I had no right to be out there." The outcome was the same when he shot 77-76 in an event at Houston and withdrew again.

The Ben Hogan of the late 1940s and the 1950s emerges out of these two dismal attempts in Texas just as the Depression began. Unlike Nelson and Snead, Hogan's rise was miserably slow and characterized by abject failure. In 1931 Ben borrowed money from his brother, Royal, and from Marvin Leonard, and tried the tour in California. He left Texas with seventy-five dollars in his pocket; soon that money was gone and he was living off oranges that he picked as he played miserably in California. His patron, Marvin Leonard, sent him seventy-five dollars more, a kindness that Hogan never forgot. This money got him to the tournament in New Orleans where he played poorly again. Years later he summed up his position: "I had to come home."

Back in Texas, Ben came up with a job at a course in Cliburn. It was a small club and the membership was not about to pay for lots of lessons and new equipment. For the most part they left Hogan alone and he used the time to practice and ponder his failure to make it on the tour. Hogan also spent much time building and repairing clubs. He developed strong feelings about how clubs should be built and how they should perform.

In part to stave off the loneliness, Ben decided to marry Valerie Fox, whom he had been courting for a while. The two had met when Valerie was fifteen and Ben was still a fourteen-year-old caddie at Glen Garden. They lived near each other in Fort Worth. It was a long courtship that culminated in their marriage on April 14, 1935. It has never been completely clear why the couple never had children. Valerie Hogan told one interviewer that she and Ben had decided to remain childless because the life of a touring pro had no room for children. Valerie and Ben Hogan, over time, became one of those tightly bonded couples that defy full understanding by anyone on the outside.

In the second half of the 1930s, Hogan confronted an uncomfortable reality. He still could not play well enough to make a decent record on the tour. Without such a record he could not get a good club job. It was also clear that he was falling behind his fellow Texans; Nelson, Guldahl, and Demaret were all doing well, or at least better, leaving Ben to wonder if he was going to be the Texan who failed.

Of course, he did make it. The question is how he shaped his inadequate game of the early '30s into one that could win. Famously, it was two pieces of advice from his wife that turned the tide. She suggested that Ben overcome his jumpy nerves by practicing to the point where he could hit important shots without thinking, without anxiety. Valerie also suggested that Ben could make more birdie putts if he simply hit the ball closer to the hole. This last bit of advice has become an arcane part of American golf talk. I played in one group that responded to anyone complaining about his inability to make birdie putts with the two words, "Mrs. Hogan."

At bottom, Hogan was an intensely empirical, scientific person. He adapted insights gained from watching other players and suggestions offered by people like Henry Picard (weaken his left hand grip and hit fewer hooks) and took them to the practice field. There he would subject ideas about the golf swing to the most rigorous testing. There were days when he would hit six hundred balls in the morning and a like number in the afternoon. For Hogan the only thing a dedicated golfer needed was "more daylight." I cannot resist noting that common Protestant doctrine holds that receiving God's grace requires that the person intensely prepare for its coming: Preparation precedes Sanctification.

The signs of coming grace began to slowly appear for Hogan in the late 1930s. In 1939 Picard told Ben to weaken his grip and learn to fade the ball. Hogan and others have suggested that during this period he unearthed some "secret" and that it was this "secret" that led to his success. I think Hogan did four things between 1935 and 1940. He weakened his grip to cut down on the hooks, and he learned to fade the ball. He practiced so much that tournament play became secondary, almost an afterthought; he also overcame his anxiety by intense practice. Entire mornings would be devoted to a single type of shot—wedges, fairway woods, or bunker play. The afternoons would be devoted to a different type of shot.

There were clear signs of progress. In 1938 Ben won the Hershey Round Robin Four-Ball. This was an eight-team better-ball event. Hogan was originally slated to play with the legendary Scot Tommy Armour, who because of a broken bone in his hand was forced to withdraw. In his place, tournament officials paired Hogan with a little-known pro from New Jersey, Vic Ghezzi. The team of Hogan and Ghezzi blitzed the field, compiling a total of fifty-three under par for the seven-round event. This win helped Ben finish thirteenth on the money list with $4,794. Hogan often called 1938 the turning point in his career; he was on the tour to stay.

Clearly, the tour, with its unambiguous scorecard—the money list—appealed to Hogan in some fundamental way. He had club jobs but never took to them as Nelson had. His biographer, James Dodson, summarized his attitude toward the duties of a club pro: "He privately commented to Valerie that every time he had to teach some bored bridge-playing bond matron or half-interested banker's brat to swing a golf club, a little bit of him withered up and died inside."

Each year he left his club job and hit the road with a keen sense of relief. He and his wife, Valerie, seemed happy on the road. What really mattered after 1938 was winning a regular tour event. In 1940, time after time, he came close, only to finish second or third. At the Texas Open, Ben was in the locker room after posting a tournament record 271, looking like a sure winner. It was Nelson who got a late birdie and forced a playoff with his childhood friend. Before the playoff, on a radio show, Ben commented that "Byron's got a good game but it would be a lot better if he'd practice. He's too lazy to practice." The Hogans and the Nelsons had become friends and traveling companions on tour. This comment by Ben shook that relationship; it was never the same after that radio interview. The playoff took place in horrible course conditions. Nelson's 70 was one stroke better than Hogan's. Second again.

When the tour got to North Carolina, in March of 1940, Ben had put together six second-place finishes in the last year and a half. All the players looked forward to the North and South Open. The weather was usually good and the Tufts family, owners of Pinehurst, treated the players and their wives well, housing and feeding them at no cost. Also the tournament had become more important after 1935 when the resort had switched from sand to grass greens.

Ben got to Pinehurst early and had meticulously prepared himself to play Donald Ross's famous Course No. 2. Just before the event began, Ben adopted a new driver. Both Hogan and Nelson were under contract to MacGregor Sporting Goods. The company had sent Nelson two new drivers and he offered the one he least favored to Hogan. It was love at first sight. On the first day of the tournament Ben did not miss a single fairway and tied the course record with a 66. There would be no last-minute disappointment this time. Hogan won easily. He won the next week at Greensboro. Quickly he also won the Land of the Sky Open. In ten days Hogan won three events, putting to an end his days as an also-ran.

James Dodson has statistically summarized the three wins and their financial impact. In 216 holes of play, Hogan was thirty-four under par. In this stretch he missed only two greens and three-putted twice. Ben raised his exhibition fee from $250 to $500 and signed to do his first print endorsement ad for Bromo-Seltzer. In 1940, he earned $10,655, putting him at the top of the money list.

Ben's rise in 1940 also led to a new kind of club job. He signed a contract with the Hershey Country Club. All that the contract required was that Hogan represent the club and the candy company on tour. No lessons, no running the pro shop, no club repair. For this Ben collected eight thousand dollars.

Ben was now established as one of the top three golfers in America. He did not know it at the time, but he was about to enter a fifteen-year period that would be dominated by the question of what might have been. Under normal conditions, Ben would have fought Byron and Sam Snead for dominance on the tour and for victories in the big events—the U.S. and British Opens, the Masters, and the PGA. However, two events—one global, one personal—derailed the playing out of normal circumstances.

He was the leading money winner in 1940, 1941, and 1942. Then the war began and Hogan signed up and trained to be a U.S. Army Air Corps flight instructor. His rival, Snead, went into the navy. Nelson, as we have seen, was rejected for health reasons and continued to play exhibitions and events. For Hogan's record, the war amounted to a blank with one controversial exception. He won the Hale America National Open, an event cobbled together to replace the usual national championship and to raise money for the USO and the Navy Relief Society. His fans have argued that this victory should count as Hogan's fifth U.S. Open. The spirit of the moment was captured when Ben put his Spalding putter up for auction — it fetched $1,500 for charity. The coming war, and Ben's inevitable draft notice, made giving your clubs away seem like a good idea.

When the war ended Hogan returned to competition and to witness much of Byron Nelson's 1944 and 1945 record-setting run. When Nelson retired, Ben rose quickly to the top of the game. He won the PGA Championship in 1946 and 1948, and the U.S. Open in 1948, leading the money list in 1946 and 1948. In November 1948, fifteen hundred top-flight citizens of Fort Worth assembled at the Colonial Country Club to honor Ben Hogan. As his family looked on, the cream of Fort Worth society stood in a receiving line to congratulate their local hero and to accord him a place at the very top of the local hierarchy. With his golf clubs and with his steadfastness Hogan had done what he could to remove the stigma of his father's suicide.

And then his rise to dominance was eclipsed by personal tragedy. On February 2, 1949, not far from Van Horn, Texas, Hogan and his wife, Valerie, were traveling home to Fort Worth when their Cadillac smashed head-on into a Greyhound bus as it was attempting to pass a slow-moving truck in the fog on Route 80. At the last second, Hogan hurled his body to the right to protect his wife, probably saving his own life. Hogan sustained massive injuries that included a fractured collarbone, a double ring fracture of the pelvis, and a broken ankle and rib. Later blood clots in his leg would threaten his life. An operation to tie off his inferior vena cava became necessary to prevent the clots from moving to his heart or lungs. The Associated Press had prepared an obituary and had distributed it to newspapers and radio stations.

Of course, he did not die. Warmed by a nationwide outpouring of concern, Hogan slowly recovered. His brave statements about eventually playing again were greeted with the sort of encouragement you tendered to someone who is not facing reality. Reality was redefined in Los Angeles and at the Merion Country Club. Less than a year after the accident, Hogan entered the Los Angeles Open and, after four rounds, Snead and Hogan were tied. It was a performance that truly engrossed a nation. That Snead eventually won the delayed playoff did not matter. This was the classic comeback story—from a prognosis that had Hogan never playing again to a reality that had him playing supremely well—all in less than a year.

Of course, the Hogan that came back was a new Hogan. He could not play as much and, in order to play at all, he had not only to prepare his game but also his body. His preround routine now included a long soak of his legs in hot water and Epsom salts, a single aspirin, deep rubs, and the wrapping of his legs with elastic bandages.

Hogan had won the U.S. Open in 1948, but the Open of 1950 was to be much more difficult. Could Hogan stand the constant pain? Could he endure the thirty-six-hole final Saturday? Could anyone play well at Merion where the greens resembled marble slabs? Ben's victory at Merion produced enough stories and legends to keep journalists in business for years. In the last round, on the twelfth hole, it looked like Ben was finished. After hitting his drive, he nearly collapsed as spasms struck in both legs. Someone, probably his playing partner, Cary Middlecoff, grabbed his arm and kept Hogan from falling. Ben may or may not have said, "My God, I don't think I can finish." After playing the thirteenth, Hogan reportedly told his caddie that they were finished, that he could not go on. The caddie, according to legend, said, "You can't quit. I don't work for quitters. I'll see you on the fourteenth tee, sir."

These stories, and more, may or may not be true. The truth was that Hogan came to the fifteenth hole in the last round with a two-stroke lead. Then his putting touch failed him. He three-putted fifteen from eight feet—one shot gone. Hogan parred the hard sixteenth. A par putt on seventeen stopped one turn of the ball short. So the limping figure of Ben Hogan came to the eighteenth and last hole of the 1950 U.S. Open needing par to tie Lloyd Mangrum and George Fazio at 287. He drove well to the middle of the fairway. He confronted a choice between his four-wood that might get him to the back right pin or a one-iron that would get him safely to the front of the green. It was to be the one-iron. It was hit perfectly and settled forty feet from the pin.

It was a shot for the ages. And its iconic status owes much to the fact that a photographer recorded it. Hy Peskin was behind Hogan as he played the fateful stroke. Steadying his camera on a fan's shoulder, Peskin captured Ben's finish as the ball was still airborne. Virtually every golf commentator has had a take on this image. Some note the thirteenth spike (most golf shoes have only twelve) clearly visible on the bottom of his right shoe. Some note the perfect form of the finish or the looks on the spectators' faces. For me, I see the small, trim stature of the man. He was in many ways the greatest small athlete of all time, and Peskin's image perfectly captures his smallness.

With that one-iron and his victory the next day over Mangrum and Fazio, Hogan left the status of mere hero and entered the realm of legend. It was a small help that someone took the one-iron from Hogan's bag and it was never seen again. Hogan had borrowed it from God, and God had taken it back? We get some sense of Hogan's move to a higher status when we review the press coverage. Writers went overboard hammering away at the comeback story and the fierce drive of "bantam Ben" to get back to the top. Many papers, including the *New York Times*, put their stories about the conclusion of the Open on the front page.

Hogan was back from the dead. In the next five years, and especially in 1953, he would only add to the legend. He would win the Masters and successfully defend his Open title in 1951. He would win the U.S. Open again in 1953. At this point Hogan faced a dilemma. For at least several years, commentators and friends had urged him to do something he had never done — go to Britain and play in the British Open. The trip had always seemed like a bad bet to Hogan. The purse was small, you had to qualify, and the expense was great. By 1953 Ben was more open to the idea that you played for something other than money. His victory at Oakmont in 1953 had tied him with Jones as the winner of four U.S. Opens. People were beginning to talk about his final record, about his legacy. They usually said that no player could be considered a truly great player who had not gone to Britain and won the British Open.

The 1953 British Open was played on the Carnoustie links. Hogan arrived early and began to prepare for what would surely be his one chance to add victory in Britain to his resume. He began a study of the smaller English ball, the grasses found at Carnoustie, and the winds he would have to deal with. As he practiced, the Scots came to understand that Hogan was more than merely a great golfer. They named him the "Wee Ice Mon," and soon the galleries for his practice rounds swelled to more than five hundred.

It's a good thing that Hogan won, for if he had failed at Carnoustie it would have been a transatlantic anticlimax. But more important than his victory was the clear evidence that Hogan had reached a status beyond "great player." A young Ben Wright recalled "an absolute aura" surrounding Hogan at Carnoustie in 1953. Wright stated that "just being near him gave one the deepest sort of thrill and chill."

It was the English writer Pat Ward-Thomas who most successfully captured the reverence that many felt about Hogan. Ward-Thomas, in his book *Masters of Golf*, celebrated many players but reserved special language for Hogan. For him, Hogan played like a man with a vengeance, determined upon destruction, and he set about it with an efficiency so cold-blooded and ruthless than even the greatest courses seemed defenseless and, in his conquering years, all other golfers became resigned to defeat.

> He [Hogan] had a rare quality of stillness, and impassivity, which was almost oriental. . . . One was aware of a cold force being generated within and also of an acute golfing brain. [On the last green at Carnoustie, having won the Open,] there was no exultant waving of the putter, no signs of joy or relief, simply the gentle bows such as a great actor might make after a long and exhausting part. Hogan seemed quite alone, humble in the presence of his mighty achievement, and indeed at that moment he was alone, on that supreme peak of greatness where, in all the history of golf, only Bob Jones had stood.

The year 1953 was not the end, of course. Ben played on, especially intent on winning a fifth U.S. Open and thus separating himself from Jones. It was not to be. He came agonizingly close in 1960 but the lingering effects of the accident were quickly eroding his ability to putt. Slowly his relentless perfectionism shifted from golf shots to golf clubs. He personally created a company and a brand that received much deserved respect. Ben continued to play and practice. He settled in at a club, Shady Oaks, built by his childhood employer, Marvin Leonard. Ben Hogan died on July 25, 1997.

There is much that we will never know about Mr. Hogan. Did he discover some secret to the golf swing? What drove him to find in a game a challenge that seemed to anger him and push him toward perfection with an intensity that can only be called religious? All I know is that in the 1950s, when I came to love golf, it was Hogan more than anyone who defined the game.

One might expect Sam Snead to be very much like Hogan and Nelson. They shared a birth year, childhoods spent in largely rural, Southern environments (Texas and Virginia), and they all experienced the life on the Depression-era golf tour and lived through World War II. Yet Snead turned out to be a very different person with a very different golfing career. He, unlike Hogan and Nelson, was never fully accepted by the USGA and the golfing establishment. Snead, for all his accomplishments, never engendered the reverence accorded Hogan and Nelson. If Nelson was the Oracle and Hogan the Pilgrim, then Snead was the Natural, known for his God-given talent and his failures, both golfing and personal.

Snead was born in Ashwood, a small town very near the resort town of Hot Springs, Virginia. His father worked for the hotel in Hot Springs as a general handyman and laborer. He would dress in a suit each day, walk to the ancient hotel (built in 1766), and change into his work clothes for a day of labor. He was an odd man with odd traits. For example, he could not abide having anyone touch his head. Haircuts were a trial.

Sam was much closer to his mother. He was the youngest of six children and always spoke with reverence of his mother, who was forty-seven when Sam was born. All the Sneads were big, strong, and athletic. It was said that Sam's great uncle John was seven foot, nine inches tall and weighed 360 pounds. Sam also inherited the musical talent that seemed to run in the family; he played the banjo and the trumpet and sang with a nice tenor voice.

Sam began to caddie at the resort at age seven. His first swings, legend has it, were with broken buggy whips equipped with iron golf heads. He always claimed that his slow, syrupy tempo was rooted in these buggy-whip swings. While golf was important, Sam played all sports in high school and was offered scholarships to nearby colleges. He decided, however, that four years of working on his golf game would do him more good than four years of college.

In addition to caddying, Sam worked as a soda jerk at a local drugstore and as a semipro prizefighter. He was paid fifty dollars a fight as part of the program put on to entertain the guests at the hotel. During his senior year in high school Sam got a job in the pro shop at the hotel course, where he learned to make clubs. He would always be an unusually good judge of clubs, able to feel poorly balanced instruments in his huge hands.

One day when he was the only person in the shop, a female guest came in looking for a lesson. Since he was alone, and the woman insisted, Sam gave her the lesson. She was impressed with Sam's teaching and told his superiors. A few days later the sports director of the hotel offered Sam the job as pro at the nearby Cascades Course. His pay was modest. As he put it, "I got whatever I could in lessons and a glass of milk and a sandwich for lunch." The move, however, gave Sam ample chance to practice, and his game developed quickly.

One important difference between Snead and Hogan and Nelson was Snead's background at a resort. Both Ben and Byron had grown up as caddies at a country club, where the pro and the membership took a paternal interest in the young caddies who came to work at their course. Sam, on the other hand, grew up at a resort with no membership to offer caddie tournaments and playing privileges on the club course. Sam developed in a world dominated by resort management, men who never saw Sam or the other caddies in a paternal way. Until he began to work for the resort as a pro, the courses were closed to him.

Snead also had little chance to gain tournament experience as an amateur. As a pro, unlike Hogan and Nelson, Sam did well from the beginning. As a virtual unknown, he placed third in the 1935 Cascades Open. He won the West Virginia Closed Professional, defeating Harry Cooper in a playoff. Later, in 1936, he went to Florida and did well in the Miami Open, winning three hundred dollars. These finishes, and the recommendation of Henry Picard (who seems to have had a part in the careers of many early pros), got Sam an endorsement contract with Dunlop that paid him five hundred dollars and a supply of clubs and balls.

The hard decision was whether to go west and try the winter tour full time. It was Sam's involvement in upper-crust gambling culture that, in large part, allowed him to try the tour. While still at the Homestead, two guests from New York decided to take Sam north to play in a high-stakes match against an amateur by the name of T. Suffern Tailer, known as Tommy. The men paid Sam's expenses and he was treated to his very first train ride.

The match took place at the Meadow Brook Club on Long Island. After Sam won the match, Tailer demanded a rematch, which he also lost. Sam later learned that his backers had won $150,000. They gave Sam $10,000 as his fee for playing so well. It was this money that made it possible for Snead to go west in January of 1937 and try his luck.

While in Florida Sam had made friends with a journeyman pro named Johnny Bulla. They decided to travel together and share expenses. To further cut costs the two stayed with Sam's uncle in Los Angeles. Johnny Bulla was one of the more intriguing figures on the early tour. Bulla was the son of a Quaker minister who did all he could to keep his son from playing golf, a game he saw as frivolous. Bulla never had great success as a touring pro. He was, however, the first to obtain a pilot's license and fly from tour stop to tour stop.

Snead was a rousing success as a tour player. He won six hundred dollars at the Los Angeles Open, won the next week at the Oakland Open, and followed that with a victory at the Bing Crosby Pro-Am. As spring approached he went on another streak, winning at Miami and Nassau. He topped off the year with one more win, at the St. Paul Open in the summer.

In 1938, just to prove that 1937 was no fluke, Sam won eight events and the astounding total of nineteen thousand dollars. The press and the golfing public loved this new golfing phenomenon. It was the classic story of an unknown player coming out of the backwoods and dominating the established tour stars. From the beginning, Sam was the untutored Natural whose skills were God given. He was simple, even a little crude, in the relentlessly civil and sophisticated world of golf. Sam quickly hired a manager, Fred Corcoran, to help him cash in on his new-found fame. Corcoran flogged the hillbilly angle for years and the golf writers were his allies in setting Sam's image as the hick who could really play.

In 1939 Sam added a second element to his image. This was the lasting reputation as a player who could not win the really big event, the U.S. Open. In 1939, at the Spring Mill Course of the Philadelphia Country Club, Sam very nearly won the Open but kicked it away on the last hole. He was in the lead as the two-round Saturday began. As the afternoon round began, he trailed his friend Johnny Bulla by one stroke. After playing very good golf for sixteen holes, he bogeyed the seventeenth and stood on the eighteenth tee not sure where he stood. He would always blame that sense of uncertainty for what happened next.

The contenders for the title were strung out behind Snead (including Byron Nelson, who would be the eventual winner) on the last nine. Without scoreboards to inform him, Snead concluded that he needed a birdie on the last hole—a reachable par five. Snead then committed his first error; he tried to hit his drive too far and hooked it into the rough on the left. His second mistake was his attempt to hit a brassy from a poor lie. This shot finished in a bunker 110 yards short of the green. A par was still possible, but he hit the sand shot thin and it hit the top of the bunker and lodged in some loose sod. The next shot finished in a greenside bunker. His next finished forty feet from the hole. Three putts completed one of the most famous eights in golf history. Sam's biographer, Al Barkow, concluded that the last hole collapse in 1939 "left a stain on Sam's psyche for the rest of his life." Sam would have a handful of chances to win the Open, but it never happened. It became part of who he was—great player, never won the Open.

A counter to his Open failures was his amazing longevity. Unlike Nelson and Hogan, who had relatively short careers, Snead's seem to go on forever. By one generous account, Snead won 135 tournaments. Of this total, 84 may be called official tour victories. Official accounts by the PGA have reduced this total only slightly, crediting Snead with 81 victories. More to the point is how well he played. In 1965, at fifty-three, he won the Greensboro Open. In 1974, at sixty-two, he finished in a tie for third at the PGA, three shots behind the winner, Lee Trevino. Trevino was born three years after Snead won his first event.

When senior professional golf began its evolution into what became the Senior Tour, Snead was a central figure. The first senior events were fifty-four-hole team events called the Legends of Golf. Sam, teamed with Gardner Dickinson, won the first event in 1978 at the age of sixty-six. Sam made six birdies in the last round. In 1982 Sam won again, this time with Don January. By 1995 the Legends tournament had expanded to seventy-two holes and, at age eighty-three, Snead, with Bob Goalby, tied for second. This was his last competitive event.

Beyond playing in the tournaments, Sam worked hard for senior golf. He was a legend and important to the success of a venture based on nostalgia. He went to all the cocktail parties and met all the sponsors. It was as if he instinctively understood how important he was in the effort to launch senior golf. Snead also understood how important senior professional golf was to the pros of his era. For them, this was the greatest do-over, or mulligan, in sports history. For many of them, unlike Sam, they simply needed the money.

This was the Sam Snead who could be generous, open, and sympathetic. There was, however, another Sam Snead whom Barkow portrays as "a very difficult man — ornery, curt, dismissive." For me, Snead is difficult to understand. It is probably impossible to get at the root causes of his self-destructive, thoughtless, and often crude behavior.

What was it about Sam that set him off from his peers? Famously, he told dirty jokes in mixed company. The jokes did not go well, even in an all-male environment. Gene Sarazen, no prude, walked out of the Masters Champions dinner when Sam started with the jokes. After Byron Nelson took over as emcee of the dinners, he limited Sam to one vulgar story per year. One evening at Pinehurst, Sam began telling one off-color joke after another. Seated at the same table was an increasingly angry Patty Berg (one of the sport's first female pro golfers and first president of the Ladies Professional Golf Association). Sam was asked to stop but he habitually brushed aside such warnings. Eventually, Patty walked out of the event. Something in Sam made him act this way in certain situations. However, he acted differently in others. He never told his jokes when his sister-in-law, Sylvia Snead, was present. If his friends, the amateur golfer Bill Campbell and his wife, were present, the jokes stopped. But the storytelling did its damage, it was part of the reason the golf establishment grew to dislike Sam Snead.

Another element in this dislike was Sam's family life and his womanizing. This requires a quick summary of Sam's married life and the sad tale of his second son. Sam married Audrey Karnes in 1940, after an off-and-on-again courtship that began in high school. Sam wanted a large family and he was nearly thirty. Their first son, Samuel Jackson Snead Jr., was born in 1944. Their second son, Terence, was born in 1952. Known as Terry, he was different from birth; clearly he suffered from some sort of mental defect.

The response to Terry's affliction was conditioned by a long-standing fear that mental illness ran in the Karnes family. Sam's mother had been dead set against Sam marrying Audrey because she believed the Karnes family was tainted by mental illness. In order to keep similar problems from afflicting another child, Audrey Snead said no more sex, no more children. They never divorced, but for the last years of their marriage they were not intimate. The burden of these family events fell on Audrey. She was left at home to care for Jackie and Terry while Sam spent much of the year on the road, where women were plentiful for a star like Sam Snead. In some sense, liberated by Audrey's edict, Sam took full advantage. Later in his career he did settle down with one particular mistress. She traveled with

Snead and, after Audrey died in 1990, they lived together when Sam was in Florida during the winter.

The PGA Tour was never a place you would send your son for training in the Christian virtues. I write this just as we are learning of Tiger Woods's lack of just these virtues. However, there never was a time when the PGA, the USGA, and golf in general did not expect a certain amount of discretion. Snead seemed incapable of exercising this discretion.

Thus there can be no doubt that Snead was deeply disliked by several very important people in the golf community. Bob Jones, from his seat at Augusta, had become the most revered figure in the game. As he grew older, and sicker, Jones became more religious, more inclined to see things in moral terms. Jones, the great amateur, did not like Snead, the new-style pro. More important, Joe Dey, the executive director of the USGA, had, for some unspoken reason, taken a dislike to Sam. Dey was a man of high moral standards, some would say too high. Sam's complex relations with women and the dirty jokes were clearly enough to set Dey against Snead. Al Barkow suggests in his biography of Snead that Dey's disapproval led him to give Sam tee times and partners at the Open that hurt Sam's chances. Furthermore, one cannot resist the idea that Snead was the living evidence that pros were taking over the game. Jones and the USGA were the great exponents of amateur golf, which by the early 1950s was losing its grip on the public mind. To men like Jones and Dey, Snead was the wrong sort of person to be the face of the game.

This conflict between Snead and the golfing establishment had one very public manifestation. By the middle of the 1960s his putting had become a serious problem. In 1966, in the middle of a round at the PGA Championship, Sam switched to croquet-style putting. He would straddle the line, with his face looking directly at the hole, and push the ball on its way. Sam was not the first to adopt this style. A pro, Bob Duden, had been using the croquet style in competition for several years. Ward Foshay, a former president of the USGA, was one of the many amateurs who putted using the style Sam adopted in 1966.

Using this technique, which some called the "squat shot" style, Sam tied for tenth at the 1967 Masters (Jack Nicklaus missed the cut). After that finish, the uprising against croquet putting began in earnest. Bob Jones took Sam aside and urged him to abandon his new putting style. Jones thought that it was a violation of the rules, but he was wrong. Jones may have talked to Joe Dey who set about getting the USGA to change the rules. By 1968 the rule was changed; you could no longer straddle a line of a putt. The USGA's rationale, that croquet style was not traditional, does little to explain why they only took up the issue after Sam Snead adopted the approach.

In the end, Sam Snead was more colorful than Ben Hogan and Byron Nelson, but some important people did not like this "colorfulness." In the years since Sam's death, on May 23, 2002, four days short of his ninetieth birthday, there has been considerable debate about his character. Tributes to Sam have been rare. There is nothing at Augusta to mark his victories. The USGA has done little to memorialize the Slammer. In the end, however, Nelson, Hogan, and Snead stand together as the men most responsible for creating the modern touring golf professional.

What exactly was it that they collectively accomplished? First of all, they kept the tour alive when it looked like fifteen years of Depression and war would crush it. This was especially true of Nelson and Snead. Nelson was the honest young Texan who could really play. Snead was the Natural from the Virginia hills, with a swing to die for and a ready-made image as the rural hick who could beat everyone. His great years in the late 1930s were critical in changing the image of tour golf. They showed that you could make a living playing just the tour. Second, during and after the war, all three made sizable contributions to keeping golf alive during its darkest days and jumpstarting interest in the game at war's end. Nelson was especially crucial during the war years. He toured the country with McSpaden and celebrities like Hope and Crosby, bringing golf to the public and to the men and women in the military. When the war was over golf could say, accurately, that the game had done its part. Nelson's play in 1945 and 1946 gave the game an enormous pop exactly when it needed it. The streak in 1946 could not have done more to revive interest in the tour and in golf generally. Lackluster local tour events of the mid-1930s became front-page news when Nelson was winning them in 1946.

Hogan, in many respects, took over for Nelson after Byron retired to his ranch. It took a tragedy, the nearly fatal traffic accident, to change Hogan from a very interesting pro athlete into a figure of consuming interest. His comeback, especially his play in the Los Angeles Open and the U.S. Open in 1950, made Hogan and golf again front-page news. From that point onward, Ben seemed to occupy a singular place in the public mind and the golf community. The press and dedicated fans talked about him using language that can only be described as religious.

All three pros were very much the creation of print media. The consuming desire of the journalists who covered the PGA Tour was for stories. Shot-by-shot accounts of tournaments did not sell newspapers. The PGA Tour, and managers like Fred Corcoran, did all they could to supply colorful stories. Famously, the longtime pro Ky Laffoon, because he looked like an Indian and the name seemed to fit, was given an Indian persona that the press loved. Laffoon played along even though he was a Walloon (not nearly interesting enough and too hard to explain).

Hogan, Nelson, and Snead were all promoted by the press using stories that were half true and half false (a good definition of myth). These stories all came with new names that somehow captured the whole story. Nelson was "Lord Byron," and the press worked hard to find words that amplified this new name. He was a gentleman — mechanical, methodical, polite, and well dressed. Snead was "Slammin' Sammy" or "the Slammer." The press worked to find words to convey the incredible grace and power of his swing. They also worked another angle: Snead could not win the big one. Hogan probably inspired more creativity from the press because he talked to them so rarely and when he did it was usually bland. They made a great deal of his small size and his grim demeanor on the course. Arthur Daley, who wrote about golf for the *New York Times,* was a tireless creator of phrases to describe players. In one story on Hogan he used all the following: "Little Ben Hogan"; "Blazin' Ben"; "tenacious Texan"; "iron-willed square-jawed scrapper"; "battlin' Ben"; "the little Texas bulldog"; "golf's mechanical man"; "the little Texan"; "Beltin' Ben Hogan"; and "the poker-faced Hogan." It was also almost universally acceptable to refer to Hogan as "the Hawk" because of the steady, somewhat hostile glare that he adopted while playing. All of this creative wordsmithing helped the public — many of whom never saw Hogan, Nelson, or Snead — become fans.

The three men were also riding a wave of cultural change of which they were not fully aware. The inexhaustible logic of specialization was transforming America. In 1895 the job of golf professional was a mix of jobs. After 1895 the job of all professionals, in the United States especially, began to fragment rapidly. The PGA, founded in 1916, helped professionalize the occupation, but it resisted, in some sense, the specialization that was already obvious. The aspect of the job that was the most problematical was the part about playing for cash prizes. Walter Hagen, almost alone, took that part of the job and ran with it.

He made the part of being a professional that was the most socially and culturally negative his own and did much to give it respectability. Why was this true? Culturally, playing a game for money was looked upon as gambling, and the culture of the early twentieth century still looked upon gambling as immoral. Playing a sport as a salaried employee was generally not considered gambling. This moral view of gambling has a long history, with its roots in Protestant and general Christian attitudes. Betting on the outcome of a contest, some thought, was at bottom to bet on the will of God. Gambling and excessive drinking were often linked as causes of ruined lives. Finally, there was the idea of a calling, an important Judeo-Christian idea that held that almost all work was sacred. The calling of gambler was an exception, since it produced nothing and it tended to tempt people into other immoral activities. In Protestant America, to think of gambling as a calling was just not possible. Golf, which took root in Victorian, Protestant America, slowly had to adjust to a more secular, less prudish culture. Hogan, Snead, and Nelson were agents and evidence of this adjustment. While it would not have been possible in 1905, in 1955 they could become nationally venerated heroes.

The rise of the PGA Tour benefited greatly from a decline in these antigambling attitudes. Hogan, Nelson, and Snead were part of this process because they acted as if what they did was not gambling. They played a game for money, but somehow it came to be seen as legitimate work, in large part, because they treated it as such.

The early touring pros, however, knew exactly what they were doing. Chandler Harper, who borrowed three thousand dollars at 8 percent to hit the professional golf tour, put it bluntly. He said, "What you did was gamble. In those early days on the tour I guess we all gambled." What we have seen in this chapter about Hogan, Snead, and Nelson suggests that they would agree with Harper. However, it's my guess that by the mid-1950s few players would have portrayed their work as gambling.

How did this transformation take place? Like all cultural shifts the causes are subtle and produce change slowly. Between 1935 and 1955 playing the tour for money went from wagering to legitimate work. There were some significant signposts along the way. It is fascinating to note that Hogan, Nelson, and

Snead all began their careers playing in shirts and ties. They ended their careers playing in what we now think of as normal golf dress. They played in shirts and ties to signal their escape from manual labor and as a way to suggest their respectability. This habit died out quickly after the war. All three of our heroes loved expensive clothes. Nelson had sixty-dollar pants; Hogan had his custom-made English shoes and Allen Solly Egyptian cotton shirts from England, and Snead was also a dandy, who took to wearing a trademark straw hat to hide his baldness. Both Snead and Hogan became associated with a certain kind of hat. Hogan wore a white cap that became his trademark. No manual worker would ever wear such a snowy white hat. Snead was just as tightly linked to his straw hat with a colorful band, and to a lesser extent Nelson was associated with a golf visor. In the end they adopted the habits of their early role models — the members of the private clubs at which they had worked and, in Snead's case, the guests at Hot Springs. Golf is the only major sport that does not have a prescribed uniform. It was Nelson, Hogan, and Snead who created the unofficial image of what a golfer should look like, and they did not look like gamblers and they did not look like manual laborers.

They abandoned the shirt-and-tie look of Walter Hagan, who frankly looked like a gambler, for the quiet elegance of country club chic. Of course, there was a minority movement. Jimmy Demaret was famous in the same years (1935–55) for his flamboyant and colorful clothes. However it was the expensive elegance of Hogan, Nelson, and Snead that won the day. It is truly remarkable how much the touring professionals of today look like Hogan of 1953.

The professional golf tour evolved between 1935 and 1955 into something new. Hogan, Nelson, and Snead were the public face of that evolution. Unlike the stars in other sports, PGA touring pros were not under contract to a team, did not receive a set yearly salary, were not representative of a city or a region (like team-based athletes), did not play a schedule set by a league, and did not derive their worth from season-long performance statistics. Instead, the PGA pro was an individual setting his own schedule and representing no one but himself and often a private golf club. Rank as a tour player was based on three things: most basically, money won, tour titles won, and victories in "majors" and other important events.

In the most general sense, Nelson, Hogan, and Snead created a new kind of work. They played a game that most of their fans played. In essence, they gambled at golf in events where other people (sponsors) put up the money. Unlike the other sports, a tour player could hit the jackpot or win nothing. Those who won nothing had to find honest work off the tour. It was not manual work, but it was not intellectual, white-collar work either. It was a very special niche in the American world of work.

The Golf Community in a New Age of Affluence

I n 1968, my father and I had a talk that I remember vivid-
ly. As a budding historian, I asked him what it was like to
live through the Great Depression and the war. His answer
was simple: "We thought that things would be awful forever."
When the war ended, he recalled, everyone he knew believed
that Depression-era conditions would return. Without wartime
government spending to bolster the economy, and with ten million soldiers returning to the workforce, unemployment would
skyrocket and the economy "would sink like a stone." My mother had worked during the war, and as a tool and die maker,
my father was exempt from military service. There was, he remembered, almost nothing to buy during the war. They saved
a huge percentage of their income between 1941 and 1945. In
1945, they thought they were going to need every nickel to get
through the coming years.

He smiled at that point and said, "But it didn't work out that
way." People began to spend their wartime savings and, after a
period of inflation, the economy took off. For twenty years, my
father made more money every year than the year before. He
shook his head in disbelief; he claimed that "just about everyone we knew was awash in money." This money allowed them to
buy things they had never heard of in 1944: televisions, a clothes
dryer, air conditioning, jet travel, a bigger home, and a college
education for the smug graduate student who was quizzing him.

My father talked about attitudes with much less conviction. Twenty-one years old in 1929, his views had been shaped in Kentucky in the 1920s. Vaguely, he said, "You can't think about people now the way we did back then." When I asked him what he meant, his eyes flashed left and right and he said simply, "Well, the Negroes, you know." After a brief silence he added, "It's up to you and your people to fix, to settle that." This topic deeply unsettled him. Never one to care much about social distinctions, my father claimed that my mother thought that "society had gone straight to hell, that no one had any respect for what was proper." My mother was happy to confirm this view.

Surprisingly, my father's comments have a lot to do with golf and the history of the golf community in the postwar era. The dominant theme was affluence. People had more money and time, and the golf community grew—more courses, more players. But affluence changed golf in other ways. There was a decline in the number of private clubs and the rise of the golf course real estate community. These massive ventures, while technically public, served many of the same functions as private clubs. As for attitudes, it became clear that the unthinking exclusion of blacks and the demotion of women to second-class status could not survive. There was no victory in either case, but after 1945 exclusion in all its forms was contested, often bitterly.

But, for the most part, it was affluence that ruled the golf community in the postwar era. The evidence clearly shows that the United States was undercoursed in 1950. Steiner, in 1930, claimed that the country had 5,800 courses and approximately 2 million players. In the early 1950s, *Golfdom*, a reliable source of golf information, put the number of courses at 5,045 and the number of players at 3.25 million. Between 1930 and 1950, the country's population had grown by 18 million. Thus the demand for courses was considerably higher in 1950 than in the late 1920s—the last years of golf's golden age.

Consistently, during the three decades after 1950, the golfing public had more money and time for discretionary activities. The gross national product (GNP) tripled between 1945 and 1965. In the 1950s alone there was a 25 percent increase in real wages. By 1960, the five-day workweek (forty hours) had become virtually universal. The average American worker received eight paid holidays and enjoyed a two-week paid vacation. One study in 1950 found that approximately one-seventh of the GNP was spent on pleasure and this rose dramatically over the years.

Out of this flood of affluence came the modern definition of retirement, which had a profound impact on the golf community. As Americans got richer, they spent—individually and collectively—much more on health. People lived longer and they stayed well and active longer. An American in 1930 who reached age sixty-five could expect 12.2 more years of life. In 2000 someone living to sixty-five could look forward to 17.7 more years. The 5.5-year difference is an extraordinary fact. The general life expectancy of all Americans in 1930 was 59.2 years, in 2003 it was 77.5.

As Americans lived longer, they worked less, especially after age sixty-five. In 1930, 58 percent of the men over sixty-five were still in the work force. In 2000, this had dropped to 17 percent. There was a similar drop for men in the age group fifty-five to sixty-four. American affluence had invented retirement—"the golden years"—a period of self-financed independence and leisure. Research into the history of retirement suggests that the expansion of retirement to vast numbers of Americans was caused by many factors: the decline of agricultural work, the rise of private pension systems and Social Security, and the spread of health insurance. But the basic cause of the new retirement was higher wages, the most basic definition of affluence. Americans simply made more during their working lives and were able to save enough to finance a substantial number of workless years at the end of life.

Golf could not have asked for better economic news. If the golf community had been a town, someone should have gone from house to house announcing that the "retirees are coming."

Of course golf had always been billed as a game for a lifetime. Senior golfers had their own tournaments or competed against players their own age in larger events. But the impact of the steady postwar growth in the number of long-term retirees was explosive. The dramatic changes that took place in the American South can, in part, be traced to the growth of retirement. By the end of the century, Florida boasted 1,228 courses, more than any other state and more than 200 ahead of second-place California. Almost every new aspect of golf that appeared after 1950, like the powered golf cart and the gated golf community, had some connection to the growth of the over-sixty-five population

Postwar affluence was not an unalloyed blessing for the golf community, however. Competition for discretionary dollars became fierce as what we now call the consumer culture shifted into high gear. Americans in the '50s and '60s confronted a world of expanding choices and products that soon came to seem like necessities. The same people who would join a golf club developed a taste for foreign products as America became the world's leading importer. This meant an expensive Jaguar instead of a Ford, a Heineken instead of a Bud. These same people came to believe that you had to have an electric clothes dryer, one of the biggest sellers in the 1950s. By 1968, 38 percent of Americans had some form of air conditioning in their home.

After the war, Americans began to travel more and to do so more expensively. Travel to Europe increased dramatically. The French, it was said, now abandoned Paris in August to hordes of American tourists. Improved prop planes and, eventually, jet aircraft transformed air travel in the '50s and beyond. On the ground, the interstate highway system gave American car culture a terrific shot in the arm. As Americans zoomed along these new, safer roads, they could stop for the night at the newly created motels. They were not back at home playing golf at their local club.

The consumer culture also produced a device — the

television—that was the clear winner in the competition for discretionary dollars and especially for discretionary time. There were only seven thousand sets in the entire country in 1947. By 1955, two-thirds of American families had a television, and by 1960, this number had risen to 87 percent. If you were watching television you were also soaking up massive amounts of advertising for national brands. Golf, and particularly the local private club, did not advertise in the normal sense of the word. Advertising that hooked people on national brands tripled between 1945 and 1960. In the next chapter we will focus on television's complex impact on the golf community.

Television, national advertising, and other factors produced a decline in localism (emotional attachment to a town or city) in the postwar era. There is much evidence to support this notion. Increasingly, people worked for large national corporations, and the very existence of local, independently owned businesses, like department stores, was threatened. More importantly, Americans became frantically mobile after the war. Atlas Van Lines, in the 1950s, estimated that members of the managerial class moved an amazing fourteen times during their careers. People joked that one of the new national corporations, IBM, meant "I've Been Moved." A substantial cause of this mobility was the opening of the so-called Sunbelt. Florida, Texas, and California grew rapidly, drawing population from the Northeast and Midwest. In 1970, one out of every ten Americans lived in California.

While there can be little doubt that the golf community prospered between 1950 and 1985, it did so in a much-altered context. It faced a number of challenges. The first was the coming of a new set of competitors for the dollars Americans had to spend on leisure. Television was the most important, but it was just the most dramatic item on a long and constantly expanding list of must-have consumer products. The second was the general detachment of families from their local areas. People moved more often, and often they moved from one newly created suburb to another. This tended to make a long-term commitment to a private golf club less likely.

But golf grew. The Korean War inhibited the construction of courses in the early fifties, but bolstered by the postwar economy all aspects of the golf community surged. The number of courses jumped from five thousand in 1950 to thirteen thousand in 1985. From just over 3 million in 1950 the number of players (who played regularly) zoomed to 14 million in 1985. There were another 3.5 million who claimed to play occasionally. In 1985, courses took up 1.5 million acres, an area twice the size of Rhode Island.

A look behind these raw numbers suggests that golf course construction was closely tied to population. Courses were increasingly built where there were the most players. However, course construction did not satisfy demand as it grew after 1945. By 1983 there were seven states with more than 600 courses: California (746), New York (739), Florida (651), Michigan (747), Ohio (642), Pennsylvania (611,) and Texas (602). All these states, with one exception, had among the lowest number of courses per hundred thousand of population in the nation. New York (with 3.8 courses per hundred thousand) and California (2.4) were especially noteworthy in this regard. Rural, smaller states had many more courses per person. Both the Dakotas had nearly 14 courses per hundred thousand. Michigan was something of an outlier with 6.9 courses per hundred thousand, exactly the same as South Carolina. The existence of rapid population growth seemed to be a key factor: golf course construction always follows population, but it tends to lag behind.

Course construction figures between 1950 and 1985 show that the private golf course was overtaken by public facilities. In 1931 almost 80 percent of courses were private; in 1985 61 percent were public (municipal or daily fee). Earlier, I tried to suggest some of the reasons behind this change. The decline of local attachments seems to me to be important. There are, however, a number of other likely causes.

Private clubs after the war faced a negative tax situation. Federal income tax rates had soared during the war and remained high. This cut the discretionary dollars available for club fees and dues, especially among the more affluent. Also during the war the tax on club dues was raised to 20 percent and remained at that level until 1966. In the three decades after 1950, clubs also faced rapidly rising property taxes. As their courses became entangled in the vast postwar expansion of urban areas, their value as house lots exploded. The clubs, depending on the state, generally confronted much higher taxes. For many clubs it was easier to just sell out.

The private club also competed against the rise of the real estate–oriented golf course. As we saw earlier, golf has always been, in complex ways, connected to real estate and land values. Groups creating clubs prior to 1930 were often acutely aware of the impact the construction of a golf club would have on the value of nearby real estate. After 1950, the situation in some sense was reversed. Land developers seeking to divide raw land into house lots and condominium projects came to see the value of golf courses. Simply put, land developers began using golf courses to increase the value of house lots they wished to sell. The courses they created were often a mix of public and private. They offered memberships to residents but also opened their courses to daily-fee play. These golf-oriented real estate ventures were one of the most important developments in the golf community over the last half-century.

It may be impossible to find the roots of this type of relationship between golf and real estate. Certainly one of the earliest examples was the late-nineteenth-century development of Tuxedo Park in New York. Developers who built suburbs prior to 1950 occasionally included a private golf club in their plans. In the years after 1950, an important pioneer was Charles Fraser and his creation, Sea Pines Plantation, on Hilton Head Island, South Carolina.

Until the early 1950s, Hilton Head was inaccessible and

produced only lumber for a few companies that controlled the island. In the early 1950s, in response to the demand for beachfront vacations, the island finally was electrified and a ferry service begun. A few people constructed vacation homes on the island's remarkable beaches. Charles Fraser, whose family was involved in the timber business, owned over three thousand acres of Hilton Head land that he would turn into Sea Pines Plantation.

Fraser reinvented the private gated community to fit the needs of postwar America. The core of Fraser's plan was the restrictive covenant, which limited builders and owners in a number of ways. Home size, the colors used, the landscaping, and more were all spelled out for owners. The community would grow according to Fraser's plan; there would be no public process or zoning controls. The result was an amazingly uniform place. Fraser made the most of his beachfront by building houses arranged in rows with paths to the beach, offering access to an increased number of homeowners. The normal approach (also seen on Hilton Head) was to build waterside high-rises with as many condo apartments as the developer could squeeze in.

Fraser, in his planning, underestimated the need for recreational facilities. His partner, James C. Self, and George Cobb, a course designer, convinced Fraser that golf could be crucial to the success of Sea Pines. They argued that golf courses could change the value of land. Golf would, they argued, also attract first-class buyers to the project. Much of Sea Pines was "interior land" that was difficult or impossible to sell as house lots or condos. However, Self and Cobb claimed that this would change if you ran golf courses through the property. Presto! The land was transformed into "golf front lots" and they began to sell briskly. In 1962 Frazier claimed that the first golf course "would have been financial folly if it were not for the fact that the course created $2 million worth of fairway lots at the same time."

Sea Pines was, and still is, a very important place. It clearly was a response to the same impulses that made the private golf club so popular prior to 1930. Sea Pines and the many developments that attempted to copy it do what the private club does; they draw a boundary between the sane and ordered world of the development and the increasingly insane and disordered world outside being created by consumer capitalism. Inside Sea Pines the roads run in looping curves (no grid pattern) and there is a false sense that land has been wasted. There is a huge nature preserve and considerable green space but, in reality, the plantation is very densely settled. There is the overwhelming sense, which the golf courses help create, that one has come to an enclave, a place of escape. This impression is formed right at the beginning, when one passes through the security gates that employ armed guards charged with keeping out those who don't belong.

Sea Pines may not have been the first golf-based real estate development but it was immensely influential. After 1970 golf became even more deeply connected to real estate. Courses were built to attract people looking for a golf lifestyle. Developers increasingly employed high-priced name designers like Arnold Palmer, Jack Nicklaus, Tom Fazio, Trent Jones, and others. As everyone sought to build the course that would attract lot buyers, costs rose dramatically. In 2000 Tom Fazio estimated that in the 1960s the average cost per hole was between $10,000 and $20,000 for new courses. By the 1990s this number had risen to $200,000 to $400,000. Total construction costs for a new course in the 1960s were slightly less than $400,000. In the 1990s they had reached as much as $7.6 million. Developers also began pumping up the size and cost of clubhouses that were not included in Fazio's estimates.

Finally, Sea Pines is important to golf because of the courses that exist there. There are four—three public and one private. All four courses are good, but one is particularly notable. The Harbour Town Links, designed by Pete Dye and finished in 1969, stands as a meaningful course in the endless debate over what makes a course great. Harbour Town is one of the great courses built after 1950. It is the poster child for the idea that a course can be short, interesting, and demanding at the same time. Lengthened in recent years, it is still short by modern standards. From the back (Heritage) tees it runs to 6,973 yards. There are middle (Dye) tees (6,603) and women's (Palmetto) tees (5,208). However, the course that is the most interesting is the one played from the Sea Pines tees and is only 6,040 yards long.

This course does at least three things to challenge and interest the golfer. The fairways are curved in such a way that the alert golfer understands that hitting the fairway is not enough, one must be on the correct side of the fairway. Find yourself on the wrong side and you discover that overhanging trees block your way. Curved fairways also define the par fives, even the longest hitters find getting to the green in two difficult. The best approach is to drive to a shorter spot and then play the curve of the fairway to the best position for your third. Harbour Town has exceedingly small greens and this puts a heavy emphasis on hitting very accurate mid- and short irons. Even the most talented players miss many greens at Harbour Town and usually the best scores are made by the best chippers and those who make all their four- and five-foot putts. Harbour Town Links stands in contrast to the general direction of course architecture after 1950. Courses in the modern era have become longer and longer, especially in the last twenty-five years. There are many reasons for this, but one of them is the failure of architects to fully understand what Dye created at Harbour Town. The average American golfer should be playing on a 5,800-to-6,000-yard course that incorporates the principles that were used to design the Harbour Town Links.

The importance of Harbour Town Links only adds to the overall historical significance of Sea Pines Plantation. It served as a model for hundreds of developments that sought to link housing and golf. By the early 1960s, the real estate sections of most newspapers were beginning to note this growing trend.

The *New York Times*, in 1964, suggested that home builders and country clubs had once been enemies, a contention that was probably not true. In any event, the paper noted that builders had come to see the value of golf courses as a device to boost sales of lots and homes. The evidence was clear: 40 percent of the four hundred country clubs started in 1964 had a real estate component. The *Times* also noted that a number of established country clubs were selling land along their fairways to builders. The driving force behind this movement was economic. Home buyers had become convinced that homes on a golf course were a better investment because such homes appreciated faster. Every survey of people who buy a home in a gated community finds that quiet, security, and freedom from crime are important motivating factors. That such communities are often overwhelmingly white suggests that race is also a factor.

By the early 1970s the sales at recreational and retirement communities had reached five billion dollars. The boom lasted until 1973 when recession, increased land costs, a saturated market, the energy crisis, and rising interest rates literally flattened the market. Recovery began in the late '70s, but over time the sales of homes in golf-related communities have been volatile, reacting to changing tax policy, limits on rental income allowed, and interest rates. By 1993 there were five states with more than a thousand "recreational subdivisions" on file with the federal government. Florida had 2,612 communities that contained 2.1 million lots covering 1.6 million acres. Texas was second with 1.2 million lots on 900,000 acres. The other states in the top five were California, Arizona, and North Carolina. In 1993 there were 22,900 recreational real estate communities in the United States; they had almost 9 million lots on 8.2 million acres. These communities were crucial in driving course construction and in defining golf after 1960. In the last chapter we shall see that the marriage of golf and real estate did end happily.

Another important aspect of course construction between

1950 and 1985 involves the distribution of private clubs by region. In general, during this period the percentage of private clubs in a region dropped below 50 percent. In New York and California the percentage of private clubs dropped to approximately 35 percent of the total number of courses. This was generally true throughout the Northeast and North-Central regions. In Michigan and Wisconsin private facilities constituted only · 22 percent of the total courses. In the South the percentages were much higher. In the mid-South private courses amounted to approximately 50 percent of the courses in each state. Some specific examples, by percentage: Virginia (57), North Carolina (47), South Carolina (46), Kentucky (51), Tennessee (46), and Missouri (48). However in the band of states running west from Georgia, the numbers were considerably higher: Georgia (63), Alabama (62), Mississippi (74), Louisiana (66), Arkansas (67), and Texas (56).

Why were private clubs so popular in the South? State laws often made forming a club easier in the South and there was probably more cheap land upon which to build clubs. However race was also a key reason for the popularity of private courses in the South. A number of court decisions in the 1950s and early 1960s effectively forced the integration of all municipal facilities, including golf courses. As this happened, white golfers, in large numbers, retreated to existing private clubs or formed new ones.

This introduces the second great theme shaping the golf community after World War II. The easy, unthinking exclusions and limitations that had characterized golf in the 1920s and 1930s were challenged on every front after 1945. No generalization adequately covers the nature and extent of this challenge. It was a messy and inconclusive process that, in many respects, is ongoing.

The golf community was obviously part of the larger American community. When that larger community turned to address the question of racial exclusion, access to the golf community by African Americans became part of a much larger movement. At its core this movement sought to overthrow the separate but equal doctrine established by the Supreme Court in 1896. In this effort, schools came first as the most crucial public facilities that needed to be integrated. Thus, the first chapter in the battle to strike down segregation in golf focused almost solely on public facilities such as municipal golf courses. The question of black access to private clubs was a separate battle that came later and is still being fought.

It is important to understand the virtually universal racism that separated black and white golfers. *Time Magazine* in 1938 found space for a story on "Negro" golf and the Negro Open. It is a golf story like any other in a popular white periodical, but with one exception — it exhibited the racial stereotyping that kept blacks from fully participating in American life.

The article does offer some interesting facts. It claims, for example, that of the twelve million blacks in the United States, "about 50,000 play golf." They play on municipal courses or at one of the "20-odd private Negro courses." Southern blacks, *Time* suggests, are much more likely to play golf than their Northern brethren because of the widespread use of black caddies at Southern country clubs and resorts.

Most of the article is a report on the Thirteenth Annual Negro Open, played at Palos Park Golf Course near Chicago. Of the 135 players showing up for the event, there were 119 men and 16 women. Thirty-four players proclaimed themselves professionals and played for cash prizes; the rest were amateurs. Many players carried their own bags, but many paid white caddies a dollar per round. All the players were extremely civil to the single white player, Charles Hlavacek. He had entered the event because he did not want to give up his habit of playing every day on the Palos Park Course. So it was just another day for Mr. Hlavacek.

As the tournament began, the favorite was Chicago grocer Pat

Ball, who had won the event three times. Other leading players were John Dendy, a "locker boy" at Asheville (North Carolina) Country Club, and Hugh Smith, an "office boy" from Thomasville, Georgia. In the end, these players lost to Howard Wheeler of Atlanta. The article took some delight in describing Wheeler as the "lanky, woolly-topped Howard Wheeler" who teed his ball on a match folder and plopped down on the green while waiting to putt. Wheeler walked "along the fairways in a Stepin Fetchit gate." Wheeler had been a professional at the Lincoln Country Club in Atlanta, one of the few black clubs in the United States. The article reported that since he lost that job in 1933 he had just been "walking around."

The article does recognize that Wheeler played very well. His play (68, 73, 72, and 71, for 284) "would please many a top-flight white golfer." His 284 netted him the first prize of two hundred dollars and set a new scoring record for the event. The Palos Park layout was "a tough hilly course" that Wheeler had never seen before the first round.

However, the *Time* article did not recognize that there was a lot more to report about Howard Wheeler. Born in Atlanta in 1918, he began caddying at a local club. He often caddied for Bobby Jones when he played at Brookhaven Country Club and was caddie master at East Lake Country Club. He grew up playing with a cross-handed grip (left hand low for a right-hander). Wheeler won tournaments as early as 1931. A few days after his victory at Palos Park, Wheeler defeated two white golfers (one was the determined Charles Hlavacek) while shooting a course record 65. In 1941, Wheeler and Clyde Martin defeated two better-known white golfers, Chuck Kocsis and his brother, Emerick, in an exhibition.

Unable to make a living from golf, Wheeler went to work for Eddie Mallory, a bandleader and golf nut. He gave Wheeler the job of chauffeuring Mallory's wife, Ethel Waters, the famous singer. He eventually left Mallory and ended up in the military for the duration of the war. He won a few events after the war but was never able to find a job worthy of his talents in the golf community.

The story of Howard Wheeler goes to the heart of what exclusion meant in the admittedly odd world of golf. By all accounts, Wheeler lived by the best values of golf; he was a civil, easy-going lover of the game who could really play. He was not a "boy," as *Time* would have it. Golf in all its literature professed to be a game open to everyone. Kings played with commoners and men played with women, but in America, Howard Wheeler could only play with his own kind. When on rare occasions he competed against whites he did well. Beginning in 1925, black players formed the United Golf Association (originally the United States Colored Golf Association). Into the 1950s, it was the UGA that provided most of the competitive opportunities for black players.

The major golf associations were, along with private clubs and many public courses, the agents of exclusion. They turned their backs on golf's inclusive traditions; the strength of American racism won the day. Blacks could not aspire to test their games against the best PGA players because the organization expressly denied African Americans membership. Hogan, Snead, and Nelson rose to stardom in a competitive field that included only white people. The USGA events, almost always played at private clubs, usually featured whites-only fields. The national Open was, in fact, not open to players who were members of the black community.

Black opposition to their exclusion from golf was never entirely absent. Most controversies prior to 1945 were local disputes about access to municipal courses. For example, there were persistent attempts by black golfers to gain access to Chicago's Jackson Park Course. There were similar attempts by Washington DC black golfers to play on the district's whites-only courses. After 1945, protests moved along two fronts. Most generally, black golfers fought to play on segregated municipal courses. On front number two, a small but growing group of black professionals sought the right to compete in professional events and for membership in the PGA.

In some cases, states took legal action before the growth of significant protest. In 1942 New York outlawed racial discrimination at golf courses and other public facilities. The conflict between equal access and segregation was most often played out in Southern cities. In most cases, these cities had made clumsy attempts to abide by the logic of the separate but equal doctrine. They constructed poorly designed and maintained blacks-only courses as some sort of balance to the town's whites-only course. In other cases, towns allowed blacks to play only on certain days or times.

Between 1950 and 1955, various cities confronted an increasing number of protests from black golfers. Until the mid-1950s the guiding principle of separate but equal, and the Supreme Court's tendency to see these issues as state matters, produced little progress. It was not until 1955 that the logic of the Supreme Court decision *Brown v Board of Education* began to alter the golf community. In the fall of 1955 the court, without comment or formal opinion, ordered the complete integration of public recreational facilities. Schools were important but so were parks, swimming pools, and golf courses. All across the South, politicians ranted and raved and promised actions to evade the court's ruling. Marion Griffin, the governor of Georgia, promised that "the state will get out of the park business before allowing a breakdown in segregation in the intimacy of the playground."

However, by all accounts, the most common response to the court's 1955 decision was local. Towns simply sold their public course to a private group that held the right to bar whomever they wished. Fort Lauderdale sold its course to a "men's golf association." Jacksonville and Greensboro also privatized their public courses. In some cases, white golfers established clubs attached to public courses for the sole purpose of excluding blacks. In a notable 1957 case, such a group attached to the

Harding Park Golf Course in San Francisco revised its membership policies and admitted seven blacks to membership.

The integration of public courses, then, probably encouraged the establishment of private clubs in the South. The example of Jefferson City, Missouri, seems significant. As blacks gained access to the town's public course, white players sought membership in Jefferson City's only private club. When a large number of applicants were denied membership they bonded together and created a new private club, Meadow Lake Acres. Something like this process occurred in a number of Southern cities.

The general movement toward black equality also deeply marked the history of the PGA between 1945 and 1960. As the group evolved, and as it spawned the tour, it was apparent that race and ethnic attitudes would be influential. Early on, fights between Scottish and American professionals were common. Gene Sarazen had to overcome the anti-Italian feelings common to Scottish pros. Apparently everyone could agree on excluding blacks and other non-Caucasians. In large part, the PGA was a professional union dedicated to limiting access to its ranks. There were only so many club jobs and those who held them were the heart of the early PGA. Eliminating African Americans as competitors made sound business sense. This does not mean, of course, that golf professionals were not in full possession of those attitudes that held blacks to be inferior and that the separation of the races was part of God's plan. There was one exception—blacks were thought to make excellent caddies. From a certain perspective this was an "unfortunate" exception; it allowed a number of African Americans to learn the game and seek to become a pro just like Hogan, Snead, and Nelson.

There was, in the immediate postwar period, a small group of black players good enough to play on the tour. We have already met Howard Wheeler, who seemed to accept his exclusion from the PGA. Unlike Wheeler, Ted Rhodes, Bill Spiller, and Charlie Sifford did not accept exclusion; they wished to test their games against the best, and when they could not, they fought back.

The most aggressive was Bill Spiller. Born in Tishomingo, Oklahoma, in 1913, he graduated from Wiley College with a degree in sociology and education. Unable to find a decent job in Oklahoma, Spiller moved west to California. For a time he worked as a red cap at the local railroad station. He did not play golf until he was almost thirty, but he was talented and quickly began to win local United Golf Association tournaments. After meeting Ted Rhodes, Spiller continued to improve. Rhodes, sponsored by the heavyweight champ Joe Louis, took lessons from Paul Mangrum (brother of Ray). Spiller went along and sat in on the lessons. In addition to working as a red cap, Spiller also worked at the Los Angeles Country Club, which allowed caddies and service staff to play on Monday and Thursday mornings.

Players like Spiller and Rhodes were not entirely isolated from white pros and golf's mainstream. They knew Sam Snead well because Snead was such a fan of Joe Louis—Snead, you might remember, had enjoyed a modest ring career and was a boxing fan his entire life. Jimmy Demaret was generally supportive of players like Spiller and Rhodes. Spiller was also helped considerably by Lawson Little. Spiller testified that MacGregor Sporting Goods gave him free golf equipment and that Wilson did the same for Rhodes.

The biggest problem for Spiller and the others was the PGA. Its constitution contained a clause that expressly barred African Americans from membership. When written in 1916, the clause was a standard part of an association's boilerplate. It accorded with the racist attitudes of the era and it barred blacks from ever competing for the club jobs that the PGA wanted to control.

In 1916 no one imagined that the PGA would come to administer a lucrative list of tournaments that by 1950 was growing into a year-round affair. In the early days, entry into tour events was informal, but slowly the PGA and the tournament sponsors became the twin forces that controlled access. Barring blacks from the events suited both; many events were played at private clubs that wished to keep blacks out and the tour players saw no reason to let black players join the tour and make it even more competitive.

There were leaks in the system. Blacks could play in a few select events. They could compete in the Los Angeles Open, the Tam O'Shanter Open, and the Canadian Open. It was the 1948 Los Angeles Open that created the circumstances that led to the first conflict between the PGA and Bill Spiller and others. Spiller and Ted Rhodes finished in the top sixty at Los Angeles and thereby qualified for the next week's event, the Richmond Open. The two black golfers went to Richmond (near Oakland), played two practice rounds, and were set to play when the PGA tournament director, George Schneiter, informed them they could not compete in the tournament. They were excluded because, as non-Caucasians, they were not PGA members and only members could compete.

In response two things happened. Through friends of Spiller, the PGA's actions at Richmond got on national radio. There was considerable negative publicity for the PGA. Second, there was the filing of lawsuits against the PGA and the Richmond Country Club. In essence, both suits claimed that the PGA and the club were denying Spiller and Rhodes a right to earn a living.

The lawyer for the players, Jonathan Rowell, believed that the PGA would drag its feet and that pursuing the case would be expensive. Some sort of settlement seemed like a good idea. Rowell worked out an agreement when the PGA seemed to promise to stop discriminating against blacks. This was rank duplicity on the PGA's part. To circumvent their promise they began to call most of their events "invitationals" and went along with the policies at private clubs that refused to invite black players to compete. They did not change their constitution that barred blacks from membership.

The issue flared again in 1952 when Joe Louis, Spiller, and Rhodes were invited to play in a charity event at San Diego. At the last moment, all three were banned from the tournament.

Again the story hit the national media. The PGA was flooded with calls and letters demanding that it change its policies.

The PGA was in a very difficult position in 1952. It was face-to-face with the reality that race relations were going to change. In 1952 the *New York Times* published an editorial condemning private golf clubs and the PGA as key elements of a sport where "the stupidity of prejudice" thrived. The editorial dismissed limited participation by blacks as inadequate and called for the complete elimination of discrimination in golf. The PGA began to run afoul of unions much larger than its own. The Congress of Industrial Organizations (CIO) harshly condemned golf's exclusionary policies. The PGA was singled out as an enemy of the idea that the workplace should be open to all, even if the workplace was a golf course. Finally, the CIO resolution struck a note that was becoming more common. It claimed that discrimination by the PGA was anti-American and turned over "a propaganda weapon for the Communists to use against the United States."

By 1960, when the issue of black membership in the PGA came to a head, a great deal of damage had been done to golf and the golf community—damage that to this day has not been undone. Again the issue arose at a California tournament. Joe Louis was invited to play in the San Diego event and Spiller and Rhodes got in by doing well in a thirty-six-hole qualifier. Just as the event was about to start, the PGA stepped in and told Louis, Rhodes, and Spiller that they could not play. Again the PGA was subjected to a much-deserved round of negative publicity, but the officials of the organization exhibited a bottomless desire to keep blacks out of the tournament and out of the PGA. The group did create an "approved player" category that allowed non-PGA members to play in some events, but blacks were still barred from membership.

Later in 1960, Spiller, who was reduced to caddying at the Hillcrest Country Club in California, was carrying the bag for Henry Braverman, who was a friend of California's attorney general

Stanley Mosk. Mosk, informed by Braverman about Spiller's situation, told the PGA it could no longer hold tournaments on California public courses unless they were open to everyone. When the PGA responded that they would play on private courses, Mosk said they could not play on *any* course without changing their rules. Mosk also wrote to most of the other states, laying out his argument. This was effective. In 1961 the PGA finally dropped its Caucasian-only clause. It came too late to help Ted Rhodes, Howard Wheeler, or Bill Spiller. It was left to Charlie Sifford and Lee Elder to forge some sort of black presence on the PGA Tour.

This situation, this stubborn refusal of the PGA to open its ranks to the few blacks who sought to play alongside Hogan, Snead, and Nelson, will never be fully explained. Deeply ingrained racism among the PGA leadership and the rank-and-file was an important factor. The fear that private clubs that allowed their courses to be used for PGA events would withdraw was also crucial. The conflict was also fundamentally a labor problem, and this side of the issue has rarely been explored. The conflict with blacks like Spiller was, at bottom, about jobs—a few slots on the tour, and more than a few slots at the private and public courses where a Class A membership in the PGA was crucial in obtaining a position. When the PGA finally eliminated the Caucasian-only clause, it kept a rule that required all applicants for Class A membership to serve a five-year apprenticeship under a PGA member. Most black golfers, no matter how talented, could not, after 1961, become a Class A PGA professional without serving a five-year apprenticeship under a white professional and obtaining that pro's recommendation.

The upshot of all this for the golf community is clear. While some obstacles to black participation were removed, it was done in such a way that black distrust and suspicion of golf in general deepened. White supporters of black equality adopted the attitude that golf was somehow inherently anti-egalitarian. It would be hard to imagine what else the golf community could have done in the 1950s and 1960s to make blacks feel less welcome while at the same time finally giving in to what was called open access to the game. The actions of the PGA did much to mark golf as a racist game, a game dedicated to exclusion. That mark remains clearly visible today.

The situation with women golfers was less heated and, we have to admit, involved a lot more people — half the number of potential players, actually. This does not, of course, mean that half of the regular golfers in the United States are, or have been in the past, women. Trying to determine how many women were regular, devoted golfers at any time prior to the 1970s is difficult. Recent surveys have suggested that women comprise approximately 20 percent of regular, devoted golfers. There is no reason we cannot project that number back into the past. The real issue was not the number of women playing, but the quality of the scores made by the women who did play. After 1940, women's golf proved to be one of the most interesting, lively, and significant parts of the American golf community. This happened because many truly good and great players emerged and found a stage upon which to perform.

There are a number of stories about good women golfers between 1940 and 1970. Some are local. At Pinehurst, there were many small informal groups that played on the resort's five courses. One such group was the Yadkin Club, which held a small number of events each year. Perhaps the most important was the Annual Medal Championship. In 1948, forty-three men and twelve women competed for the trophy. The winner was Martha Platt. Her 73 on Course No. 3 was two shots better than her nearest competitor, male or female. Her husband, James Platt Jr., was far back in the field, with a 90. Events like this wear away at the idea that while women may play golf, they should nonetheless give way to men as generally the superior players.

This lesson was illustrated on an international scale. In early

1951, Fred Corcoran was in England to set up a series of exhibitions for a group of American women pros. He had recently helped found the Ladies Professional Golf Association. In England he ran into Leonard Crawley, a golf writer and a fine amateur player, who had played for England in the Walker Cup matches. Crawley asked Corcoran how good the American women were. Corcoran suggested that his women could beat any team of British amateurs Crawley could assemble. Crawley never blinked; the match was set for July 15, 1951, on the West Course at Wentworth.

Corcoran's team included Babe Zaharias, Betty Jameson, Peggy Kirk, Becky Bush, Patty Berg, and Betsy Rawls. In the morning foursome matches, the British men did well, winning two and halving a third. It was, however, the six afternoon singles matches that defined the event. In each case, the American woman won her match; the British amateurs did not put up much of a fight, and no match made it to the eighteenth green. The match between Zaharias and Crawley has received the most notice. The Babe was five up after eight holes and won easily. The story has been told that the Babe induced Crawley to promise to cut off his mustache if he lost. Babe reportedly chased the defeated Crawley across the parking lot attempting to collect on the bet but was unsuccessful. To many, the victory of the American women suggested that some sort of quiet revolution was afoot. To the more thoughtful and insightful, it simply proved that in golf women could fully share the spotlight, that they could be very good players, good enough to put on a show worth watching.

Of course, it was the rise to prominence of just such a show between 1950 and 1970 that did much to redefine women's golf. Before World War II there were few women professional golfers. Women like Helen MacDonald stumbled into the pro ranks in order to give lessons or run a pro shop. MacDonald's husband owned the Golf Studio in the Chicago Loop. It was a place to take lessons and buy equipment in an urban setting. When the couple separated, in 1931, Mrs. MacDonald took over the business.

One of the early pioneers was Hope Seignious, who was the head pro at North Shore Country Club in Milwaukee. She wanted to build the number of open events for women into something like the men's tour. In 1944 she founded the Women's Professional Golf Association (WPGA). Seignious labored mightily to make her idea work but she was a bit too early. Nonetheless, she was able to lengthen the very short list of tournaments in which professional women could play. In 1946 she enlisted the support of the Spokane Athletic Roundtable to put up the money for a United States Women's Open. In 1954 the USGA took over this event and made it a regular part of its annual schedule.

By 1949 the WPGA was failing. In January of that year a meeting was held at the Venetian Hotel in Miami. Patty Berg, Babe Zaharias, her husband, George, and Fred Corcoran were the sole attendees, and they decided that the WPGA needed to be replaced by a new organization. After obtaining some legal advice, Corcoran came up with the Ladies Professional Golf Association, a name that avoided any difficulties with the fading WPGA. In the next six months there were more meetings that established Corcoran as the tournament manager and elected a slate of officers. Patty Berg was the first president.

The general consensus is that Corcoran got women's professional golf off the ground, but this is true only up to a point. Corcoran could do his promotional magic only if there were people willing to put up the money to fund the tournaments and to pay Corcoran's salary. In looking for the deeper reasons behind the rise of the LPGA, you find men who wished to sell their products (golf equipment and women's sport clothing) by connecting those products with women's professional golf. L. B. Icely, president of Wilson Sporting Goods, was the first to contact Corcoran and ask him to help organize the LPGA. In the beginning, it was only Wilson providing support, but soon the LPGA was also getting support through the Athletic Institute, "a cooperative promotion agency" composed of athletic equipment manufacturers. As Corcoran recalled, the idea was simple: if women could see women playing golf well and having a lot of fun, then they might go to their local sporting goods store and buy the clubs and balls they saw the pros using. L. B. Icely might have been thinking that his company could double their sales.

But of course it was not just Icely who had such thoughts. Corcoran noted that the founding of the LPGA "touched off a national storm of indifference." This changed somewhat when Corcoran heard that Alvin Handmacher, the owner of Weathervane, a maker of women's sportswear and golf attire, was interested in investing in women's pro golf. Corcoran heard about Handmacher from Herman Barron, the pro at the Fenway Club, and one of the few Jewish men to make it on the early PGA Tour. Corcoran referred to Handmacher as "the Angel from Seventh Avenue."

Corcoran claims that he sold Handmacher on the idea of a cross-country tournament. The ladies would play four events (San Francisco, Chicago, Cleveland, and New York) in the Weathervane Transcontinental Tournament. Corcoran scheduled these events around the few existing Open events, and the women had what looked like a substantial schedule of tournaments. The 1949–50 list of events was so substantial that amateurs like Betsy Rawls and Peggy Kirk decided to turn pro and play for the money. Of course, Weathervane created an advertising campaign that was tightly tied to the new events. The company also signed Babe Zaharias and paid her ten thousand dollars to wear Weathervane products.

However, by 1953 the arrangement with Handmacher began to sour. Corcoran, who had had plenty of problems dealing with the male pros, recalled that "the situation became insane when I had to deal with the girls." He had found a way to deal with Handmacher but there was, according to Corcoran, no way of dealing with the lady pros. As he recalled, after the players staged a sit-down strike at a Weathervane event at Whitemarsh Country Club, Handmacher withdrew his support in disgust. This parting of the ways came too late to fatally damage the tour. The women's professional tour was established and would grow slowly over the next two decades. No doubt the support of manufacturers was crucial, but it was also true that the LPGA had attractions that people would pay to see.

At this point, we run into a fundamental issue. You can go back into the journalism of the late thirties and after and find countless stories that portray women golfers as monstrous deviations from the idea of true womanhood. You can also find an equal number of stories extolling female skill and competitiveness. The women who founded and developed the LPGA did so in a world that at the same time supported and condemned their endeavors.

There were two women at the meeting in Miami that founded the LPGA. The most famous was Babe Didrikson Zaharias. She was perhaps the most important female in modern American sport history. Her career illustrated the ambiguous quality of public opinion concerning women in sport. Born Mildred Ella, on June 26, 1911, in Port Arthur, Texas, she picked up the name "Babe" in her youth because of her home-run-hitting prowess. Writing about Babe is not easy. There is still, for example, some controversy over her date of birth. It's almost surely 1911, but Babe herself gave it as 1913 and occasionally as 1914. She also changed her maiden name, or allowed it to be changed. At some point "Didriksen" became "Didrikson," and she never changed it back. People disliked and even feared her because of her mannishness and her refusal to embody the characteristics of some notion of "true womanhood." People also adored her, found her fascinating, and paid good money to attend her exhibitions and tournaments. Well, which was it? Of course it was both. However, the question I am concerned with is her place in the evolution of the golf community. The answer to that is really very straightforward.

Babe grew up in a lower-class Norwegian family in Texas. Her father was a truck driver. Sports and performing dominated her life from the very beginning. It would be easier to list the sports and activities she never tried; she even entered and won competitive sewing contests. There is no evidence that she ever seriously tried football, but everything else was fair game. American Athletic Union competitions provided an outlet for her skills in basketball and track and field. In the 1932 Olympics, Babe won three medals, two gold and one silver. Olympic rules at the time limited women to only three events. By the midthirties Babe was groping for some way to make a living from her talents; she barnstormed with touring basketball and softball teams. For a time she tried vaudeville and even cut a record. She was a professional-quality harmonica player and there was a brief fling at pocket billiards, but clearly she was no Ruth McGuinness.

Babe first played golf when she was sixteen but did not become serious about the game until 1933. At first her natural skill and strength carried her along, but she could not really play. She made a decision to devote herself to the game and took lessons from Stan Kertes, hitting thousands of practice balls. By 1935 she began entering major amateur events and the gossip and malicious talk followed her into the golf world. After she won the Texas Women's Amateur, officials of the women's Southern Golf Association asked the USGA about her eligibility, and her amateur status was questioned. She was declared a nonamateur for having played other sports as a professional. The USGA made its decision based on the precedent set in the 1920s in the case of Mary K. Brown. They had declared Brown ineligible to play in amateur golf events because she had played tennis professionally.

Even while being slapped down by the USGA, Babe was making the decision to focus her athletic efforts on golf. Wilson hooked her up with Sarazen for a series of exhibition matches. Two things came out of this experience. She learned a great deal about golf and the golf swing from Sarazen, and this began the process of refining her into a much better player. Second, the Babe began the masquerade that would define her life until her death in 1956. The decent fees she collected for the exhibitions suggested to her that in golf, unlike basketball and track, there was a living to be made. Golf had a tradition of celebrating talented female players like Glenna Colette and the great British amateur Joyce Wethered. All this was advanced when Wethered turned pro in the mid-1930s and came to the United States for a series of exhibitions.

From 1935 to 1949, and at the meeting in Miami, Babe followed a twisting path, always trying to promote herself as a golf attraction. She played in open tournaments and exhibitions; she regained her amateur status and then gave it up again. Through it all the Babe and her husband, George, simply hustled and felt their way toward the day that a woman could make a living playing golf.

Every modern American sports star engages in a masquerade of sorts. The public that buys the tickets and the companies that sponsor the events and extend the endorsement contracts want the player to be colorful, unique, and talented while never crossing any number of vague boundaries that, taken together, add up to "socially approved."

Babe made it work by skating close to these boundaries. She was crude, aggressive, and competitive enough to be controversial and to make people line up to buy tickets to see a woman do things they had never seen a woman do. At one event she assembled a cordon of women around her on the course and removed a slip that was restricting her swing. Major-league baseball teams booked her to hit some golf shots before the game began. The Babe, after putting on her golf show, would often grab a glove and take infield practice with the team (in a dress!). One night in New York she lured Joe DiMaggio out of the dugout and threw him a few pitches that he could not hit. The reality was that she was a barnstorming whirlwind, making a living from exhibitions and appearances wherever Fred Corcoran or her husband, George, could find people curious to see the Babe put on her show.

After the founding of the LPGA, the Babe's life changed to some degree. The list of sanctioned events gave her year more structure and the prize money was decent enough to lure her away from the backbreaking schedule of exhibitions. By 1953, the LPGA was playing twenty-four events with $120,000 in total prize money. There can be little doubt that Zaharias was the main draw, but it would be wrong to give her sole credit for the success of the women's tour. Corcoran recruited backers like Handmacher and others. But what made the LPGA different from the WPGA was the growth in the number of women pros on the tour. At the WPGA events in the late 1940s there would be fewer than ten professionals in starting fields of over one hundred. The galleries were there to see the local amateurs play in an event that was local, not part of a national tour with nationally recognized players. The LPGA, with more national publicity, drew an increasing number of players into the professional ranks to join Patty Berg and the Babe. The quality and number of the women professionals grew so quickly that the USGA recognized the existence of a critical mass of women professionals and took over the staging of the Women's Open in 1954.

There were many significant events in women's golf in the 1950s, but none transcended the import of the 1954 U.S. Women's Open. In 1953, Babe had been playing well but was experiencing abdominal pains. She had put off seeing a doctor for a very long time. When she finally had a physical the news was bad—stage three colon cancer. In a Beaumont hospital, doctors performed a colostomy and Babe began her recuperation. Amazingly, she returned to the tour in 1954 and played very well. Her target was the U.S. Women's Open to be played at the Salem Country Club in Massachusetts.

The Babe played herself to a seven-shot lead after two rounds. She then confronted the thirty-six-hole final and there was every chance that her strength would give out before the finish. After a 73 in the morning round, Babe took a nap in the clubhouse. As she came to the final holes with a huge thirteen-stroke lead, Babe began to fade. Her drives began finding the rough and the trees, but she finished like a champion. The comparison to Hogan's heroic finish at Merion is obvious.

In 1954, talking publicly about cancer, especially colon cancer, was not done. To her undying credit, Babe talked at length about her experiences. After her win at Salem, the Babe said, "I wanted to show thousands of cancer sufferers that the operation I had, a colostomy, will enable a person to return to a normal life." She had received thousands of letters from people suffering from the same disorder, and her victory in the Women's Open was an elegant reply.

She would win one more tournament—the Peach Blossom Open in South Carolina. The cancer returned. On September 27, 1956, Mildred Didrikson Zaharias died at the age of forty-five. Always controversial, usually crude, approaching vulgar, she was certainly more than a golfer; her life was significant in the gender history of the twentieth century. Her dear friend Bertha Bowen said of Babe, "Her life was really hard and rough. She faced not being welcome, not being wanted, and she was determined to break that barrier. She was fighting a system and she won."

There was another player at the meeting in Florida that started the LPGA. She was inevitably overshadowed by the Babe and the controversies that followed her wherever she went. The other woman was Patty Berg.

Born into an affluent Minneapolis family, Patty Berg was destined to be the model for the woman golf professional. For more than thirty years she would be present at all the turning points, she would know and support all the women pros, and she would turn over the role of the female golf professional to a new generation of women who would build on the achievements of the founding mothers.

Patty began playing golf at age twelve. She took lessons from Willie Kidd at Interlachen Country Club, where her family had a membership. Later she would become the pupil of Lester Bolstad, the coach of the University of Minnesota golf team. Golf hooked her in an unusual way. Her first tournament was the 1933 Minneapolis City Ladies Championship. After shooting 122 in the qualifying round, Patty lost her first match 10 and 8, a humiliation that set off a firestorm in her head. She promised herself that she would play and practice every day for the next year, and that when the tournament was held again, she would redeem herself. In 1934, in the Minneapolis City Ladies Championship, Patty Berg was the medalist and won the championship.

Unlike the Babe, Patty benefited from her parents' social and economic position. She played at a fine country club, and even during the heart of the Depression, the whole family enjoyed golfing vacations to Florida. They could also afford to send Patty off to national amateur events. In 1935 she was runner-up to Glenna Collette Vare in the USGA Women's Amateur. This was a match of some symbolic importance. In it Glenna passed off to Patty Berg the responsibility for representing the highest level of women's golf in America. Colette Vare did it as an amateur, and Berg would do it as a professional.

In 1938 Patty entered thirteen amateur tournaments and won ten. She also had gotten a taste of what doing exhibitions was like when she put on golf demonstrations to raise money for the University of Minnesota. We know little about her decision to turn pro in 1940. Apparently she was invited to do so by the ubiquitous L. B. Icely of Wilson Sporting Goods. Her job was to show women that golf was a sport they could play and that they could play it better with Wilson equipment.

Just as Zaharias had discovered, Patty knew that there were few tournaments for women pros before the war. There were, in essence, three: the Western Open, the Titleholders, and the Asheville Invitational. In 1941 playing in tournaments became the least of Patty's problems. She was in a serious traffic accident that left her with a badly damaged left knee. It looked as if she might never play golf again. The knee never fully healed, but a long painful rehabilitation with prizefighter Tommy Littlejohn got her back to playing golf. During the war she spent two years doing public relations work as a member of the U.S. Marine Corps.

Patty Berg's take on the postwar years and the founding of the LPGA is considerably different from that of Babe Zaharias. It seemed that wherever Babe went controversy followed. Patty Berg's view of the period between 1948 and 1954 is intensely, maybe impossibly, positive. She claimed that she "never got ragged for being an athlete," and that the criticism leveled at Babe never came Patty's way. She stated that she never saw the crude Babe Zaharias. For Patty, Babe was "a wonderful athlete" and "someone with a lot of class," who as a player with a big name helped the LPGA get off the ground. Patty also had nothing but kind words for male pros. Johnny Revolta and Sam Snead were two of her favorites. Patty Berg was a relentlessly positive person.

The LPGA succeeded for many reasons, but one that is often neglected is the fact that the women put on a good show on the golf course. This was true as early as the 1951 Weathervane Transcontinental Tournament. The tournament, up to the very end, worked just as Corcoran and Handmacher had planned. There would be four thirty-six-hole events and interest would build as the overall winner would be decided in the late spring of 1951. After the first three events (Dallas, Pebble Beach, and Indianapolis), Zaharias led Berg by two shots—450 to 452. This two-shot lead was based on an amazing 66 Babe had recorded in the second round of the Weathervane event at Dallas. She had shot 83 in the first round.

When the women arrived in New York for the last of the four Weathervane events, they got their fair share of space in the city's sport sections. Could Babe hang on and win the five-thousand-dollar bonus as the overall winner? Plus, the pros with the lowest cumulative scores in the four Weathervane events would receive an all-expense paid trip to England and Europe. This was the team that would defeat Crawley and his chums at Wentworth.

The LPGA arrived in New York featuring a hot competition between Berg and Zaharias. Beneath this headline, the ladies tour was improved but was still a very thin, close to marginal, affair. The event in Indianapolis had had the largest field of all the Weathervane events. There were thirty-seven players in the field and twenty of them were amateurs. Clearly a good number of these amateurs were playing with no hope of really competing for the title. Six of the twenty amateurs shot 180 or higher for the thirty-six-hole event. The Babe won with a total of 145.

Babe held a two-stroke lead over Berg as the first round began at Knollwood Country Club in White Plains. Patty ended the day one shot ahead. She had picked up three shots on one hole. Somewhat miraculously, Berg had holed out her three-wood second shot on the tenth hole for an eagle two, while Babe recorded a five. In the second and concluding round the Babe was able to make up the one-shot deficit but no more. She had to birdie seventeen and make a heroic par on the eighteenth to do it. The two women ended the cross-country 144-hole contest in a flat-footed tie, both with a total of 601.

The rules called for a thirty-six-hole playoff. The two rounds were scheduled at the Scarsdale Country Club and at the Deepdale Golf Club. Both players turned in fine scores of 71 on the first day at Scarsdale. The second day at the more difficult Deepdale course began when Berg birdied the first to gain a stroke and took a two-stroke lead on the second when Babe three-putted. The rest of the day was a seesaw affair, but Patty never gave up the lead she had acquired on the first two holes. Babe picked up a shot on the last but it was not enough. After 180 holes of golf, Patty Berg had won by a single shot.

It was very dramatic stuff, but delays for rain and other matters set the playoff back to the second week in June. The men were playing the Open at the recently redone Oakland Hills in Detroit. Hogan would win, bringing the "monster" to its knees. One upshot of Hogan's dramatic victory was that the playoff between Berg and Zaharias got very little coverage. This illustrated a key reality in the golf community. Women might get a tour together and lure a sponsor like Weathervane to support them, but they were clearly a marginal enterprise compared with the men's tour. No matter how exciting women's golf was, it would always take second place to the men. The LPGA would have to take care not to compete directly with the men's tour.

The LPGA would struggle and survive in the 1950s and 1960s. The Babe and Patty Berg turned over what they had created to a new generation that came on the scene in the late 1950s. The pioneers of the late '40s and early '50s had made for themselves a place to play and compete. The women who followed on their heels were of a very high quality. The LPGA quickly lost its image as a thin rank of twenty professionals playing in fields filled out with noncompetitive amateurs. By the mid-1950s a new generation of female players began to arrive on the scene. There was, of course, Louise Suggs, who was joined by Betsy Rawls, perhaps the best-educated professional golfer of note, male or female. After graduating Phi Beta Kappa in physics from the University of Texas, she thought that pro golf would be more interesting than a career in science, and she never looked back.

But the period after the Babe-Berg era would be dominated by two women who defined the modern female touring professional. Mary Kathryn "Mickey" Wright joined the LPGA tour in 1955. Kathy Whitworth joined her in 1958. Wright would win eighty-two LPGA events; Whitworth would win a record-setting eighty-eight. Together they proved, beyond debate, that women could play golf worth watching, worth celebrating.

Kathy Whitworth was born in Texas, in 1939, but will always be associated with Jal, New Mexico, a small town for which she often expressed her deep affection. By her own account, golf hooked her from day one. She took lessons from a local pro, Hardy Loudermilk, until she felt she needed advanced instruction and was sent to Harvey Penick, in Austin, Texas. The local ladies golf association helped Kathy get to amateur events where she honed her competitive skills. When Kathy was seventeen, she won her first big amateur title, the New Mexico Women's Amateur. After a year at Odessa Junior College she turned pro in 1958.

She was no overnight success. In 1960 she won slightly less than five thousand dollars and was elected the most improved player on the tour. She also changed her image by dramatically changing her weight. At one point Kathy had weighed 215 pounds. At the beginning of her professional career, she stood five feet nine inches tall and weighed 175 pounds. In her first two years as a professional she lost over thirty-five pounds. Every dedicated fan of women's golf sees Kathy Whitworth, in their mind's eye, as the elegant rail-thin player she was after 1960.

Whitworth was a tireless campaigner. She dominated most of the statistical categories in the late 1960s. She won the Vare Trophy for lowest scoring average three times running, between 1965 and 1967, and then again in 1969. Whitworth won the LPGA Championship in 1967, 1971, and 1975. She reminds one mildly of Sam Snead when you review her near misses at the U.S. Women's Open. Whitworth never had the gigantic collapses that haunted Snead, she simply could not shoot the lowest score. She finished second twice.

Whitworth's game declined in the late 1970s. In 1979, she failed to win a tournament for the first time in eighteen years. She returned to Harvey Penick and her game got a little better. By 1981 she had regained much of her old form and confidence. As she played into the mid-1980s she began to break a number of significant records. In 1982 she set the mark for the number of LPGA wins when she passed Mickey Wright's total of eighty-two. She passed Snead's all-gender record of eighty-four victories. She would eventually record eighty-eight professional wins.

Kathy Whitworth had a remarkable run. There is no way we can estimate the impact of the constant travel, the boring motels, or the physical impact of playing so much golf for so long. She also served as LPGA president for four terms. This meant, in addition to playing, Whitworth confronted the inevitable cocktail parties, dinners, and endless rounds of soul-destroying meetings.

Whitworth believed that she was not the best woman golfer of her era. She awarded that honor to Mickey Wright. Kathy Whitworth went so far as to claim for Wright the title "best ever"—man or woman. However one might come down on this debatable claim, it is clear that Mary Kathryn Wright, together with Whitworth, stabilized and built the LPGA into a vital ongoing enterprise.

But Mickey Wright was more than just a competent woman professional golfer. Talking about her, debating her greatness, brings out the people who are in the golf community and those who are not. The real golfers have the sense that the differences between men and women really do not exist. They ignore the fact that men play longer courses and shoot lower scores. They know that a few women belong on any list of "Fifty Greatest Golfers" and they know that Mickey Wright belongs in the top ten, if not the top five.

There is not much published about Mickey Wright. There are few exhaustive interviews to draw from; there is no autobiography (but there should be). Born in 1935, to a father who had hoped for a boy, Mary Kathryn became forever, and for everybody, Mickey. At age seven, her father, a successful California lawyer, gave his daughter a set of toy plastic golf clubs. Mickey swung them so hard and so often that she broke them all. Golf, for some inexplicable reason, got to her, engulfed her. She grew up playing all sports, but she was only truly happy at the driving range with her own bucket of balls, swinging as hard as she could.

The father quickly understood that his daughter was more

than a little nuts about golf. Mickey demanded to play the La Jolla Country Club course where her parents belonged. They purchased their daughter some lessons with Johnny Bellante, the club's pro. At eleven she broke 100; at fifteen she shot 70 at the Mission Valley Country Club in San Diego. She began to win junior events, and as she did, she attracted the interest of Henry Presser, the professional at San Gabriel Country Club. Presser was, in some sense, Wright's finishing school. He taught her to keep the clubface square throughout the swing. She also learned to roll her weight from her front side (left) to the inside of her back foot (right) during the backswing. It was during these lessons with Presser (for which he never charged) that Wright developed the swing and the feel for the swing that would make her technically perhaps the best there ever was.

Mickey was a good student and was set to go to Stanford to major in psychology. But golf would not let go. In 1952 she won the USGA Junior Girls Championship. Later Mickey admitted that this win "got me all fired up about golf." Stanford is a good school, and a college degree is essential, but these bits of wisdom had no chance against a young girl who later said, "I was determined to make golf my career."

In 1954 she persuaded her father to let her take a term off from school and to finance a try at the LPGA's winter season in Florida and the Southeast. She did well enough to convince her father to finance her travel to a few of the larger summer events for women. Mickey was the winner of the amateur division at the Tam O'Shanter All-American and World Championship in Chicago. She then had an experience that stands as one of the most significant passing-of-the-baton of events in women's golf. She was the low amateur in the 1954 Women's Open Championship. She was Babe's playing partner during the triumphant final round. In the fall of 1954, Mickey became a professional golfer.

There were no Hoganesque struggles. However, Mickey was convinced that she could play better. She took lots of lessons, even making the almost obligatory trip to Austin to consult Harvey Penick. By the late fifties, she had put together the swing and the mental skills that drove her to the very top of the women's game. Between 1958 and 1964, Wright won the LPGA Championship and a U.S. Women's Open each four times. During the same period, she won the Western Open three times and the Titleholders twice. In the end, health problems, particularly with her feet and hands, and burnout shortened her career. By 1971 Wright was all but retired, playing only in a few events after that. But for a period of ten years, 1958 to 1968, she dominated her sport.

It is clear, however, that Mickey Wright's significance to the golf community transcends her competitive record. For a truly committed golfer the game is many things, but at bottom it is the swing. It is the hitting of a ball using a complicated action of the human body. It just might be that Mickey Wright had the best swing. Rhonda Glenn, in her *Illustrated History of Women's Golf*, presents the testimony of experts. She quotes Ben Hogan: "She (Wright) had the finest golf swing I ever saw, man or woman." Byron Nelson also made a similar claim. It is interesting to note that Bob Jones thought that Joyce Wethered had the best swing (any gender) he ever saw. It is not known if Jones ever saw Mickey Wright play.

Wright was also significant to the golf community in ways that are only tangentially related to the swing. Her book on golf, *Play Golf the Wright Way* (1962), conveys elements of the game with the economy of a haiku. Single sentences jump off the page. For example, "When I play my best golf, I feel as if I'm in a fog." This takes us back to William Garrott Brown and his "dreamy" feeling. Wright claims — building on advice from Betsy Rawls — that in her best year, before every shot, she said to herself, "This is your own responsibility. Do as well as you can but make no excuses for yourself." Her book also makes plain the role of repetition in learning the swing. One can be told the correct technique, but only countless repetitions (and corrected incorrect attempts) can ingrain it so that it will work under pressure.

Finally, there was something about Mickey Wright that tells us something very important about golf. While she compiled an amazing competitive record, people who saw her play, and people who have read her book, understand that the wins and the money were not the ultimate rewards. Rhonda Glenn, I think, put it perfectly when she wrote that Mickey Wright "viewed golf as a form of self-expression rather than a contest between people." Americans, particularly, find it hard to approve of the idea that women can and should express themselves with their bodies, with their physical talent. They also find it hard to affirm the idea that women should profitably engage in contests that are essentially gambling games. But thankfully, golf was there in the early fifties for Mickey Wright to have as a means of expressing herself. Looked at this way, issues about true womanhood, male versus female, money in sport, and all the others fade. At the heart of the golf community, in all its neighborhoods, is the idea that the game is a form of personal expression that millions find compelling and deeply meaningful.

In no way do I mean to let golf off the hook for its social practices. I do mean to suggest that bias and exclusivity in the golf community are abhorrent most fundamentally because they are limits on expression, because they prevent people from making of their lives what they will.

A brief portrait of a golf heroine will make clearer the point. Just as Mickey Wright was turning pro and beginning her evolution into one of the game's best all-time players, Ann Gregory was making history of a different sort. Ann Gregory's basic biography is not one that usually includes a passionate commitment to golf. She was born in Aberdeen, Mississippi, on July 25, 1912 (the Hogan/Nelson/Snead year). Both her parents died when she was a young girl, and she eventually landed with a white family who raised her. She also served the family as their maid. In 1938, over the family's objections, Ann married Leroy

Percy Gregory and moved to Gary, Indiana. Always a good athlete, Ann's first sport was tennis, and she became the Gary city champ.

Her husband, known usually as Percy, was addicted to golf. Before the war, Ann played the role of frustrated golf widow. When Percy entered the navy in 1942, Ann took up his clubs and gave the game a try. Quickly she understood why Percy spent so much time at the course. She joined the all-black Chicago Women's Golf Club (CWGC) and began a long career playing in amateur events. At the beginning she played mostly in local tournaments that were usually all-black events. Eventually she began to compete in United Golf Association (UGA) tournaments. In 1950 she won the national UGA Women's Championship played in Washington DC. Between 1950 and 1956, Gregory became a dominant force on the female side of the UGA.

In 1956 the CWGC decided to apply to the USGA for membership. The USGA approved the application, making the club the first black organization granted access to the association's list of approved clubs. This also allowed Ann Gregory to enter national USGA amateur events. In 1956, at Meridian Hills Country Club in Indianapolis, she became the first African American woman to play in a USGA event. She lost her first-round match to Carolyn Cudone, 2 and 1.

For more than twenty years, Gregory competed regularly in USGA events and in the all-black UGA events where she had begun her career. This often created awkward situations; if Ann played in a USGA event that was scheduled opposite a UGA event, she was criticized for abandoning the organization that gave her a start.

In 1959 Ann confronted one of these awkward situations. She decided to compete in the USGA Women's Amateur at the Congressional Country Club in Bethesda, Maryland. This meant that she could not play in a UGA event also being held in the Washington DC area. The problem arose when Congressional Country Club decided that while it would allow Ann Gregory to play on its course, it would not allow her to attend the player's banquet and eat the club's food. Unwilling to face Gregory directly, the people who had decided to exclude Ann Gregory sent Joe Dey of the USGA to tell Ann that she was excluded from the dinner. Gregory took the slight with a grace and decency that the people who excluded her would never know.

She had some measure of revenge when she got on the golf course. Ann won her first-round match and faced the Georgia state champion, Mrs. Curtis Jordan, in the second round. In front of a large gallery that included Gregory fan Frank Stranahan (long considered one of the world's top amateur golfers in the decade after World War II), Gregory made a birdie on the last hole to win one up.

Ann Gregory's story says a great deal about golf in the two decades after the war ended. Journalists tell her story as if the meaning were self-evident. It was a story of American racism, and of a woman struggling against the forces stacked against her. In some sense this approach misses the obvious. Ann Gregory represents the growth of golf in the postwar era. It says a lot that an orphaned black girl, once a maid in a Southern white household, could come to Chicago, start a family, and take up two "white" sports, tennis and golf. She broke down barriers in the first place because she got a chance to play and love the game. In this she symbolizes the spreading affluence of the period and the impact of that affluence on golf. The Gregorys, a black family from the Midwest, had enough resources to send Ann to a number of tournaments each year, where over time she became a much honored and respected competitor.

But of course the incident at Congressional, where Ann was barred from the competitors' dinner, and other racist incidents, deserve their place in the story. Unfortunately we do not know enough about what happened at Congressional. Was Ann kept from the dinner by an overwhelming vote of the membership, or did the majority bow to the demands of a minority determined to keep this black woman in her place? I suspect it was the latter. After the tournament, the manager of the club told Ann that she could play at Congressional anytime she wished. Ann Gregory rejected that offer. We have no reason to suspect that the offer was anything but sincere, that it might well have been an attempt to counter a minority in the club who excluded Gregory from the dinner. To me, Ann Gregory suggests something central to the history of the golf community. At the center of golfing tradition is the idea that all should have access to the game. Especially when it comes to formal competition, open access should be the rule. In the era between 1950 and 1970, this tradition found broad expression. It confronted, especially in the cases of African Americans and women, deeply ingrained traditions that ran counter to open access. The machinations of the PGA to keep African Americans out of golf were the best example of these efforts. There was progress, but no final victory. Certainly golf has come a long way since the 1920s, but the culture-wide beliefs that teach a separate and inferior status for women and blacks are immensely powerful, and anyone who thinks that golf can make them go away is simply deluded.

Golf and the Age of Television

By the early 1960s, when we look closely at the evolving golf community, at least two things are clear. First, there was an established definition, or cultural configuration, of the game. This definition had taken deep root between 1890 and 1930. Golf was a game, and a social and cultural institution, dominated by white businessmen. Its most important institution was the private country club, and this institution put the game into the real estate business. The members of the golf community defined their game — its essential qualities — in several simple ways. Amateur golf was the heart of the game. Professional golf was interesting but marginal. Golf offered unique benefits for hard-driving businessmen; it was seen as medicinal. Golf would never be, in any substantial way, a spectator sport like baseball or boxing. Golf was a walk through a pastoral setting, a walk that relieved stress and reconnected the player to nature. American families came to value their golf club as an extension of their home, as a place that gave them access to activities, to a social life, and to the kind of status they could not have in any other way. This definition reached some sort of perfect expression in the person of Bobby Jones.

This definition of the golf community slowly became a conservative, establishment position. Nearly twenty years of economic depression and war were crucial in pushing the older view of golf to the right. However, by the early 1960s, it was clear that postwar affluence had unleashed other forces that were quickly and fundamentally transforming the golf community. African Americans and women challenged the white male dominance in golf, and egalitarianism in its many forms would attack exclusion and bias in golf just as it did in the larger community. Meanwhile, conservatives would defend the older view that Americans had a basic right to form private associations and to include and exclude as they saw fit.

This chapter, however, will focus on two other developments that arose in the 1950s and would reshape the golf community to the present day. The first of these developments was the politicalization of golf. The second, and most important, was the continuing influence of technology.

It is true that golf has always been political. Famously, Teddy Roosevelt warned William Howard Taft not to let the public see him playing golf. Taft ignored this advice and became a vocal champion of the game. In a letter to the *New York Times*, Taft stated that golf was not "a rich man's game. . . . It is a game of all classes." Journalists joked about presidential golf, but in a fairly muted way.

By 1950, something had changed as politicians began slowly to experiment with the idea that hanging golf around the neck of your opponent was a winning strategy. In 1950, William C. Campbell was an early victim of the politicalization of golf. Bill Campbell was one of the most prominent amateur golfers in postwar America. After serving in World War II, he earned a degree in history from Princeton. He would play in thirty-seven U.S. Amateur Championships; in one stretch (1941–77) he participated in thirty-three in a row. Campbell served in a number of positions for the United States Golf Association, including president in the early 1980s. In 1987 he was named captain of the Royal and Ancient Golf Club at St. Andrews. From the early 1940s to the 1990s, Campbell was one of the most prominent competitors and officials in amateur golf.

As a member of a wealthy and influential Huntington, West Virginia, family, he was drawn into state politics and was elected to the House of Delegates. In 1950 he decided to challenge the incumbent, A. R. "Snooks" Winters, for the Democratic nomination for the state senate seat in Campbell's home district. Through the summer of 1950, Winters and Campbell hacked away at each other. Campbell accused Winters of personal corruption and of being an important cog in the corrupt state political machine. Winters countered by claiming that he was in touch with the average American. Portraying Campbell as an elitist was not hard; he had attended Phillips Exeter and had been captain of the Princeton golf team. Winters made much of Campbell's devotion to golf. He suggested that there was a link between golf and the big corporations that oppressed the working class. A big part of his campaign was to refer to his opponent as "Country Club Campbell" and to broadly distribute a picture of Campbell playing golf, in Bermuda shorts, at the Greenbrier Golf Club. Winters defeated Campbell in a close election that may have been less than honest. Campbell demanded a recount, but Winters's victory by 309 votes stood.

This was merely a local warm-up for the coming of golf as a political factor on the national scene. Golf arrived as a national political issue when Dwight Eisenhower moved into the White House in 1952. There was little doubt that Ike was a devoted, even an addicted, golfer. He would routinely leave his White House office to hit practice shots (mostly eight-irons) on the South Lawn. These outings at first created traffic jams and sizable crowds of onlookers, but soon the novelty wore off. Americans quickly came to understand that their president was a golfer.

It was not so clear what the meaning of Eisenhower's golfing addiction would be. His advisers had struggled to keep their man's golfing under wraps during the campaign. As president this caution melted away and Eisenhower routinely took long golf vacations at Augusta National, where he would eventually become a member and have his own cabin. In Washington he played on Wednesday afternoons and Saturday mornings at Burning Tree Golf Club. He also belonged to Gettysburg Country Club, near his farm in Pennsylvania. In the summers he often left Washington for Denver and rounds of golf at Cherry Hills.

Critical comments about all this golf began almost immediately. It was clear, however, that the public took little offense. A 1953 Gallup poll found that 73 percent of the Americans surveyed felt that Eisenhower was not taking too much time away from his duties for golf. Seventeen percent thought his golfing excessive, and 10 percent had no opinion.

Eisenhower and his advisers mounted the classic defense of the game. Repeatedly, the president's doctor, Major General Howard Snyder, would supply reporters with the ancient rationale for golf: Ike was under stress and worked too hard, and any doctor would prescribe more exercise and relaxation for such a patient. The president's golf vacations and his weekly play were exactly what he needed. It was common for others to second the doctor's recommendation. The Rev. Dr. John S. Bonnell, of the Fifth Avenue Presbyterian Church in New York City, was one of several ministers who approved of Eisenhower's love of golf. After noting that the president had been severely criticized for "periodically turning aside from his work to golf or fishing," Bonnell stated that instead of being critical of Ike, "Americans would do well to learn from the president's balanced mode of living."

There was much evidence that Americans were influenced by the president's "balanced mode of living." While there is no way to quantify his impact on the growth of golf, it was clearly substantial. In 1955, recognizing his deep influence on public opinion concerning golf, the Golf Writers Association of America awarded Eisenhower the William D. Richardson Award for his contributions to the game.

In some cases Eisenhower's influence on the golfing public

seemed trivial, if a bit alarming. In July 1955 the president played a round of golf at the Gettysburg Country Club in a pale-pink golf hat. This set off a brief but intense fashion fad. Dubbed "Eisenhower pink," the color took off. Especially in the Gettysburg area, golfers, both men and women, began showing up for their rounds in shirts, golf dresses, and hats in the dusty pale-pink color.

But in the long run, Eisenhower's golfing was a serious issue. His frequent retreats to Gettysburg, Augusta, and Burning Tree were fodder for anyone opposing his policies. They could simply imply that Ike was not working hard enough, was not fully on top of the issue, whatever it might be. Golf, for Ike's critics, became a sign of indifference and even laziness.

Much of the criticism came from Democratic labor officials. A persistent critic was Jack Kroll, the director of the Congress of Industrial Organizations' political action committee. After 1955 the Eisenhower administration faced serious charges of corruption involving federally funded power projects and mink coats provided to administration officials. Kroll complained that while all this was going on, the newspapers protected Eisenhower: the newspapers "continue to tell us how popular his ideas are, what his golf score is, and where he is vacationing this week."

Over time the criticism of Eisenhower's addiction to golf began to stick. In his first term, such criticism was largely ineffective. This was, after all, the man who had liberated Europe and had won the presidency by a substantial majority. However, in his second term, when he confronted a number of serious issues (farm prices, unemployment, the Cold War), the constant golfing became a liability. In March 1958, the Gallup poll announced that Eisenhower's popularity had fallen to its lowest point since he took office in 1952. People in the poll cited three reasons for their disapproval of the president's handling of his job. The second most important reason was "irritation with the president's vacations to play golf."

In the end, Eisenhower's eight years in the White House had

a profound influence on the golfing community. As a figure of undeniable popularity, he helped golf to grow in the 1950s. On the other hand, the criticism of his frequent golf vacations had a lasting impact. It made golf seem controversial and partisan. It became easy for some Americans, especially Democrats and those in the laboring classes, to see golf as frivolous, as essentially a Republican sport. Remember also that this was the period in which golf was bitterly portrayed as exclusive and inherently racist.

This was not lost on other national political figures. John Kennedy was a much better player than Eisenhower, but he made great efforts to keep his affection for the game a secret. Kennedy much preferred to publicize the family's touch football games and other non-elitist sports. When *Sports Illustrated* published a story on "sport on the New Frontier," golf received only a brief, passing mention. While playing the game, and apparently enjoying it, Kennedy understood that golf and golfing could be cast in a negative light. In what must be his most quoted reference to the game, Kennedy, while still a senator, employed a line from T. S. Eliot's poem *Choruses from "The Rock."* Kennedy used the line that reads, "And the wind shall say: 'Here were decent godless people: Their only monument the asphalt road and a thousand lost golf balls.'" Many interpreted this as a veiled criticism of Eisenhower and a challenge to the American people to aspire to something higher than a national highway system and endless golfing.

By 1960, some sort of pattern had been set. Golf would flit in and out of political discourse. Some politicians would brazenly golf, others would not, but the game had clearly become an issue. Particularly on the left, golf would become a sign of bad character or, at least, bad politics.

Even Barack Obama was not immune. In its December 2009 issue, the *New Republic* advised the president to give up his newly acquired affection for golf. The magazine claimed that "golf is a dubious pastime for any decent, sane person, much less this particular president." The author of the piece, Michelle Cottle, asked why a president seeking to change politics-as-usual, "to shake up Washington," would "sell his soul to a leisure activity that screams stodgy, hyperconventional Old Guard?" Cottle also seems to have a pipeline to the American mind and its image of golf. She claims that "in the popular imagination, golf is the stuff of corporate deal-cutting, congressional junkets, and country club exclusivity. And, unless a president is very careful, a golf habit can easily be spun as evidence of unseemly character ranging from laziness to callousness to out of touch elitism." Toward the end of her piece, Cottle just piles on. Obama should steer clear of golf because "it remains largely the province of reasonably affluent white guys." Finally, she notes that "golf is a dying game — on the skids for nearly a decade." The piece ends with a question: "Does President Obama really want to be associated with a game so antithetical to modern life?"

Actually this attack on Obama and his golf addiction is merely the most recent example of the politicalization of golf that first took firm hold with the criticism of Eisenhower in the 1950s. Something that might be called "the antigolf doctrine" has become a small but enduring part of American cultural discourse. This position has two central elements: it attacks golf for its connection to political conservatism and for the continuing importance of the private golf country club as a venue for the game.

Golf, from the antigolf perspective, is old-fashioned, old hat. Thus Michelle Cottle can state that the game is a leisure activity "that screams stodgy, hyperconventional Old Guard." In 1998 Bruce McCall, in *Esquire*, could ask, "Who wants to snuggle up to a game — a culture — that exudes at its loftiest and most exalted levels all the gaudy human panache of the 1909 summer picnic of Boston's biggest law firm?" The rules of conduct that are such a big part of the game — silence and stillness when others are playing, player enforcement of the rules, and so on — McCall calls "golf's sourpuss rules of decorum."

Civil rights activists and feminists have launched a more

substantial and influential attack on the golf community. They have done so by focusing on the private golf club and its exclusionary policies. Eisenhower had played much of his golf at Augusta National and Burning Tree Golf Club. Both are all-male bastions that feature mysterious and exclusive membership policies. Remarkably, Eisenhower largely escaped criticism for going to, and playing at, such exclusive clubs. But the time was coming when these types of clubs would come under relentless attack.

It's difficult to pinpoint exactly when the assault on the private, exclusive club began. It may well have begun in 1959 when Dr. Ralph Bunch, diplomat, educator, and Nobel Peace Prize winner, was denied membership in the Westside Tennis Club in New York City. This denial focused attention on private clubs and their admission policies. The *New York Times* launched a survey of local private clubs and it failed to turn up even one African American member. Most clubs also barred Jews from membership. There was considerable attention given to Winged Foot Golf Club; it had just been the site of the U.S. Open in June 1959. The club had no African American or Jewish members. The club manager, Thomas Farley, explained that new members were nominated by a member and seconded by another member. The candidate then collected letters of recommendation that were passed on to the admission committee and eventually the board of directors for final approval. Clearly, given such a system, no explicit exclusionary rule need appear in the club's constitution or by-laws.

In the fifty years since 1960, the pressure on private clubs has been steady and unremitting. On the legal front, with the Bunch case as a starting point, the clubs have lost their nearly sacred place in the American social system. The attack on them has come from several angles. In 1983 Burning Tree Golf Club became the target of a couple, Stuart Bynum and Barbara Rentschler, who sought membership in the club. When the all-male club rejected the couple, they sued in Maryland, seeking to have a tax break enjoyed by the club revoked. Burning Tree had an agreement with the state that awarded the club a substantial tax reduction in exchange for the club's promise always to maintain its grounds as open space. In the end, the club lost and was forced to pay much higher taxes in order to remain an all-male club. This was an example of the typical route taken by those seeking to expose and abolish exclusionary policies at private clubs. They argued that such clubs should not receive any state support (tax breaks, liquor licenses, etc.) so long as they continued to discriminate.

There was another front in this war on private clubs. The issue arose when Shoal Creek Country Club in Birmingham, Alabama, was about to stage the 1990 PGA Championship. The association had played its annual championship at Shoal Creek in 1984 and had no reason to expect trouble in 1990. This was true until the founder of the club, Hall Thompson, began talking, very honestly, to the press. He claimed that the club admitted all sorts of people (Jews, Italians, Lebanese) but had no black members and would not have any. Thompson claimed that the "club was our home, and we pick and choose who we want."

Thompson's remarks put the PGA in a difficult position. Civil rights groups like the Southern Christian Leadership Conference threatened massive demonstrations during the tournament. Corporate sponsors, which had become crucial to the event's success, pulled or reduced their support. The tournament was saved when local officials convinced the club to accept a single black member, Louis J. Willy, a nongolfer. The controversy at Shoal Creek convinced the PGA to change its policies. They announced that their tournaments would no longer be played at clubs that discriminate. Several clubs, Cypress Point and Butler National, most notably, rejected the conditions put forward by the PGA and were excluded from the list of approved courses. At a number of courses, the Shoal Creek controversy set off a search for African American members. In California, O. J. Simpson agreed to join Sherwood Country Club; he told

Sports Illustrated that Shoal Creek would be remembered as "almost like the Boston Tea Party." Instead, it is accurately recalled as one of those modern controversies that set off a flurry of tokenism and little else.

For the partisans in these conflicts the issue was clear. On one side was freedom of association, on the other a commitment to egalitarianism. Freedom of association was the establishment, conservative stance while egalitarianism, energized by years of civil rights protests and progress, was the modern, liberal view.

In my view, it took a professional golfer, Tom Watson, to address the issue in a novel and meaningful way. Watson had resigned from the Kansas City Country Club (where he had played since age six) because they rejected the application of Henry Block, a founder of H&R Block, tax accountants and preparers. Block was denied membership ostensibly because he was Jewish. Watson was not Jewish, but his wife was. Watson believed that if Block's membership had come before the entire membership he would have been admitted. The problem was the membership committee, where bigotry ruled. A small group of bigots had held the entire membership hostage; this same group had made the entire club seem anti-Semitic.

Watson put his membership where his mouth was; he withdrew from the club and sent off an op-ed piece to the *New York Times*. His argument was elegant and compelling. He admitted that "golf in America, has been largely the sport of the privileged, a game for white, Protestant men to learn and master at private clubs." In recent times, the problems of bias and exclusion within these clubs had become visible; he cited Shoal Creek as an example. Instead of opting for either freedom of association or equal access, Watson admitted that he was passionately devoted to both. His solution, deeply influenced by his recent experience at the Kansas City Country Club, was to advocate openness. Clubs may do as they wish but they must be open about their policies. If they are going to be racist or anti-Semitic, "just let them own up to it, not hide it." Finally, he was certainly right to suggest that in the debate over private clubs there had been hypocrisy on all sides and that tokenism was no substitute for real progress.

Watson's essay was very nearly the last word in two years of passionate discussion about golf and private clubs. After 1991 private clubs, which had been in retreat for three decades, became institutions non grata in American life. No candidate for public office could maintain membership in a private club of any sort. Barack Obama plays his golf at air force bases or public courses, and he plays at considerable risk to his popularity. Recent scandals, especially the Abramoff-DeLay affair, in which free golf trips were employed as payoffs, have simply created a negative aura around the game. A round of golf—forget a membership—at Burning Tree or Augusta National would be a huge political mistake. *If* you play golf, and especially *where* you play, remains a political issue for most Americans.

At the same time that this politicalization was evolving into a cultural reality, the golf community and the older, established view of the game was being transformed by technology.

If you ask a devoted modern golfer about the influence of technology in the game, you will get a semilearned discourse on the graphite shaft, cavity back irons, titanium driver heads, and video swing analysis. A truly addicted player will know something about advances in the machinery that allow architects to alter land and push around unbelievable amounts of dirt. He or she may also know something about the recent history of the ball. Old timers fondly recall "the wound ball." It was a simple object: thin rubber bands wound around a small elastic core and covered with balata. These objects varied in compression and roundness, and they cut easily. The leading edge of an iron could put "a smile" on your ball and ruin your day. The advent of the solid ball covered with a synthetic substance (at first, Surlyn) changed all that. Balls lasted longer and, in relative terms, became much cheaper. There is little doubt that changes in the ball have made the game more enjoyable for the average player. For the top players, the changes in the ball have been more dramatic. In the last twenty years on the PGA Tour, players have dramatically increased the distance they can hit the new balls. This has made courses, once thought long, into sitting ducks for the new long hitters.

Technology has also led to a transformation in what dedicated players think of as "their clubs." In the 1950s a set of clubs was standardized and the emphasis was on the set being matched, or identical in style and balance, from club to club. The standard set included four-woods, eight-irons, and a putter. Usually the player picked up a wedge to fill out the fourteen-club set. Today there is no standard set, as technology has particularly transformed the driver, the putter, and wedges. These clubs are invariably purchased separately and usually at much greater cost than in the 1950s. The standard iron set of two through nine is also changing as so-called utility clubs are rapidly replacing the two-, three-, four-, and even the five-iron. Few players carry four-woods. Instead, one- or two-woods have been replaced by specialized wedges or utility clubs.

However, these technological and commerce-driven changes are relatively minor compared to the transformation in the golf community promoted by the advent of the golf cart and the impact of television.

Of the two, the golf cart was the least important. This does not mean that the power cart did not dramatically transform golf. The invention of the small, two-seat electric golf cart (and of, eventually, the gas-powered version) was spurred by gas rationing during World War II. With gasoline in short supply, it just made sense that American inventiveness would turn to electricity. It is probable that the first carts were built by Merle Williams and his firm, the Marketeer Company, in Redlands, California. Large-scale production of electric golf carts did not begin until the mid-1950s. The EZ-Go Company began production in 1954 and Cushman followed soon after in 1955. In

1957 the industry produced only five thousand carts; by 1967 yearly production approached fifty thousand.

The reasons behind the rapid adoption of the power golf cart are fairly straightforward. It solved several structural problems that have long been part of the golf community. The most central was the caddie problem. Of course, the caddie has an honored place in the golf community, but at clubs and resorts they posed a dilemma. In the North, caddies were generally available during the months when school was out. However, in the spring and fall, they were in short supply, and on weekdays they were often simply not available. This was particularly true in the South where, as air-conditioning became more common, the golf season lasted all year. Furthermore, the training of caddies and their administration (hiring a caddie master, maintaining a caddie shack, etc.) was a cost that produced no profit. Many clubs saw the caddie program as a costly headache.

Carts were the answer. They worked all year and they produced a profit for the club or the professional who invested in a fleet of the carts and then rented them to players. Caddie shacks could be torn down or put to some profitable use. A cart never said anything rude to a golfer who had just hit two balls into the creek ten yards away. A cart never quit in disgust or complained about a lousy tip. Golf courses came to depend increasingly on the income carts provided. Carts also induced people to play in very hot weather, increasing the profitability of courses, especially in the South.

The move to carts began when clubs allowed their use for elderly or ill golfers. The movement gained momentum when it became clear that Eisenhower often used a golf cart at Augusta and elsewhere. While playing in Scotland, Ike employed one of the two carts in the whole country. Slowly the restrictions that limited their use to only the old and the lame were lifted. In 1956 the Metropolitan Golf Association announced that golfers in their senior tournaments could use power carts. Some sort of line was crossed in July 1960 when a Riviera (California)

Country Club employee, Merle G. Hanmore, was crushed to death by an overturned golf cart. He became, as far as I know, the first casualty of the cart era.

There were, of course, other losses. People charged with caring for golf courses were, at first, appalled by power golf carts. Courses simply were not designed to handle the damage caused by the carts. The main problem was compaction of the soil and the inevitable death of turf where compaction was the most severe. Courses had to be retrofitted to make carts less destructive. This meant the laying of miles of cart paths that dramatically changed the look and playing characteristics of most golf courses. It soon became apparent that caddies were important to the health and playability of the golf courses where they had labored. They raked traps, replaced divots, and repaired ball marks. People in carts often forgot to do these things.

Some of the damage done by carts was more subtle but perhaps more important. The job of caddie had introduced thousands of young boys (and a few girls) to the game of golf. The cart slowly squeezed shut this pipeline into the game. The few African Americans who came into the game usually came by the caddie route. As caddying died, the trickle of blacks into the game dried up. The image of golf as inherently racist deepened.

The death of the young caddie was a boon to other sports, however. Aided no doubt by rising affluence, young boys in the early 1950s had a tough choice (at least it was for me) between golf-caddying and baseball. As the caddie job died, baseball was a big winner. Little League baseball, founded in 1939 by Carl Shotz, grew luxuriously in the fifties and sixties. Pop Warner football dates back to the 1920s, but did not go national until after World War II. Between 1950 and 1970, the league grew rapidly; in 1970 there were three thousand teams and over three hundred thousand participants.

The cart also undercut a good part of the long-standing rationale for golf. The golf cart reduced the exercise one received from a round of golf to near zero. For seventy years the heart of golf had been a walk, either carrying your bag or having someone else do it. Since 1960, increasingly, the heart of golf has been a ride. It is truly amazing that if you examine golf art in the last forty years you will rarely see a golf cart or a cart path. It is as if photographers and artists know that the cart has ruined the aesthetic of golf. The idea that golf can reunite the player with nature and produce a stress-reducing experience has been profoundly undercut by the ubiquitous cart. Anyone who says they are playing golf for their health and plays in a cart is simply deluded.

The power golf cart has done much to change the game. It has changed golf's financial landscape, transformed the actual landscape, and driven almost all the caddies from the game. Quite an impact for what is really just a very simple technological innovation.

Television, in the long run, was more important. It was the central technological advance during the early years of the age of affluence. It had, from 1950 onward, a profound influence on American habits. A look at some statistics regarding discretionary time from Stanley Lebergott's fine book *Pursuing Happiness: American Consumers in the Twentieth Century* (1996) can give us a sense of television's impact. Based on a survey taken in 1975, the data show that Americans spent approximately forty-six hours per week working. This was a sum of the hours worked on the job and at home. Men spent more time (thirty-three hours) at the job, while women did most of their work at home (thirty hours). The number of hours spent in "recreation" was thirty-three hours for men and thirty-two for women. Of this total, each gender spent approximately fourteen hours on "sports, entertainment, travel, and hobbies." There were also small allotments of time set aside for meals out and taverns. The survey showed that Americans spent slightly more than fourteen hours per week watching television. Roughly speaking, television absorbed nearly half of the time available for recreation.

On average, Americans, in 1975, watched television approximately two hours per day. In the years since 1975, other surveys have shown that the hours devoted to television have grown. There is little doubt that watching TV, in one form or another, takes up more discretionary time than any other nonwork activity.

The advent of television had an impact on all aspects of American life. Golf was no exception. Golf and the private golf club were seen by many as extensions of the home, and so the game and the club at which it was played were valued because they expanded life, recreationally and socially. Television blunted, but did not totally destroy this role for golf. Television did keep people at home, though. It hurt not only golf but any number of other activities that took people out of the home and into the world and into society. Television produced a rapid drop in movie going and a reduction in attendance at athletic events. Robert Putnam, in his book *Bowling Alone*, concluded that "nothing else in the twentieth century so rapidly and profoundly affected our leisure."

The combined influence of television and affluence produced a dramatic change in the nature of the American home. Especially among the classes where rising affluence was the most pronounced, the homes began to grow. A survey in 1950 showed that the average American home contained slightly less than a thousand square feet. And only one in twelve featured more than one bathroom. Since the mid-1950s the American home has steadily grown. By one estimate, the average American home grew from 1,500 to 2,330 square feet between 1970 and 2001. In 1971 only 9 percent of American homes were larger than 2,400 square feet, and in 2001 38 percent surpassed the 2,400-square-foot mark. The ballooning of the American home was widespread; even starter homes increased from 1,440 to 1,570 square feet.

These numbers suggest a profound transformation in American habits between the mid-1950s and today. A good name for this transformation is the privatizing of leisure. To understand this change it helps to look at some individual examples. Take, for example, the home of Michael Frisby, once a correspondent for the *Wall Street Journal,* who in 2006 ran a public relations firm. His home was in Fulton, Maryland, not far from Washington DC. This home contained eleven thousand square feet, was three stories tall, and stood on three and a half acres. There was an English garden, a music room, a gym, a sauna and steam room, and a business office. It also featured an entertainment room with a ten-foot-wide screen for movies and the best projection equipment money could buy. When asked to explain why he had such a huge home, Mr. Frisby said he believed "that you can live out your fantasy." Unfortunately he did not precisely define what that fantasy was.

Obviously the growth of homes into minimansions had some basic economic roots. There was simply more discretionary income available to pour into homes. Also the tax benefits that came with huge mortgage payments and the tax-free conveyance of the profit on a home were, and are, important. Many individuals, when asked about their extravagant homes, note that a home is a good investment. This was the general economic wisdom until 2007, when wisdom turned into stupidity.

But there was clearly something else that promoted the lavish expansion of American homes in the last fifty years. A desire for privacy seems important when you consider the huge increase in the number of bathrooms per home. The lure of either attached or semiattached "amenities" also seems crucial. Tennis courts and pools, either as part of the home or as available in the gated communities where many of these homes are located, were also important. It's only a modest oversimplification to suggest that the new massive American home was a combination of the smaller home bonded to facilities once found at the private country club. In some sense, the home had become a resort. People like to feel that coming home is like going on vacation.

A considerable amount of the time once devoted to golf and

the golf club was slowly absorbed by television and the attractions of the new ever-expanding home. No one thought of golf as exercise or as a way to reduce stress. Exercise was something done at a "fitness center" or in your own home gym, following the new rules that emphasized aerobic fitness. Hello treadmill. You played golf in a cart.

All this did not mean that golf, in some sense, did not benefit from television and the new utopian home. Golf would become a product molded to fit these new realities: it would get on television; it would become a television show. The bonding of golf and television was a slow process. Many in the PGA thought that television offered little to tournament golf. Horton Smith, a longtime power in the PGA hierarchy, said in 1947 that TV was "a gimmick that wouldn't last." Broadcasting golf was also very difficult and expensive. Football, baseball, and the other major sports have relatively small confined fields. Golf, and particularly the actions that determine a golf tournament's outcome, take place over acres of space and are unconfined by the usual time constraints.

The first golf shows were local, filmed products that mixed competition and instruction. A central figure in getting the shows on the air was Joe Jemsek, owner and operator of several public daily-fee courses in Chicago. The first was *Pars, Birdies, and Eagles*, a thirty-minute show that included instruction from Johnny Revolta. This program led Jemsek and others to create *All-Star Golf*, a program that featured filmed matches between pros.

George May was the first to put an actual tournament event on television. Born in rural Illinois in 1890, May became the most inventive and promotionally creative operator of a tour event after the war. May sold Bibles and had many other jobs early in his life, but eventually he became a consultant to other businesses when he established George S. May International.

May owned his own country club, the Tam O'Shanter Golf Club, in Niles, Illinois. From 1941 to 1958, he put on a tournament that featured both pros and amateurs and was more like a festival than a golf event. He tried every promotional trick that he or his staff could conjure up. The prize money increased every year, eventually reaching fifty thousand dollars. He installed bleachers at key vantage points and once demanded that the players wear numbers so the fans could easily identify the contestants. He hired clowns to entertain the children.

May seemed to be aware of the few experimental attempts to televise golf; there had been a crude broadcast of the British Open in the 1930s and a local broadcast of the U.S. Open in 1947 at St. Louis. In 1953 May agreed to pay ABC thirty-two thousand dollars for televising his tournament, then called the Tam O'Shanter World Championship. In 1954 the network sold the show to a number of advertisers and May got his television coverage free.

Perhaps one million Americans saw the last day of May's 1953 event. There was only one camera and it could only show the play on the eighteenth hole. As the tournament played out, only two players had a chance for the twenty-five-thousand-dollar first prize. Chandler Harper was finished and enjoyed a one-stroke lead over Lou Worsham, the only competitor who could catch him. Worsham hit a good drive on the last and was faced with a 120-yard shot to a back pin. His approach, hit with a Mac-Gregor "Double Duty" wedge, hit on the front of the green and ran nearly sixty feet and into the hole for an eagle that gave him the championship and the first-prize money. Surely one can argue that this was a sign that the golf gods approved of the game on television. However, people and institutions (networks) responded slowly to what was perhaps a sign from on high.

Golf on television grew slowly after 1953. In 1954 the USGA put their Open on the airwaves. In 1955 the Masters made its first television appearance. Regular tour events, however, made it to national television only after 1960. The networks could see the Open, the Masters, and the PGA Championship as events that they wished to broadcast. The rest of the tour, for the most part, still had "a quaint ring to it," as Al Barkow has put it. There was an event in Texas called the Rio Grande Valley Fruit and Vegetable Open and an event in Indiana called the Speedway Open. Broadcasting essentially local events made little sense to the networks.

In the standard view, Arnold Palmer was the catalyst for the rapid growth of televised golf in the 1960s. After winning the U.S. Amateur in 1954, Palmer turned pro and did well in the late fifties; he won a number of tour events—Insurance City, Azalea, Rubber City, Pepsi Opens—and bigger events, the Canadian Open and the Masters in 1958. But 1960 was his coming-out year. He won nine events; but the real fireworks came at the Masters and the U.S. Open. In both tournaments, Palmer produced last-round heroics that made for compelling television.

At the Masters, Palmer birdied seventeen and eighteen to snatch the trophy from the hands of Ken Venturi. At the Open at Cherry Hills, in Colorado, Palmer's comeback entailed the entire final round, especially the first nine. As the last round began, Palmer was seven shots behind the leader, Mike Souchak. No one gave him a chance. He began the last round with a titanic blast on the first hole into the thin Colorado air; it reached the green on the 342-yard hole. This ignited a blazing front nine of 30. He played the back in 35 and won by two. No one had ever produced such a low final round or overcome such a huge deficit to win the U.S. Open.

Much has been written about Palmer's rise to the top of professional golf between 1958 and 1960. No one has summarized that rise with more clarity and grace than Herbert Warren Wind. For him, Palmer

> made golf seem as exciting as any contact sport, and many sports buffs who had hitherto scoffed at the game became ardent converts after watching Palmer in action on television. When his fans met their hero in the flesh they were seldom if ever disappointed. He had the innate politeness and patience to treat

people as individuals in handling their endless requests for autographs and answering their repetitive questions. . . . Success did not change him. . . . He was equally at home with presidents, ad men, caddies, students, tycoons, farmers, and small-town radio interviewers eager to tape a close-up with him.

I believe that Wind has touched the heart of Palmer's contribution to golf. He lured nongolfers and people uninterested in the game out to the tournaments and into what was called "Arnie's Army." For the most part this was wonderful, and certainly Palmer's comebacks made great television. But some of these new fans did not fully understand the values of the golf community.

This became clear when Jack Nicklaus arrived to challenge Palmer as king of the hill. Some of Palmer's fans took an immediate dislike to Nicklaus and far too often gave voice to that dislike. They yelled insults, usually making some reference to his weight—"fat boy," "fat Jack," and "blob-o" were popular. This behavior indicated that Palmer had lured into the game fans who were not part of the golf community and had not internalized the rules of decorum central to golf. Bobby Jones had done something similar in the late 1920s. People came to see the great Jones, as if he were some amazing temporary celestial phenomenon. They stampeded around the course, delayed play, and influenced the outcome of more than one tournament. Arnie's Army did much the same thing. This illustrated that there is a considerable difference between a golfer and a golf fan.

The Palmer-Nicklaus duels made tour golf seem like a more salable product; and television, as it grew in the 1960s, had an insatiable appetite for product. It helped that Palmer and Nicklaus were joined by a notable list of challengers. The most important was Gary Player from South Africa. Player won his first American event in 1958—the Kentucky Derby Open. When he won the Masters in 1961, and the PGA in 1962, he became very nearly the equal of Palmer and Nicklaus. Journalists began to refer to the trio as the Big Three. Player's presence also gave the evolving tour an international tone. There had always been foreign players in PGA events, but Player was different. After his success, the stream of international stars would be incessant. Certainly the arrival of competitors like Player aroused the old nationalist fervor that had always stimulated interest in golf.

It is always more interesting to think that an individual like Arnold Palmer was the cause of television's love affair with golf and the rapid rise of the official PGA Tour. But Palmer's popularity provided only a partial explanation for TV's adoption of golf as a weekly staple. Clearly more important was the split between the tour players and the PGA that occurred in 1968.

There had been grumbling by tour players as early as the 1930s. The administration of the tour by the PGA, essentially a trade association of club professionals, made little sense. From the mid-1950s to the late 1960s, television slowly increased the amount of golf available to viewers. The major events were televised and the networks created their own events. Regular shows such as *Shell's Wonderful World of Golf*, which ran from 1961 to 1970, and CBS's *Match-Play Classic* taught the networks that golf was a viable, profitable product. Regular, nonmajor, tour events began to appear on television in 1960. Produced by Dick Bailey and Sports Network, these productions of tournaments like the Los Angeles, Phoenix, Tucson, and Western Opens also convinced network executives to do more golf.

The PGA turned to Martin Carmichael as their man to negotiate with the networks. He had learned the intricacies of the business while working for CBS and *Match-Play Classic*. Carmichael did something very important. He locked up corporate sponsors first and then went to the networks to sell the PGA weekly tournaments. In 1966 he was unable to get suitable bids from the networks so he sold the events to Bailey, who broadcast twelve events on Sports Network.

In 1967 the three major networks made offers, and all three broadcast some PGA golf. Altogether they paid slightly more than one million dollars to the PGA. In 1967 the PGA events were on the tube for a record number of hours. The PGA canceled its deal with CBS for *Match-Play Classic* and also ended its arrangement with ABC that gave that network the right of first refusal to carry any tour event. This set up competitive bidding between the three networks and prices soared.

By 1968 it was apparent to everyone that PGA events were much more valuable than they had been only five years earlier. The question was why. First, the Palmer, Nicklaus, and Player–led tour was compelling television. All three had their fans, and events in which they appeared simply were more valuable. Second, the arrival and rapid spread of color television in the late 1960s made all sports more valuable, though one could argue that golf, with its varied and pastoral venues, gained the most from color telecasts. Third, by the late sixties the PGA was finally putting its reputation as a racist organization behind it and golf, on the participant level, was growing steadily.

But in the end it was the corporations and television that made golf tournaments so valuable. Since the inception of the tour in the 1920s, most tournaments had been local affairs, designed to promote cities like Los Angeles, Phoenix, or San Antonio, or resorts like Pinehurst. Televised tournaments on a national network instantly made the Los Angeles Open and others national events. Large corporations saw the opportunity to associate themselves with golf and with tournaments that had a deep history and a certain amount of prestige. The first companies to step up were Goodyear, Bell Telephone, and Chrysler, but they were certainly not the last.

None of this was lost on the players. Led by Marty Carmichael, the players quickly came to understand the value of the tournaments in which they performed. The crux of the matter was the ownership of the right to broadcast the tournaments. Traditionally, these rights were owned by the tournament itself. For example, Bing Crosby owned the rights to his event and sold them as he saw fit. The tour players thought they should own the rights to what they saw as their performance. The event sponsors (producers of the production) thought they should own the rights. The parties initially compromised on this issue: the players got 25 percent of the rights, the PGA got 25 percent, and the sponsors received 50 percent, but had to promise to put some of that money into the purse for the tournament.

It was this deal that began the rapid increase in the total amount the pros played for each year. Between 1958 and 1961, Palmer's best years, purses on the tour increased approximately $150,000. From 1961 to 1967, they grew about $300,000. In 1968, the year of the split, the total yearly purse skyrocketed. In that one year the annual total purse increased by more than $1 million.

It is important to acknowledge that more than broadcast rights were an issue in the conflict between the touring pros and the PGA. The tour had evolved in a way that has no parallel in the history of sport. An organization made up of approximately six thousand teaching and club pros elected officers to control their substantial operations. They ran an annual championship and the biannual Ryder Cup, controlled the complex program that licensed club professionals, issued instructional materials, ran an employment service, and administered a number of other minor programs. In the end, the core of the PGA was to serve their members, the club professionals. By 1965 the fact that they also ran the tour was a glaring anomaly. Yet clearly they did. The executive committee of the PGA had absolute veto over the actions of the tournament committee that ran the tour.

Max Elbin, the head pro at Burning Tree and president of the PGA in 1968, never wavered in his position that the PGA should control the tour. In June 1967, Elbin told the *New York Times* that the PGA would compromise on some issues "but we positively will not compromise on control and think this is the crux of the whole matter." He suggested that player control of the tour would lead to "chaos." One cannot read the journalistic accounts of the nearly year-long conflict between the players and PGA officials like Elbin without coming to the conclusion that they simply did not like or trust each other.

On December 14, 1968, the two parties announced that they had resolved their differences. The players had won their independence. The tour would now be controlled by a new, completely autonomous committee. It would have ten members: four players, three PGA officials, and three members from the business community. It was clear at this point that the key figure in the new arrangement would be the man who took over the post of tour director. Soon it was announced that that person would be Joe Dey from the USGA. Dey had the respect and trust of the entire golf community. He would serve the new organization from early 1969 to February 1974, when Deane Beman took over. There will be more about Beman in the next chapter.

By any measure, 1968 was a watershed year in American history. There were violent antiwar protests, the Nixon victory, and the passions aroused by the conflict between middle-class culture and its critics. This has obscured the fact that it was a revolutionary year in sport as well. Across the world of sport there was a seeming explosion of interest and controversy. Jean-Claude Killy won his third Olympic medal in skiing when "the apparent winner got lost in an alpine fog." Bob Goalby won the Masters when Roberto de Vicenzo made a bookkeeping error. The winner of the Kentucky Derby, Dancer's Image, was brought up on drug charges and disqualified. UCLA and Lew Alcindor dominated college basketball, and two competing leagues fought for control of the pro game. Tennis began the open era—pros played with amateurs. Americans were getting familiar with the idea of a Super Bowl—the Packers won again. Over fifty-two thousand college basketball fans watched Houston defeat UCLA in the Astrodome. Everyone paid attention to figure skating because of Peggy Fleming. From out of nowhere, Lee Trevino won the U.S. Open and joined the world of golf stars at the very top. Arthur Ashe, an amateur, won the first U.S. Open

Tennis Championship. Denny McLain won thirty-one games for the Tigers. The Tigers spotted the St. Louis Cardinals a three-to-one lead in the World Series and won the next three games and the last real World Series championship. Early in 1969 Joseph Durso of the *New York Times* clearly saw the motor driving the revolution in sport: it was "the great god television, which broadcasts sports with all their wonders and woes for the largest audiences in history."

Looking back on 1968, it seems as good a year as any to mark the spot where sport, and especially sport on television, began to truly dominate the American psyche. Sport, in all its forms, would grow and spread and create. Corporations, awash in money and convinced of the power of advertising, would rush to sponsor it all, and television was the medium whereby Americans got to see it all. The distinction between sport and entertainment dissolved. Previously, the golf tour began the year with visits to California towns. By 1970 the tour began its annual trek with events hosted by Bing Crosby, Bob Hope, and Andy Williams.

Fueled by corporate cash, the networks would spend ever-increasing amounts on their coverage of golf events. In 1966 ABC telecast two hours of the final round of the U.S. Open at the Olympic Club in San Francisco. They employed seventeen cameras to record Arnold Palmer's historic collapse and Billy Casper's eventual victory. Viewers saw action on only four and a half holes and missed many of Palmer's biggest mistakes. In 2010 NBC deployed forty-nine cameras on all eighteen holes in their broadcast of the U.S. Open at Pebble Beach. For the week, viewers could watch thirty hours of coverage; there had been only four in 1966. Viewers now get a much closer look at the action. Lighter, more portable cameras take us right down onto the green where we can see every spike mark and lip out. Slow-motion cameras show the point of impact between club and ball with amazing clarity. This growth was expensive, but corporate sponsors were there to pay the bills.

In some ways, the history of the LPGA in the 1970s is the best illustration of the process I am trying to describe. In the 1960s the LPGA survived, but lacking real star power and corporate interest, it lagged behind the men's tour. In the early 1970s, the average purse at a standard LPGA event was only thirty thousand dollars. The LPGA Championship offered a total purse of fifty thousand dollars.

In 1972 the LPGA attracted the interest of a very big, iconic corporation — the Colgate-Palmolive Company. The company's CEO, David Foster, saw in women's golf a vehicle to sell his products. The big splash was in the United States. Colgate sponsored the Colgate–Dinah Shore Winner's Circle Tournament with a total prize purse of $110,000. The first playing of this event was a smashing success. Dinah Shore lured her friends into playing in the pro-am, and the network television broadcast got good ratings. I remember that my mother watched every minute; my father stated that his wife "would pay to watch Dinah Shore boil eggs."

Foster had big plans for golf and his company. In 1974 he sponsored a fifty-thousand-dollar women's event at the Sunningdale Golf Club in England and a similar event, called the Colgate Far East Open, in Australia. In 1975 Colgate created a tournament called the Triple Crown, with a purse of fifty thousand dollars and a field of only ten women players.

Few know that Colgate also owned the Ram Golf Company. Foster signed many of the best women players, paying them substantial sums to become part of what came to be known as the Ram Team. Other club makers were forced to scramble to keep up, and the money flowing to women players for endorsement contracts jumped significantly. Foster and Colgate were only doing what other equally big corporations were doing: they wanted their products associated with golf and were willing to pay handsomely to get it.

The LPGA did well, but it never was anything like the equal of the men's tour. When the male players took over their tour from the PGA, a number of commentators wondered if the women's game could keep up. The issue was money. Lincoln Werden, the *New York Times* sports columnist, wondered if the jump in men's purses in 1969 would diminish the women and the LPGA. He noted that the year's opening men's event, the San Diego Open, had been transformed. The prize money had jumped from $66,000 to $150,000 and the event had a new host, the singer and television star Andy Williams. Werden wondered, "Can the women compete with such affluence and influence?"

Part of the answer was provided by David Foster, Dinah Shore, and Colgate. Another answer was provided by Shirley Englehorn, a fine player and the president of the LPGA in 1968. She thought women could not compete with the power game of Nicklaus and Palmer. Instead, the women should move up to the women's tees, play shorter courses, and post lower scores. Englehorn also noted that the women's game had more in common with the golf played by the average male than the power game on the PGA Tour—a point that is truer today than when Englehorn made it in 1968. She also thought that women should dress to attract an audience. She stated that "if miniskirts or minishorts will do it [attract an audience], let's wear them now." The growth of women's golf on television made this potential use of sex appeal seem all the more attractive. For the last fifty years this issue of using attractive sexy stars, or not, has been part of LPGA life. Golf, in so many ways, had become show business.

Finally, any discussion of television, golf, and sport in general has to confront the relationship of spectating and participation. Did the exposure granted professional golf by television increase or inhibit general participation by average Americans? In some sense this is the wrong question. Watching golf on television may or may not have stimulated interest in the game, but the really important question concerns the impact generally of televised sports. There can be little doubt that the time spent watching the vast array of sport on television cuts into the time people devote to actually playing games—golf being only one such game.

As the age of affluence matured in the 1970s and the 1980s, televised sports became one of its central institutions, and professional golf was a relatively small part of a much larger development. The American calendar, once organized by months and seasons, came increasingly to be ordered by televised sporting events. Viewers divided a year using "must see" sporting events. From the World Series (conveniently played at night for a bigger TV audience) to the Super Bowl, to the Masters (announcing the arrival of spring in America), to the NBA Finals, to baseball's All-Star Game and the opening of the college football season. Between these landmarks there existed a bounty of everyday games. Soon television began bringing to America virtually everything about sports. The draft days—when college students became professional football, baseball, or basketball players—were transformed into television programs. Minor sports and newly invented ones were used to spackle the few empty spots on the sports calendar.

The fans for this tidal wave of televised sports were continually produced by an expensive and expansive program of school sports. From the earliest grades, students moved through a system that inevitably created a vast audience of passive fans. In American schools, the events that profoundly engaged the passions were the big games. From high school onward through college, for the few who play in these games or for the many who watch them, nothing will ever match the emotional excitement or the sense of total involvement. These big games are almost always football or basketball games. As people grow older, playing these games becomes less and less realistic. But being a fan fits the bill. Trained in school to care deeply about the outcome of certain games, it's hardly surprising that they move easily into the role of passive consumer of television's long calendar of equally big events. Get me a beer and pass the chips.

For the most part, games that one can play for a lifetime—golf, tennis, swimming—are minor events in the school-based program to train fans. There are no big golf games; audiences at school golf matches are usually "friends and family." As Americans leave school, the conflict between spectating and participation is decidedly tilted toward spectating. That is where the emotional intensity, the commitment, resides. Television makes being a fan, and connecting with that intensity, easy and cheap. Being an actual player of a game, in contrast, seems hard and expensive.

In the end, the golf community that had flourished unimpeded between 1890 and 1930 found itself in a very different world after 1950, and particularly after 1968. Postwar affluence changed everything. People stayed home in houses that grew larger every year. They could watch an ever-increasing stream of television programming on one of their three or four televisions. The pressure to consume, created by advertising, poured discretionary income into second homes, third cars, and expensive vacations. Americans became detached from where they lived. They changed jobs more often and this often meant leaving one anonymous suburb for another. For some it meant exchanging one gated community for another.

After the war, the golf community was forced to confront the bias and exclusivity that were defining elements of the pre-1930 game. African Americans and women found an enlarged place in the golfing community, but this place was not all that it should be, and the price of carving out that place was far too high. Oddly, the arrival of the powered golf cart was influential in slowing the egalitarian movement. The cart all but destroyed the caddie. The caddie's role had been more than a job; it had been an avenue into the game for lower-class blacks and whites. As measured by the number of African Americans on the PGA Tour, the growth of racial diversity in golf has actually been blunted.

In the years after 1980, it has become apparent that the golf community is split in two. On the one hand there are the conservative defenders of pre-1930 golf—suspicious of change and determined to preserve the true and lasting values of the game.

Arrayed against the conservatives, is the modern party, a group determined to adjust the golf community so that it might better fit a new and rapidly changing economic and cultural context. In the next chapter we will examine golf under the two-party system.

Golf and the Two-Party System

Powerful organizations always exaggerate their reach. Officials put up speed-limit signs but most speeders are never caught. The tax collector rarely collects all the money due. In the golf community things are no different. The majority of American golfers play using rules devised, for the most part, by the players themselves. They take mulligans, ground their clubs in hazards, and the use of so-called winter rules in all seasons is widespread. More than a few golfers play to keep their handicaps as high as possible so they may do well in net competitions.

However, once we leave the world of the casual recreational player the situation changes dramatically. Any sort of meaningful competition, from weekend money games at the club to a national open championship, calls for a complicated and fairly enforced set of rules. One of the most important traits of a full-fledged member of the golf community is the full acceptance, the internalization, of the rules of golf. In the United States these rules have been written by the United States Golf Association (USGA). Each year they produce a little book called *The Rules of Golf.* It is, as far as I know, one of the most commonly reproduced rulebooks in all of sports. It is to golfers as the Bible is to Christians.

But the governance of the golf community requires more than codified rules. In this *The Rules of Golf* makes a substantial start.

The little book begins with a section called "Etiquette." It is a charming essay that states that its goal is to lay out guidelines on the manners essential to the game of golf. The "overriding principle" of these manners "is that consideration should be shown to others on the course at all times." Some of this "consideration" involves safety—the time-honored tradition of shouting "fore" when your shot endangers other players, for example. Golf etiquette is based on the idea that all players should do everything possible to allow others to play the game completely free of influence from other competitors. These rules are what Bruce McCall called "golf's sourpuss rules of decorum."

The codified suggestions called etiquette provide substantial informal governance of golf. In formal competitions a player may be disqualified for repeated breaches of etiquette. Again, a true member of the golf community accepts and internalizes these informal rules, these manners. After playing for a few years the dedicated player follows the formal and informal rules instinctively. Golf is an arduous community imposing all sorts of restrictions. Many clubs still enforce a dress code on players that bans the wearing of denim. Western culture seems to have adopted denim jeans as the all-purpose pair of pants. Only at some private clubs do they still carry a stigma strong enough to get them excluded as improper golf attire.

Golf, acting through the USGA, has done an excellent job of establishing a uniform set of rules. There have, however, been substantial disputes. The United States and Great Britain, for much of the twentieth century, played the game by slightly different rules. For many years there was a British ball and an American ball. In the past there have been a few bitter dust-ups about equipment, especially when the British outlawed the center-shafted Schenectady putter used by Walter Travis as he won the British Amateur in 1904. Golf antiquarians enjoy tracing out the differences between golf in the two countries and their resolution. These historians point to 1951 as the year in which golf took its biggest step toward worldwide uniformity. The USGA and the Royal and Ancient met several times to iron out their differences regarding rules. A new uniform code was announced in 1951 and was formally adopted in 1952. Today *The Rules of Golf* states that "this book contains the rules of golf as approved jointly by the United States Golf Association and the R&A." Every four years the two groups meet to revise the rules.

In the governance of a popular game such as golf there is much more to consider than the codified rules. There are many issues not covered by the written code. One important consideration is the nature of the golf course and how it should be maintained. And there are other issues as well. What kinds of competitions are best? What should be the relationship between amateur and professional players? What or who should monitor the products of companies that produce golf clubs and balls?

The answers to these questions come from two sources — the United States Golf Association (USGA) and the Professional Golfers' Association (PGA). Since 1968, the professional golfers have, of course, been divided into two groups: touring pros and club pros. As one looks back at the record of the last sixty years, it would be easy to quote numerous statements expressing mutual admiration and pledging cooperation between the USGA and the pros. And, indeed, in many ways they do work together to advance the game. But in the end, they are very different assemblages of people with very different visions for golf and its future.

The two organizations emerged from World War II at loggerheads about the rules. It was the USGA's position that, particularly during the war, the PGA had begun to play by its own rules. In 1946 Francis Ouimet, who had become chair of the USGA committee that conducted championships, wrote a letter to all the entrants into the Open Championship. He contended that in the five years since the last Open, an unfortunate trend to disregard the rules had developed. "The game must be played by the rules," he insisted. "It is no game at all if the accepted code is not observed."

It was clear that Ouimet's letter was aimed at the PGA, though he did not say so. The PGA, for some time, had conducted its tournaments using a slightly altered set of rules. Some variations were technical. PGA players had been altering the markings on the faces of their irons to increase the spin a player could impart to the ball. The USGA objected to these variations. Other PGA deviations from the rules were more basic; since 1938, for example, the PGA had played golf events allowing players to carry more than fourteen clubs.

This conflict between the USGA and the PGA was more bitter and fundamental than most have admitted. The PGA ran events in all types of weather and often invoked winter rules to improve the quality of play. On some occasions conditions were so bad that players carried mats or squares of carpet from which to play their shots. The pros noted that the USGA ran only one tournament, the Open, in which pros played, and this was conducted in the summer, usually under ideal conditions. While no one admitted it, the pros saw the fourteen-club rule as an arbitrary limit on the main business of a golf professional in 1948—selling golf clubs. They may well have thought that a jump in the limit from fourteen to sixteen would translate into increased club sales.

By the spring of 1948 the issues that existed between the two groups were settled, at least for a time. They were resolved at Augusta National Golf Club. The president of the USGA was Fielding Wallace, a member and secretary of the Augusta Club. The president of the PGA was Ed Dudley, the head professional at Augusta. Dudley was, in some sense, Wallace's employee.

Apparently, the PGA voluntarily withdrew its objections to the USGA rules. However, a letter sent to Dudley by Wallace (and published in the first edition of the USGA Journal in spring 1948) suggested the depth of the differences between the two organizations. Wallace, speaking for the USGA, stated that "our divergence from your views is accounted for by a difference in general approach to the game." For the USGA golf was "essentially a recreation and a sporting test of skill," but Wallace saw that for the PGA, golf was "a program of intensive competition among professionals for money prizes." Wallace believed that the changes (the increase in the fourteen-club limit, for example) "would tend to soften the game and to make for artificially low scoring." Wallace argued that touring professionals who advocated the changes in the rules had interests that were "quite special in that they are constantly competing for money prizes." Wallace bluntly stated that the interests of touring pros did not "necessarily represent the best interests of the game as a whole." As an example, Wallace addressed the suggestion that the club limit be raised from fourteen to sixteen. He rejected this idea because of the increased cost. Every golfer would want to add clubs to his set and the cost of golf would rise.

There was one issue between the two groups that did not involve the rules of play. The PGA wanted the USGA to increase the prize money offered at the Open Championship. The prize money at the Open had grown from six thousand to ten thousand dollars since 1946. Wallace thought this increase more than adequate. However, his attitude toward this issue was shaped by larger concerns. He pointed out that any increase in the prize money paid to pros would require the USGA to cut its budget in other areas. He also noted that the Open was run by amateur volunteers. If these volunteers were to be paid for their services, it would cut drastically into the prize money. In the end, Wallace wrote that the prize money was not a big issue at the U.S. Open because "it is not a commercial event for advertising purposes."

The dispute between the USGA and the PGA, and Wallace's summary letter in 1948, laid out most, but not all, of the differences between the two organizations. As time passed, the two groups settled into an uneasy peace. The PGA agreed to play its events by USGA rules. The USGA ran its U.S. Open as a profit-making venture, which funded much of its growing program. The USGA, in most respects, remained the master of amateur golf, especially amateur competition.

In one area — control of the rules that govern equipment and the ball — the USGA and the pros have continued something that looks like polite warfare. Golf ball and equipment manufacturers have, over the last century, come up with balls that go farther and spin more or less; they have invented new club designs that drive the ball farther and that actually straighten poorly hit shots. The vast majority of these advances have been beneficial, especially for the average player. The USGA has the job of determining when change has gone too far, when the new design "softens" the game, to use Wallace's term from 1948. Particularly in the area of driver design and the grooves on irons, the USGA has decreed that things have gone too far. It should be noted that the professional game has been the target of these decrees, and the average amateur has been largely unaffected.

Unfortunately these arcane debates about grooves and rebound effect have obscured the more fundamental differences between the USGA and the PGA. After the two groups resolved their differences in the immediate postwar era, larger, more general differences slowly evolved. Much of this was the work of USGA officials who took offense at the direction golf slowly began to take in the mid-1950s. In essence, these officials articulated a conservative and critical approach to the game as it evolved in the age of affluence. The most outspoken of these officials was Richard Tufts.

Richard Tufts was certainly one of the most important people in the twentieth-century golf community. To a great extent, he owed this status to his father and grandfather. James Walker Tufts, Richard's grandfather, had founded Pinehurst in North Carolina, in 1894, as a refuge from northern winters and as a place where those with lung disorders could recuperate. When the initial plan for the resort did not work, Tufts turned to golf, about which he knew nothing. He did not see his village fully adopt golf before he died in 1901. Not long before his death, however, James Walker Tufts hired Donald Ross to build golf courses and to establish a golf program.

Pinehurst was largely the creation of Leonard Tufts, who inherited the village in 1901. From 1904 to the mid-1930s, Leonard Tufts directed Pinehurst and shaped it into one of America's most prominent winter resorts. His son Richard, after attending Harvard and service in the U.S. Navy, came to Pinehurst after the war and helped it grow rapidly in the 1920s. Richard took over in the 1930s, steering the business though the Depression and World War II. This experience imbued Richard with a profound conservative bent. After the war, he became deeply involved in USGA affairs. He was particularly interested in codifying the rules of golf and was a central figure on the American side in the meetings with the R&A that created a unified set of rules. Between 1946 and 1955 he served on the USGA executive committee and as vice president. In 1956 he became president for two one-year terms.

Tufts was an unusually productive figure at the USGA. Beyond his work on the rules, Tufts is credited with creating the modern approach to setting up courses for the U.S. Open. After the war the difficulty of the Open setups, done by the host club, varied widely. The punishing setup at Oakland Hills in 1951 was a sharp contrast, for example, to the relatively benign conditions at Riviera in 1948. Along with Joe Dey, Tufts created a definition of the standard Open setup—tightened fairways, graduated rough, and hard, fast greens. Tufts was also involved in modernizing the handicap system and in transforming the Green Section into a service that visited clubs and courses, providing the most up-to-date advice.

During his years at the USGA, Tufts wrote a great deal for public consumption. Using the newly created *Golf Journal* as his pulpit, he left a substantial written record. He also wrote two books, *The Principles Behind the Rules of Golf* and *The Scottish Invasion*, a short history of golf in the United States. In these books and in his *Golf Journal* essays, Richard Tufts laid out a conservative view of golf. He did not like what he saw in the golf community in the 1950s.

One compelling theme in the Tufts view of golf was a decided distaste for gambling. During his presidency of the USGA, the organization waged a campaign against gambling in conjunction with tournaments. The main target was the Calcutta tradition. It was common for a tournament, from local affairs up through PGA tour events, to hold a Calcutta auction in conjunction with the event. Players or teams would be auctioned off to create a pool that was paid out to those who owned the winners. This added considerable excitement to what might be a normal club event. Once a player or team was purchased, a market was created in which teams and players could be sold and resold. If a club player had a three-foot side-hill putt to win the Fourth of July Best Ball, it added something if a bettor stood to win a thousand dollars if the putt went in.

In 1956, with Tufts as the driving force, the USGA passed a resolution against gambling in golf. The resolution argued that "golf is a game to be played primarily for its own sake, especially amateur golf." When gambling becomes involved, "evils can arise that endanger both the game and individual players." The USGA noted that gambling, particularly Calcuttas, spawned abuses. Players, with real money on the line, could find ways to enhance their handicaps. Players entered events under assumed names and with bogus handicaps. Tufts concisely summarized his position in a 1956 *Golf Journal* essay: "Golf should be played for its own sake and not for profit."

Richard Tufts saw a connection between his views on golf and the state of American culture. He could rail darkly against the commercialization of amateur sport, and he clearly saw this commercialization as connected to a general decline in American life. In an essay from 1956, entitled "A Sense of Values in Amateur Sport," Tufts saw rising affluence as the core of the problem. He noted that "more people have more money and more leisure time to spend it in than ever before in the history of man." But, of course, we Americans often "spend our money on our leisure time in a bad way." One of these bad ways was "the commercialization of amateur sport." Tufts noted the rise of bribery, gambling, and the payment of expenses to amateur athletes. It was so bad that Tufts reached for the standard analogy used by conservative critics for centuries: "It has been said that one of the first steps in the decline of the Roman Empire was the commercialization of her amateur sports."

Tufts seemed to think that amateur competition should be limited to those who could afford it. He thought it "a common conviction" that any golfer with ability was entitled to compete in "all sorts of competitions." He stated that "if the player has the means, they can compete in any event for which they are qualified." If a player does not have the means, "he must then apply himself to more useful pursuits than playing golf." In this, Tufts was in part reacting to the dramatic change in the USGA Amateur Championship. It had once been a meeting of affluent golfers who could afford to compete. After the war the signs were clear. Young, ambitious college golfers would take over the championship, driving away older, more affluent, but less skilled golfers who were also the core of Pinehurst's clientele. Some of the young winners of the U.S. Amateur in the 1950s were Sam Urzetta, Billy Maxwell, Gene Littler, Arnold Palmer, and Jack Nicklaus. All of whom made the Amateur a stepping-stone to a pro career. As time passed, this trend would become even more pronounced.

It is also clear that Tufts did not like the increased prestige accorded professional golf after the war. His distaste would eventually transform Pinehurst and the professional tour. To understand this claim we need to understand what happened at the 1951 Ryder Cup played at Pinehurst and at the North and South Open held immediately after the cup was won by the Americans.

Pinehurst had staged the North and South Open since 1902, playing the event even during the two world wars. The point, from the resort's perspective, was advertising for the resort and entertainment for its guests. Pinehurst provided room and board for the pros and a modest purse. The championship had become

a staple on the budding tour; it was often the last big event before the pros headed north to resume their club jobs. For many
it announced the beginning of spring and the resumption of
the golf season in the North after a long winter.

By 1950 the PGA was changing. It had passed a resolution seeking a minimum purse of ten thousand dollars for all tour events.
Tufts removed his offer of free room and board and raised the
purse, but he was not happy. He had agreed to host the 1951
Ryder Cup and planned to hold the North and South immediately after the cup was decided. Clearly he hoped that many, if
not all, of the members of the two teams would remain in Pinehurst and give the North and South one of its best fields ever. It
did not work out that way. The pros were offended by the schedule of the Ryder Cup competition. Tufts arranged that there
would be no play on the Saturday of the competition weekend.
Instead, the players traveled to Raleigh for a lunch and attended
the University of North Carolina football game. One can only
surmise what the pros thought about this. The most important
international professional competition stopped for a day to attend a football game.

But the real problems arose with the North and South Open.
Offended by their treatment, the American Ryder Cup team
held a meeting and a number of the players agreed not to play
in the North and South. Notable players who skipped the event
were Hogan, Demaret, Burke, and Mangrum. Only one player from the team, Henry Ransom, played all three rounds. In
several cases the behavior of some of the pros who did play was
questionable and unsportsmanlike.

While Tufts never uttered a word of criticism that made it
into print, he was clearly done with professional golf at Pinehurst. After the debacle of 1951 there would be no more North
and South Open. Pinehurst gave up the tournament that for
many had marked the beginning of golf in the North. His act
was of great benefit to a struggling club just south of Pinehurst
in Georgia. Tufts vacated the spot that the Masters, eventually,

was more than willing to fill. Augusta National, not Pinehurst No. 2, would become the most widely recognized golf course in the land. From the early 1950s onward, it would become an American site of memory. Golfers and nongolfers would come to see Augusta National and the Masters as the most important course and tournament in the United States.

I have never known what to make of Richard Tufts. By all accounts a shy and reclusive man, he nevertheless found a voice that gave expression to his misgivings about the changes in golf being wrought by 1950s affluence. He did not like gambling, changes in the rules, professional tour players, and the declining importance of amateur golf. He came to believe that professional golfers had become the leaders of the golf community, that they had replaced gentlemen like him. Finally, as we might well have guessed, he really hated the advent of the powered golf cart.

I do know, however, what happened to his beloved Pinehurst. As the 1960s began, he confronted two problems. Much of the resort dated to 1900 or before, and maintenance and updating (read air-conditioning and a place to park the powered carts) were very real and expensive problems. Second, he had lost control of the stock in Pinehurst Incorporated that his father had distributed at his death. By the late 1960s, the other owners were demanding a sale and Richard could not fail to meet their demands. In 1970 the resort passed into the hands of Diamondhead Corporation. In a little less than a decade, Diamondhead ruthlessly commercialized Pinehurst. The thousands of acres of vacant land that once surrounded the village were divided into lots and sold. Larger chunks of land were sold for condo developments. Debt piled upon debt, and by 1980 Diamondhead was bankrupt. It very nearly broke Richard Tufts's heart. He remained in Pinehurst growing more depressed and reclusive each year. He wrote the USGA and asked them to remove his name from their mailing lists. He died in Pinehurst in December 1980. He was eighty-four.

Tufts had made a start on defining "old golf." It was amateur golf, played by affluent gentlemen who hired caddies and hated carts. They never played winter rules (or as it came to be known "lift, clean, and place"); if you had mud on your ball it was just bad luck. They did not like the rise of professional tour golf. The public largely stopped listening to men like Tufts; instead men like Ben Hogan and Arnold Palmer had, apparently, become the kings of the game.

Tufts had a more than worthy successor. His name was Frank "Sandy" Tatum. Raised in California, Tatum attended Stanford, where he won the NCAA individual golf title in 1942. He was a Rhodes Scholar at Oxford, where he played on the golf team and absorbed the British golfing traditions. After obtaining his law degree at Stanford, Tatum began to climb the ladder in both the world of law and golf administration. He became a partner in a highly regarded California law firm and began working his way up to the USGA presidency in 1978 and 1979. In this office and after, Tatum has refined and revised the conservative position I have called "old golf."

Unlike Richard Tufts, Tatum has, to my knowledge, never made an issue of gambling and golf. He did, however, share some of Tufts's passion about the growing tendency to soften the rules. On the issue of winter rules, which by 1980 had been enshrined in the rules of golf as a suggested local rule, Tatum was blunt and unequivocal. For him, this local option should be abolished. This is certainly a central element of the "old golf" philosophy. Tatum admits that luck plays a substantial role in golf. Balls end up in divots, they collect mud, and roll into very bad lies in the middle of the fairway. Winter rules, or "lift, clean, and place," were invented to counter the perceived unfairness created by unusual conditions. Tatum responds to this by employing the ancient argument, "Who said golf was supposed to be fair?" No one, to my knowledge, has ever responded to this query with an equally valid one: "Who said golf was supposed to be unfair?"

Tatum has been, like Tufts, concerned about the fate of amateur golf. Again, by 1980, the rise of college golf, and especially the rise of golf scholarships, gave many young men and women the means to use amateur and scholastic competition as a way to prepare for a professional career. For Tatum, this had a serious effect on the competitive balance in amateur golf. In short, the young ones won all the big tournaments on their way to the professional ranks. Tatum wondered what was going to happen to the player who worked for a living and played the game as an avocation, when, at all levels of competition, they have to compete with young players funded by scholarships. More generally, Tatum defended the idea that "knowledgeable, dedicated amateurs should determine and interpret the rules of golf." He seemed to fear that if amateurs lose this role, rules would be made and interpreted according to "what may or may not be the commercial consequences of a given rule or its interpretation."

This obviously brings us to the issue of the ball and the equipment used to play the game. Tatum has confronted important transformations in the ball and clubs that clearly make the game easier. Professionals, and especially equipment manufacturers, want few if any restrictions on their ability to apply technology in an attempt to make the game easier. This has been one of the most dramatic developments in golf since 1960. However, the impact has been almost entirely at the professional level. Everyone seems to have a theory. Professional golfers in the last thirty years have become bigger, stronger, and better conditioned. Instruction, sometimes very expensive, has improved dramatically. Young golfers work their way up through a series of increasingly difficult competitions; those who survive are ready to compete with anyone. In short, today's professional golfers are incomparably better athletes than those of fifty years ago. Given all this, it is probably impossible to determine exactly what effect improved equipment and balls have had.

Tatum wants to limit the ball. He would mandate a ball that could not be hit more than 280 or 290 yards. He believes, as he put it in a 2002 interview, that such a ball would "put shot-making values back into the game" and reduce the growing role of pure power. If golf does not do something, Tatum believes that the day of the four-hundred-yard drive is "well within contemplation, and then the fundamental character of the game would be lost."

Perhaps the most striking element in Tatum's critique of golf concerns the modern American golf course and what might be called the American "version" of golf. He believes that American courses are designed and maintained to play the game in the air. Americans learn to hit high pitch shots that spin and stop. Tatum points out that originally (in Scotland) golf was played along the ground, requiring the player to have a keener imagination and better judgment. He would have Americans give up the airborne attack and learn to play more low-running shots.

For him the airborne nature of the American game is rooted in the construction and maintenance of our golf courses. As he put it in 1980, "The problem, simply put, is one of too much water! This has been endemic to this country for a long time." He notes that Americans seem to care more about how a course looks than about how it plays. Americans have come to accept a brand of golf that is played from one mushy lie to the next until you hit the green where even poorly hit shots stay where they land. Tatum is undoubtedly right about the overwatering of American golf courses, but he has no explanation for why this state of affairs has come to pass.

Sandy Tatum hates golf carts. In 1980 he wrote that "anyone who cares about the game has to look upon the use of these miserable machines as a perverse development which has to be reversed." He would allow them for "people who otherwise would not be able to play." His critique of golf carts is full and convincing. They waste energy, the gas version fouls the air, cart paths destroy the beauty of courses, they increase maintenance costs, and they drove the caddie from the game. On this last count he is especially passionate. Tatum sees the disappearance of the caddie as "an irretrievable loss, both for the game and for the young people in this country."

Finally, we must discuss Tatum's role in shaping the modern U.S. Open Championship. In this he followed in and extended the footsteps of Richard Tufts. Every year the contestants gather to play for the national title. The contest is quite egalitarian; there are open qualifying rounds, and the field is chosen without bias or favoritism. Each year the USGA goes to great lengths to choose and nurture a site that will be seen as consummately difficult and challenging. Each year some contestants complain that some aspect of the course is too difficult. It was Tatum who uttered what has become the standard USGA reply: "Our objective in setting up Open courses is not to humiliate the best players in the game, but rather to simply identify who they are." (There have been several versions of this statement. I have used the version from Tatum's 2002 book, *A Love Affair with the Game*, page 158).

This issue concerning the difficulty of Open courses has become a stock debate in the golf community. Each year players complain and some USGA official utters some version of Tatum's statement. No one ever replies, "Well, what does it mean if you do humiliate players?" Or, "Are Open courses anything like real courses?" "Could you regularly maintain Shinnecock, Pinehurst, or Winged Foot, or whatever course, as you have for Open week?" "Is number sixteen at Pinehurst a par five, as Donald Ross thought it was, or is the USGA right and it's really a par four?" In any event, Sandy Tatum was a crucial figure in creating this debate that shows no sign of going away anytime soon.

Tatum and Tufts were leading figures in the conservative party that developed after 1950 and grew into a substantial presence in the golf community. In limited ways they continued the demands for simpler golf and for simpler golf courses that has always been a part of the discourse on golf. Certainly the USGA is the institutional home of this party. As I have tried to emphasize, there are a number of issues and they have changed over the years. However, the conservative party does not like the changes that have transformed the game in the last fifty years. There is a clear desire to roll back the impact of technology on the playing of golf. Tatum would ban carts. They would like courses to be harder, faster, and cheaper to maintain. They want the caddie back. They think amateurs should run the game and make the rules; but they believe, deep down, that professionals have already usurped their position as the dominant force in the game.

Affirming this view, Richard Tufts, in 1961, wrote that the average golfer saw the PGA "as the governing body of golf." He thought that this was based on the growing popularity of a few touring pros. In this he was largely correct. However, it was not merely the figures of Hogan, Palmer, Casper, and Nicklaus that gave the PGA its growing power with the people. In order to fully understand the other major party in the modern golf community, we need to understand the postwar history of the PGA.

At the 1951 Ryder Cup that so upset Richard Tufts, the PGA, that conducted the competition, published a book called *The Book of Golf.* In this slim volume, every national golf organization in the Anglo-Saxon world received space in which to explain itself. The PGA, then thirty-five years old, was especially eager to promote itself to the growing postwar golfing public.

The PGA listed the services it offered and the programs it controlled. At its core the PGA worked to help club pros. It provided life and other types of insurance and a fund to help needy members. It had created a bookkeeping system tailored to the needs of golf professionals. There was also an employment service and monthly magazine that helped members keep up with the latest golf news and developments in teaching and "merchandising techniques." Of course, there was the tour, which they called "a $600,000 tournament schedule which serves as golf's greatest advertising and promotion vehicle and a school for players who are desirous of obtaining competitive experience." In 1950 the Tournament Bureau of the PGA conducted forty-two tournaments. It also promoted competition through an annual PGA Championship and, every two years, the Ryder Cup Matches. Finally, like most golf organizations, it had entered the real estate business; the organization owned and operated its own course in Dunedin Isles, Florida, and inevitably there were home sites for sale along its Donald Ross–designed fairways.

The PGA in 1951 was interested in dispelling some misconceptions. It was, they stressed, "a voluntary, unincorporated, not-for-profit association," organized to advance the mutual interests of its members. It was not, "contrary to the popular impression that prevails in some quarters, a commercial organization, and its major source of income is the revenue which it receives from the dues of its membership." The PGA was run by a small slate of officers (Joe Novak was president in 1951) and a large executive committee of fourteen. Finally there was a national advisory committee, which included a number of businessmen and several show-business figures such as Bing Crosby, Bob Hope, and Fred Waring. In 1951 the organization collected dues from 2,916 members. In 1929 there had been 2,022 members, but this number dropped to a Depression-era low of 1,009 in 1933. In the postwar era the PGA grew with the game, and in 1974 membership reached 7,392. Today the organization claims approximately 28,000 members.

It is amazing how foggy some public relations publications can be. You can read about the PGA in *The Golf Book* of 1951 and still not understand the organization. To cut through the clutter, let's assert that the PGA in 1951 had two jobs. First, it sought to support the nearly three thousand club pros who were, at the same time, small retailers and the face of the game for the golfing public. Second, the PGA was, as Harlow had baldly stated in 1935, in "show business." The Tournament Bureau of the PGA in the early 1950s ran a traveling show that made forty-two stops, putting on forty-two performances annually.

Today, of course, the PGA no longer runs the tour, but it still administers and profits from a number of important events that include the PGA Championship, one of golf's majors. And every two years, they bring golf fans the Ryder Cup Matches. These matches have become the most important international team golf competition on the growing schedule of important golf events.

In addition to running important and profitable tournaments, the modern PGA is also involved in a number of other golf-related activities. For much of the 1990s it was in the golf exposition business. The PGA has, of course, come to own some golf courses in the late 1990s. The organization opened three public courses at what is known as the PGA Village in Port St. Lucie, Florida. The PGA would clearly like to own a site that would become home to its annual championship. This was probably the motivation behind the purchase of Valhalla Golf Club in Louisville, Kentucky, in 2000. Attached to the courses at the PGA Village, the organization opened education, instructional, and historical centers on the same site.

All of these endeavors, however, are peripheral to the PGA's main job today, which is to license or credential PGA professional golfers. In reality the barriers facing anyone who wishes to call himself or herself a golf professional are very low. Anyone can play in tournaments with a money prize or announce themselves to be a golf instructor and give lessons for a price. What the PGA does is run a program that gives a person the right to call himself a PGA professional. The association offers, at considerable cost to the participants, two avenues to the status of PGA professional: the Apprentice Program and the University Program. Both pathways involve coursework, the passing of a playing ability test, and work or internship experience. A young man or woman who wishes to become a golf professional must navigate substantial tests and bureaucratic requirements equal to obtaining the necessary permits to build a junkyard in a protected wetland. In essence, the PGA, since 1916, has thoroughly professionalized an occupation that had no entry requirements other than a desire to be a professional and the skills to beg your way into a job at a golf course. The usual start of a professional's career was as a caddie, but alas, not anymore.

So once you make your way into the category Class A PGA professional, what is it that you do? There are many jobs in the golf industry but the crucial one is club pro. Of the twenty-eight thousand members of the organization, some hard-to-determine percentage run the golf programs at golf courses — either public or private. In this position they are the priests, rabbis, and ministers of golf. Just like those selling religion, club pros are there at the point-of-sale, running junior clinics, giving lessons to adult beginners, and talking frustrated hackers out of giving up the game. Their main job is to grow the flock, increase the number of the saved, of the redeemed.

The USGA may write the theology (the rules of golf), but the club professionals are largely responsible for instruction and enforcement. The USGA may create rules officials for its own events, but across the country, at thousands of other golf tournaments, most of which are local, it is the club professional who keeps the competitive play within the rules. The professional, particularly at a private club, is usually in a very odd position. Hired by the membership, one of his jobs is to teach and discipline the people who hired him. When a club pro has to tell a prominent member that we are no longer playing winter rules or that the member has just been disqualified from the club championship for signing an incorrect scorecard, we are staring conflict of interest straight in the face.

Over the years, a number of pros have fulfilled these job requirements so well that they deserve the title of "saint." Certainly the best-known golf saint was Harvey Penick, of the Austin Country Club. Born in 1904, Penick began as a caddie at the Austin Club in 1912. He became the head professional in 1923, a job he held for fifty years. After 1973 he remained at the club giving lessons until his death in 1995. He taught a glittering list of players: Tom Kite, Ben Crenshaw, Mickey Wright, Kathy

Whitworth, and many others. He was the very successful coach of the University of Texas golf team for more than thirty years.

In 1992, with Bud Shake, Penick wrote *Harvey Penick's Little Red Book*. It has had the largest sale of any golf book in history. This publishing success led to four additional books based on Penick's teaching notes; all sold well, but nothing like *The Little Red Book*. In fact, all a golfer needs in the way of instruction can be found in this volume. It is, however, a big help if you buy the related DVD. You will also learn from this book what it means to truly love the game and what it means for a person to find in a game and the teaching of that game a means of personal expression that lasts a lifetime. When I reread *The Little Red Book*, I always think that no one ever loved golf more than Harvey Penick. Few present-day club pros possess Penick's devotion, and even fewer will have such a long and profitable career.

An increasing number of PGA professionals hold jobs outside the world of the private club. They work at large sporting-goods stores, at resorts, and at daily-fee courses where the opportunity to develop a long-term relationship with a membership does not exist. In the last two decades, the number of golf schools or academies has grown sharply and many professionals spend their entire careers as instructors in such schools.

The PGA professional exercises a number of governing functions in the game of golf. Some are obvious, some not. As we have already noted, the pro is called upon, in a number of settings, to explain and enforce the rules of golf. They often have a role in making decisions about the care, design, and daily set-up of golf courses. Less obvious, but perhaps more important, the local pro serves as a role model for those who wish to know what the term *golfer* means. Their behavior, dress, and deportment deeply influences new golfers. Young golfers, especially, look to the pro for clues about how to look and behave. In the simplest possible terms, the local PGA pro is the face of golf for most players. This all makes a bit more sense when we understand that the pro controls the first tee at his course. Players with improper equipment or dress, and players with insufficient skills to play the course, are often stopped by the pro who then must explain the ethos of golf to people who do not fully understand it. The pro must also deal with bogus handicaps in a net competition; in this he must again be a better-than-average diplomat.

The local pro's life is complicated by the fact that he or she is also in the business of golf. They have to be diplomats, teachers, and advisers while, at the same time, they are often running a small retail business selling clubs, balls, shoes, and golf clothing to a small, limited clientele. A good portion of their time is spent caring for and renting golf carts. They also sell instruction, and their skill as a teacher is one of their most valuable assets. They are often called upon to promote events and tournaments at their courses that are profit-making ventures or serve some charitable function. Local club pros often find themselves in a real bind, caught between wanting to be in the shop selling and promoting, while at the same time, down on the range, the free junior clinic (twenty potential lifelong golfers) is waiting for him to explain the game to them. Finally, all these obligations keep the pro from playing as much as he or she wants. For, in some sense, playing skill is the pro's most important credential and it easily erodes if neglected.

Of course they have one other problem. Increasingly, the public does not see the local pro as the face of the game. Since 1968, what has come to be known as the PGA Tour has grown rapidly as a governing party in the golf community. In essence, to govern in a community like the Kingdom of Golf entails the power to define the game. From the point of view of the PGA Tour, the game is defined by its fan base. If it is growing, the game is growing. Since 1968, by almost any measure, the fan base, the number of people willing to watch, in person or on television, a PGA Tour event has grown faster than the number of people who actually play the game. There are many people who equate the health of the tour with the health of the game. The game becomes the sum of those who play and those who watch.

The history of the PGA Tour since 1968 is a story of rapid growth built on world-class marketing skill. Joe Dey ran the tour very successfully until 1974, when he was replaced by Deane Beman, the man who redefined spectator golf in the twenty years he was at the helm. Born in 1938, Beman gave up a business career to become a touring professional—he collected five tour titles. This came after an amateur career in which he won two U.S. Amateurs and was a member of four Walker Cup teams.

According to figures from Beman's World Golf Hall of Fame profile, the PGA Tour had assets of only $700,000 in 1974. When he retired in 1994, those assets had grown to $800 million. In addition, Beman is given much of the credit for nurturing the Senior Tour into a massively successful endeavor. He also developed the idea of a developmental tour, at first named after Ben Hogan but now known, for the moment, as the Web.com Tour. Beman is also credited with the idea of a World Golf Village that would put together exemplary golf courses, a Golf Hall of Fame, and a PGA Learning Center. Of course, all of this was surrounded by a massive real estate development. The PGA Village opened in 1998.

One of Beman's most influential ideas was the creation of the Tournament Players Club (TPC) and the building of TPC courses. The first, and most important, of these courses was TPC Sawgrass, which opened in 1980. Today there are over thirty TPC courses. The growth in PGA Tour assets has been substantially rooted in the TPC course concept.

In order to understand this concept, we have to remember a basic rule of golf—whatever happens in golf usually involves real estate. Owning courses made a great deal of sense for the PGA Tour. One nagging problem for the early tour was securing courses upon which to play events and to secure them as cheaply as possible. A number of tournaments are now played on TPC courses. The most notable, of course, is the event owned outright by the PGA Tour, the Players Championship, played every year at Sawgrass. By creating its own courses, the tour, by its own estimate, has saved over $50 million, which has helped to boost purses and has increased the money that tournaments can give to charity.

The PGA Tour's involvement in real estate is more apparent at some TPC courses. At least five such courses are part of master-planned communities. Summerlin and the Canyons in Las Vegas, and Eagle Trace and Heron Bay in Coral Springs, Florida, have become successful, highly rated golf communities, as has Wakefield in Raleigh, North Carolina. The tour has created a subsidiary to run this real estate called PGA Tour Golf Course Properties, Inc.

Beman's most obvious success, however, has been the expansion of the tour itself. He inherited a very lush set of circumstances in 1974. Nicklaus, Player, and Palmer were proven draws. Nicklaus, especially, was important; by the early 1970s he had become golf's version of the Yankees. Whenever he played in an event he was the favorite. However, the tour and Beman were lucky to have a colorful and talented group of players who could and did beat Jack. Palmer still played well enough to draw fans and, at some point in the 1970s, it became clear that his fans would turn out no matter how well or how long he played.

Perhaps the most notable arrival on the scene was Lee Trevino. A product of municipal courses and driving ranges in Dallas, Texas, Trevino was one of a kind. He was one of the last great American players to begin his career as a caddie. His impoverished Mexican American heritage, his incessant chatter on the course, his homemade swing, and his ability to play his best golf in the big events on hard courses made Trevino unique in the world of touring pros, a world that was growing more guarded and homogeneous each year. He literally came out of nowhere to place fifth in the U.S. Open in 1967. In the 1968 Open, Trevino produced four rounds in the 60s and beat Nicklaus by four. In 1971 Trevino and Nicklaus staged a memorable battle at the Open at Merion. On the last day, only three men had a realistic chance to win. Jim Simons was the big surprise. He was an amateur, the number-two man on the Wake Forest golf team. Simons had surged to the top of the leader board with a 65 on Saturday. This gave him a two-shot lead over Nicklaus and a four-shot lead over Trevino.

On Sunday Trevino made a crucial birdie on the twelfth hole that put him into a tie with both Nicklaus and Simons. I can still remember Trevino's shot to the twelfth green — an eight-iron that landed perhaps twenty feet beyond the hole and spun back to less than two feet from the pin. Trevino made a difficult twelve-foot putt on fourteen to assume a one-shot lead, which he held until he missed a makeable par putt on the eighteenth. Nicklaus came to the home hole needing a birdie to win. But his birdie putt barely missed left. The heroic Simons had hung in all day until a six on the final hole left him three shots short of a tie with Trevino and Nicklaus.

It was a fascinating playoff. It pitted the gold standard in golf — Jack Nicklaus — against a chunky ethnic upstart with a funny swing. The Yankees versus Detroit. This time the Yankees lost. After a wobbly start, both players settled down to a contest that featured very good golf, and Trevino proved to be the superior player that day — his 68 bested Jack's 71. It would be hard to overestimate Trevino's accomplishments. Very poor as a child, he did not play golf in any real sense until he entered the U.S. Marines and played on its golf team. After the service he worked tirelessly to create a game that would hold up under pressure. Late in the 1960s that game emerged as one of the two or three best in the world.

The Open and the resulting playoff exhibited exactly how compelling professional golf could be. The silent, vaguely Germanic Nicklaus with a classic, amazingly powerful swing hitched to an unearthly ability to concentrate, to focus on the task at hand, against Trevino, the Super Mex, with a weirdly effective loopy swing and the desire to talk to anyone within earshot. Trevino talked incessantly to his caddie, to the fans, and to himself.

These were the sorts of contests and personalities that Dean

Beman inherited in 1974 when he took over the PGA Tour. It was his job to use the fan interest created by major championships to sell the weekly tour events. Of course, it wasn't just Trevino and Nicklaus. In 1972 Tom Watson became a full-time member of the tour and, in some respects, replaced Trevino as Jack's primary foe. In 1977 Watson and Nicklaus famously locked up in a last-round duel at Turnberry to determine who would win the British Open. Lost in all the talk of the personal duel was the fact that Watson shot 268, a score that smashed the old record total by eight shots. Beyond Watson and Trevino, the tour benefited from the arrival of a number of interesting and talented players—Johnny Miller, Tom Weiskopf, Raymond Floyd, Tom Kite, and Larry Nelson.

Beman took the materials handed him and vigorously promoted them; and he had considerable help from the professional agents who had begun to represent an increasing number of tour players. In this, Palmer's agent, Mark McCormack, and his company, International Management Group, was the model. The rise of these agents changed player's lives and incomes dramatically. As the tour got more popular, the players reaped the benefits in nontournament income arranged by creative and tireless agents. Gary Player once estimated that a talented agent could earn his player approximately four times the amount of his tournament winnings. As the players were promoted and became brands and household names, it greatly benefited the tour in general.

At the heart of the tour's expansion and Beman's success was money—especially the amazing growth in money a talented player could win. The tour reached a notable landmark in 1988 when Curtis Strange became the first player to win one million dollars in a single season. Some today might say that a million dollars is not what it used to be, but in 1988, the word *million* still had magic. Imagine, people said, travel around the country, play golf, and win a million bucks!

What drove the dramatic increase in the size of the checks

collected by touring pros? Beman was an important factor. When he took over in 1974, he understood that the product—weekly tour events—was undervalued and underpromoted. In appraising his own career, Beman has stated that he "looked at what the other professional sports [were] doing, especially the NFL and how it marketed itself. I thought that the tour was underpromoted." This was particularly clear when it came to television. Beman claimed that when he took over in the early 1970s, "We didn't really understand the value of our product." What Beman and his coordinator for television, Steve Reid, did was expertly to extract the hidden value in regular tour events—their product.

In extracting this value, Beman benefited from the growth of corporate wealth and the willingness of corporations to spend vast sums on promotion and advertising. Between the year of the split with the PGA (1968) and the year Beman retired (1994), corporate wealth soared. The year 1968 began with the S&P 500 Index at 95.04. On the last day of trading in 1994, the same index finished at 459.24. In the four years of Joe Dey's control, and the twenty years of Beman's rule, the market capitalization of American corporations had more than quadrupled. With this success, corporations began to look for new ways to advertise, to promote themselves, to become brands. Golf tournaments were an obvious answer. By 1988, twenty-nine of forty-four tour events contained a corporate name in their title. As newspapers and television dropped the ban against using corporate names in its daily coverage (it was free advertising), the rush to sponsor golf tournaments was on. All the evidence shows that being the title sponsor of a tour event is worth the expense.

When Beman retired in 1994, his responsibilities passed to Tim Finchem. Born in Illinois in 1947, Finchem attended high school in Virginia and the University of Richmond before law school at the University of Virginia. He practiced law and worked in the Carter White House in 1978 and 1979. In the early 1980s, he founded his own company, National Marketing and Strategies Group in Washington DC. He went to work for the PGA

Tour in 1987 and became the deputy commissioner and COO in 1989. In 1994 he replaced Beman.

Virtually everything you might say about Beman is also true of Finchem. He has grown the PGA Tour by marketing it as a product with which American and international corporations wish to associate themselves. On the PGA Tour website one can find a list of what sponsoring a tournament, becoming a "title sponsor," means to a corporation:

Brand association with winning the values of golf
Multichannel marketing opportunities
Unparalleled relationship-building opportunities
Substantial public relations coverage
Positive community impact
VIP access to tournaments
Worldwide brand exposure
Premium hospitality
Pro-Am spots
Local and national promotional opportunities

Between 1974 and 2008, this list of benefits proved irresistible to a growing number of corporations, especially financial services companies. The growth of the tour as measured in dollars, since 1994 particularly, has been huge. The million-dollar mark has lost its magic. In 2010 the winner of the Players Championship, Tim Clark, received $1.71 million for that tournament victory alone. The final 2010 money list contained five players who each won more than four million dollars. Matt Kuchar topped this group with $4.9 million. Ninety players collected more than a million dollars. All the businesses begun by Beman have grown under Finchem's hand. The number of TPC courses has passed thirty; a number of partnerships with credit card companies and other ventures have done well. The PGA Tour logo has been branded into the minds of Americans.

And Finchem, like Beman, has benefited from a very friendly economic environment and the rise into professional golf of compelling players. When Finchem took the helm, the s&p 500 stood at 457.63. It closed the year in 2007 at 1468.36. For thirteen years, then, Finchem, like Beman, enjoyed a heady rise in corporate wealth. In recent years, the tour has also enjoyed increased sponsorship from international corporations like Barclays Bank, Deutsche Bank, and the automaker BMW.

Together with a rich corporate environment, in 1996 Finchem received the gift of Tiger Woods. Destined to become the most well-known athlete in the world, Woods provided the tour with an attraction certainly the equal of Palmer, Nicklaus, and Player. His very first tournaments were the sort of events of which marketers dream. Overlaid on tour events like the Greater Milwaukee and the Las Vegas Opens, you had the arrival of the "manchild into the promised land" of million-dollar purses.

Finchem had openly worried about the lack of diversity on the tour. Tiger was the answer to this worry. The press, with some exceptions, deemed Tiger to be African American; he became a black golf genius in the very white world of corporate country-club America. The press granted to Woods amazing causative powers. He would transform the tour; he would transform the game of golf. He would bring minority children to tournaments and compel them to take up the game.

When Tiger turned pro in 1996 and quickly established himself as the favorite in any event he entered, it set off what can only be called cultural hysteria. In 2000 *USA Today* concluded that Tiger Woods "is revolutionizing the game of golf. Not content with rewriting the record books Woods is on a mission to spread the game's reach." His father fueled the hysteria by calling his son "the Chosen One" and "an interracial Pied Piper." It was the collective journalistic wisdom that Tiger had made the game cool. He had ripped it from the hands of aging white men and made it acceptable to the young and to minorities. Michael Caruso, editor of the short-lived magazine *Maxim Golf*, claimed that golf had "undergone this great people's revolution led by Tiger Woods."

People in the golf industry struggled to find statistics that supported the notion that Tiger was drawing people into the game. But the boom, according to some of the same people, had already begun. In 1989 Kit Bradshaw, from the National Golf Foundation (a group that provides golf-business research and consulting services), stated that "golf is the fastest growing sport in America." A *New York Times* article claimed that "women, blacks, and younger players are fueling the boom." No one asked how much of this increase was due to rising affluence and simple population growth. However, it is undeniable that Woods dramatically increased the number of African Americans interested in golf. It is also true that Woods fed off the media and the media fed off Woods. Golf writers were suddenly interpreters of the national racial drama. Tiger made what was happening in golf seem broadly important, and golf periodicals briefly had their day as organs of cultural analysis.

Tiger became more than merely an asset for the PGA Tour. Pundits engaged in a frenzied quest to explain how a multiethnic, handsome young man had come to sit atop the golf world and had become one of the most recognized and bankable faces on the planet. This quest to explain Tiger's rise included considerable criticism and carping. For some he was not black enough or political enough, for others he was arrogant.

By 2000, much to my surprise, I began to feel sorry for him. Oddly, Tiger had come to resemble Babe Zaharias. They both were forced to live their lives in disguise; their lives were vexing, complex masquerades. The Babe hid her sexuality, her true self, behind a carefully constructed image that presented her as a normal woman and wife who was also a very competitive athlete. Whether Tiger was ever allowed to develop an authentic personality is open to question. Whoever he really was or could have become was lost under a mountain of myth. His father, Earl, engaged in mythmaking about his son so relentlessly that, from an early age, Tiger felt enormous pressure to live up to his father's notions that Tiger was the "Chosen One" and the "multiethnic Pied Piper," destined to lead the world to the promised land. It was an outrageous burden to place on a young man's shoulders.

Also outrageous was the money. Between 1997 and 2009 it literally rained money on Tiger Woods. He, more than anyone else, benefited from the increase in purses on the tour; he, more than anyone, enjoyed the huge cash premium put on winning. Prestigious corporations paid Tiger obscene sums to endorse their products. It was the grand finale for the age of affluence and no one—not on Wall Street—was a better symbol for the age than Tiger. The end of the age of affluence, of higher and higher home prices, higher and higher executive salaries, higher and higher first-place checks, and Tiger's fall from grace came at very nearly the same time. Late in 2009 the American public learned a good deal about what lay behind the mask. Tiger was not a faithful husband, and his complex sexual life was hung out in the press like so much dirty laundry. Racists and the borderline insane took to the Internet to vent their view that putting an African American at the top of the golf world had been, after all, a mistake. Since the winter of 2009–10, Tiger Woods has been attempting to redeem himself. There was a truly weird televised apology to friends, family, and the nation. No one, especially the PGA Tour and Tim Finchem, wanted anything to do with this event or with the ugly details (a hugely expensive divorce) that defined the early stages of the redemption process. But the core of redemption is in the game; Tiger remains, through it all, truly addicted to the craft of golf and the drug of competition. Therein lies his salvation.

Tiger Woods is not done. Most of the fans and the honest commentators cannot wait to learn what he will be able to do with what amounts to his life's third act. There is nothing as exciting as watching the fallen rise and try again.

It was the combination of Tiger and television that drove, by one limited measure, the recent growth in the game. Woods was an incredible spark for the PGA Tour. It was professional golf that benefited the most from the arrival of "the Chosen One." In 1996 the average purse at tour events was $1.12 million; that year four players surpassed the magic million-dollar mark. In 2007 the touring pros competed for average purses that soared to $5.81 million, and 99 of the 125 fully exempt players topped the $1 million mark. Over the same period, Finchem's salary rose from $900,000 to $5.2 million. This massive rainstorm of dollars was driven by increased television ratings and the apparently bottomless pit of corporate dollars willing to sponsor tour events.

By 2001 Finchem had probably become the most aggressive and ambitious sports executive in America. He was the dominant voice in organizations of golf organizations such as the World Golf Foundation and Golf 20/20. As the new century began, Finchem was quoted as saying, "We should consider as our [golf's] first goal to become the number one sport in fan base, surpassing the NFL by the year 2020 and reaching 177 million fans." With Tiger rising to demigod status and corporations spewing cash, Finchem seemed to have the sports world by the tail.

His rosy view of the golf world ignored some important trends that should have given him pause, however. For example, in 2001, Lawrence Donegan, writing in the *Scotsman*, saw golf in America as hitting "a rough patch." He noted that in Myrtle Beach, South Carolina (more golf holes per capita than any town in the United States), the golf boom was over. There was talk of "bankruptcies, empty tee times, and golf courses being bulldozed to make way for shopping malls." The Links Group, a leading course management company, had filed for bankruptcy.

From Donegan's Scottish perspective, the decline in golf had obvious causes. First, the cost of golf in the United States was too high. Daily-fee courses in or near large urban areas were charging eighty dollars for a single round. Second, slow play had made the game too expensive in terms of time. In Scotland, Donegan claimed, a foursome could play eighteen holes in three hours. In the United States, a similar foursome often took three hours just to play nine. He noted that, sadly, "Wagner's operas are snappier than a round of golf this side of the Atlantic." Third, in America you were inevitably pushed to rent a cart, called "buggies" in Scotland. If you ask to walk, the pro "looks at you as if you've just announced that you're bin Laden's brother." Walking on American courses has become a nightmare defined by "an epic trek from green to tee." Too many courses have been built to sell real estate not to be played enjoyably by the average player.

All in all, Donegan found American golf in horrible shape. For him the growth in the fan base for PGA events was not a plus. The most powerful sign of this was the apparent triumph of spectating over participation. He quoted a National Golf Foundation (NGF) survey that concluded that on any given Sunday the number of people watching golf on television was triple the number of people actually playing the game.

This same sense of decline was also evident to some American observers. Blaine Harden, in the July 22, 2001, issue of the *New York Times*, noted that the television networks had just agreed to pay 50 percent more than ever before to televise golf tournaments. However, participation was another story. The demographics seemed good; baby boomers were beginning to flood into their fifties and they should be turning to golf. But the evidence was clear: growth in the numbers of players had dried up. Harden focused on the fact that while golf gained players each year, it also lost very nearly an equal number. Establishing a long-term commitment to the game by players was proving difficult. For many people he talked to the problem was the new golf course. It was too hard, had too much sand and water, and cost too much to play. When you found a happy golfer it was at simpler, easier, and cheaper golf courses. Finally, Harden noted that the new courses were designed to promote real estate developments. He quoted Darrin B. Davis from the NGF, who said, "What you had was an almost crazed influence of real estate development without paying close attention to the marketplace."

By 2001, it looked oddly like golf was going in two directions at the same time. Televised golf was growing rapidly; Finchem's tour was hot, and the other non-PGA tournaments like the Masters and the Ryder Cup were just as hot, if not hotter. Golf course construction was booming, fueled, in part, by the demand for homes with a "golf course view." In 1999, 509 courses opened in the United States. This was the fifth consecutive year that had seen more than 400 new courses completed. Approximately 450 courses opened in 2000. On the other hand, the number of golfers had flat-lined and had begun to shrink. Between 2000 and 2006, about two million golfers stowed their clubs in the garage and gave up the game.

This failure to keep the supply of courses aligned with demand had a number of apparent causes, but much of the blame rests with the government of the golf community. As the governors of the golf community, the USGA and the PGA Tour engaged in some activities that actually suppressed participation. The USGA operates an Open Championship each year from which it makes a great deal of money. Much of this money is used to conduct an array of tournaments for amateurs of all sorts. It puts on championships for juniors, seniors, public-links golfers, mid-amateurs, and regular amateurs. The USGA loses money on these events. It also probably loses money on its commitment to provide valuable advice on course maintenance issues through its Green Section.

The USGA golfer is the dedicated, competitive amateur. This golfer looks to the USGA for a number of things beyond competition. They need and get good advice on establishing a fair handicapping system. For many years the organization published *Golf Journal,* which published unbiased news of the game and notable articles on golf history. Inexplicably they suspended publication of this fine journal. The USGA also maintains a museum and library in Far Hills, New Jersey, that are dedicated to celebrating and explaining the history of golf in the United States. Finally, the USGA is the organization charged with establishing, in the broadest sense, the rules. This has had only a marginal effect on amateur golfers and has, for too long, pitted the USGA against the professionals and the equipment manufacturers. Their disputes about grooves, driver construction, and the ball have, in the end, diverted everyone's attention from larger issues, like declining participation.

Unfortunately, the model USGA course is not established by the agronomists in the Green Section. Instead, in the public mind, the USGA course is the Open course chosen each year. In what has become a silly ritual, the USGA picks the course and sets it up to defend par against professionals who grow more talented each year. This forces the USGA to establish conditions so difficult, so contrived, that the average golfer looks at his or her local course as pitifully easy, as somehow not golf, as somehow inauthentic in the context of USGA Open courses. The distance between what the average golfer experiences on his or her home course and the Open Championship course has grown so large that one can legitimately ask, What is "authentic golf"? No one in the golf community can authoritatively answer this question.

The power of the golf that people see on television is hard to overestimate. I live in Pinehurst, North Carolina, and play on the six courses at Pinehurst Country Club. One of these is Pinehurst No. 2, where the Open has been played twice in recent years. I have often played with guests at the resort who have come to play No. 2, "the Open course." On one occasion I was paired with three golfers from Toledo who all had handicaps around 15. This meant they shot in the middle to high 80s on their home course.

At Pinehurst, instead of playing from the white, or member, tees, they and their disgusted caddies marched back to the championship tees. One remarked, "We want to play where the pros play." It was a long day. They meticulously kept score, holing out on every hole (stretching the round out to nearly six hours), and the totals were: 111, 114, 118. For my part, I kept track of the bunker shots until, so horrified by the carnage, I gave up. One gentleman, through thirteen holes, had visited eleven bunkers and had taken seventeen shots from the sand. They hit drivers on all the par threes except on nine, where Mr. Sandman hit a bunker shot out of bounds. On number ten, normally a short, interesting par five, none of the visitors reached the white tees with their drives from the Open tees—one player barely made it in two. It was at this point that the eye rolling and the suppressed laughter by caddies reached a high point.

These golfers had paid more to play this one round then I pay in monthly dues. They did not, in any sense I could understand, enjoy it; but at the end of the round, they engaged in the same banter that soldiers who survive a firefight share. As they drank their postround beers, one of them said he thought the fees at his home club were too high and that he might give up his membership. There is an important point to this story. Golf on television, particularly the U.S. Open and the Masters, sets up expectations for fast greens and super conditioning; they establish a model that is deeply counterproductive to long-term participation by average players. It creates the sense that the only authentic golf is played on 7,500-yard courses, with lightning-fast greens, 500-yard par fours, and bunkers as deep as coal mines. Anything that falls short of these standards is deemed inauthentic; and if modern Americans crave anything, it is the authentic.

In this, the PGA Tour is also a primary cause. Unlike the USGA, the PGA Tour owns courses that profoundly influence the definition of what is a proper golf course. The TPC courses that are used to stage events are designed not only to play golf on, but they are also designed to make watching golf easier. This is the so-called stadium course concept. The template for this concept is the TPC at Sawgrass, especially the Players Stadium Course. On its website we learn that at TPC Sawgrass there are

"36 professional holes," created "by the legendary Pete Dye," who we assume also designs amateur holes. The Stadium Course "is revered as the home of one of professional golf's most prestigious competitions: the Players Championship." You are invited to "face the same challenges that have tested the skill and resolve of the game's greatest players—including the formidable par-three 17th island green." The idea is to make golf at Sawgrass seem so unique, so authentic, that you'll not notice the mind-boggling green fees. The authentic experience, the real thing, costs a lot of money; island greens are not cheap. The place was built on swamp that was drained to create a golf course.

In this drive to define the "authentic" golf course, the USGA and the PGA Tour have a notable ally in Augusta National Golf Club. Each spring golfers tune in to the Masters and are treated to visions of a fairyland golf course that has evolved over the years and is the product of vast sums of money lavished on a nearly perfect site. The beauty and the order, the other-worldly tidiness of Augusta, creates in visitors to the tournament and television viewers a definition, an image, of the golf course that can never be realized at the local courses on which the vast majority of golfers play. After watching the Masters (or the Open, or a tour event), a visit to your local club or public course is bound to be disappointing: where are the azaleas, the island greens? At some point, golf is consumption, and the pressure to see "revered," much-hyped courses as the purchase of a lifetime is immense. A round of golf at Sawgrass or Whistling Straits or St. Andrews can, we are told, create memories that last a lifetime. They can also cost up to half what the yearly membership at a simple private club might cost. How does one compare aping the habits of the super rich for three days to playing a hundred rounds on a simple local course?

The point is simple. Neither the USGA nor the PGA Tour do much to encourage participation on local courses. In fact they do some things that probably discourages participation. Not only does televised golf take up valuable discretionary time that could be used to actually play the game, it also creates the powerful impression that authentic golf is played elsewhere on spectacular, expensive, and unique courses.

Is there anybody working to advance participation on a large scale? One candidate is a program called the First Tee. This enterprise, begun in 1997, is essentially a creature of the major powers in golf (the Masters Tournament, the USGA, PGA of America, the PGA Tour, and the LPGA), bolstered by donations from corporate America. The essence of the program is to provide places for young golfers to play. This inevitably puts the focus on local sites and local volunteers. The program also has an even larger goal: "to promote character development and life-enhancing values though the game of golf," (as the First Tee website puts it).

The program, in its brief history, has become huge. It operates at over seven hundred locations, has recruited over three thousand volunteers in fifty states, and has touched approximately 3.5 million participants. This level of success suggests that American life as a whole had not been creating, organically, the opportunity for children to learn about golf, to come into contact with the game. In some ways, the First Tee program is a substitute for the caddie programs that served as a conduit into the game for many young men. The program is also a way to make up for the minimal commitment to golf by school sports programs. Golf in schools is overwhelmed by the massive emotional and financial commitment made to the "major sports," especially football.

It will take some time before we can render any final verdict on First Tee; the key will be the role of early contact with the game. Golf, as presented to young people by First Tee, competes in a world rich with alternative ways to expend spare time and energy. We should look at this situation as very much a struggle in which the enemy is television, video games, computers, the mall, and the image of golf as only for white, rich people. We shall discuss this issue in more detail in the last chapter.

A second candidate as a vital stimulator of participation in golf is the local, state, and regional golf associations. The best list of these associations comes from the USGA. The various local associations may align themselves, for various purposes, with the USGA, and 280 have done so. These vary greatly in size and scope. There are heroic, small organizations like the Anchorage (Alaska) Women's Golf Association and enormous, complex groups like the Western Golf Association. The Florida State Golf Association is in some ways typical. Founded in 1913, it has eight hundred member clubs and approximately 180,000 individual members. On 325 days each year, the association conducts some sort of tournament somewhere in Florida. It conducts twenty-five various state championships and administers the Florida Junior Tour, a series of events for young golfers.

The larger, statewide associations are very much like mini-USGAS. Their central job is to conduct amateur championships and, like the USGA, they often stimulate interest in the game by maintaining a state hall of fame or museum. They also produce newsletters that tie golfers in their state together. Several state associations produce local television shows like Kentucky's *Inside Kentucky Golf.*

A complete portrait of local, state, and regional associations would be sleep inducing. However, to understand the golf community you have to understand that these associations play a crucial role in the lives of individual golfers. The USGA has created a handicapping system: the Golf Handicap and Information Network (GHIN). This system is made available to local clubs and courses through the state organizations. The state association is often the vehicle for administering the USGA rules on amateurism and the USGA course-rating system. In this way the USGA promotes broad participation in ways that the PGA Tour never can. The USGA, in substantial ways, nourishes the local associations that promote play by average golfers.

Beneath all this administrative clutter lies another crucial task carried out by local associations. Many, but not all, carry out a program of weekly tournaments at the courses in their state. This program serves several important functions. It drives play at courses willing to turn over their facility for a day in exchange for a good-sized field of paying guests, many of whom eat big lunches and drink too much beer. Since many of these events are both net and gross competitions, they draw contestants from all skill levels. These events are also important socially; they bring together golfers from around the state and do much to create a sense of community among golfers.

This brings us back to a difficult, but crucial, issue: the role of gambling and the golf community. The program of weekly events run by state and local associations usually works something like this—the players pay a fee to the association, which in turn pays the local club a fee for use of the course, and the remaining money goes into a prize pool divided among the net and gross winners. The prizes are not paid out in cash; instead the winners receive certificates or credits redeemable at one or more local pro shops. Usually players are allowed to accumulate these credits for a year or more. This system exists because the USGA *Rules of Golf* (specifically, Rules of Amateur Status 3-2) allows amateurs to accept a "prize voucher" if it is less than $750. Building on this exception to the notion that amateur golfers may never play for a cash prize, golf associations of all kinds have made their events attractive, have drawn a field, by offering vouchers or actual merchandise to the winners. Local charity golf events also often use the voucher system as a way to draw a field. Of course, this system also redounds to the benefit of the local pro shops that redeem the vouchers.

This sort of event, whether for charity or not, has quietly become a staple in the golf community. Avid players establish a foursome and plot out their golfing seasons around regular play at their home course and "away games" at other courses in the region. In the Carolinas, the Carolinas Golf Association posts a schedule of forty-six one-day tournaments; the first 2010 event was on January 16 and the last on December 12. For a relatively

modest fee, players can play some of the country's finest courses, meet other golfers, and maybe win a few dollars to spend in
the pro shop.

Not all local golf is so competitive. There are countless local
leagues and groups that collectively have golf their way. One
typical, very informal group is the Oakland County (Michigan)
Hacker's Tour. Founded by Mike Godoshian (director of operations) and John Kowal (director of competition), the tour begins in April with two "preseason" events. From late May to late
August the group plays five regular events followed by a "Tour
Championship" in September. Each event features fields of fifteen to twenty golfers. Scores are generally high (there are points
awarded in both gross and net divisions), ranging from the high
70s to an alarming 159 posted by one player. The championship is determined by an inexplicable point system that seems
to be part of the fun.

The Oakland County Hacker's Tour suggests that the two major parties, the USGA and the PGA Tour, may dominate the news
by dominating television exposure while, at the local level, golf
carries on an unimaginably rich program that cares very little
what the big national organizations are up to. Tim Finchem might
worry about the size of the fan base for tour events. The USGA
might worry that the golf ball goes too far or that the grooves
on wedges are too deep. What they should worry about, and the
USGA does to some extent, is the vitality of golf at the regional,
state, and local level. All politics is local.

We have seen that the American golf community is governed
by two loosely organized parties. The oldest and smallest party advocates "old golf" and draws its values from the game as
it existed before 1930. It believes in caddies or carrying your
own clubs. It still thinks that the private club is a good idea and
that the heart of the game is the dedicated amateur. Its ideal
course is the Scottish or Irish links course. The newest and largest party has created "new golf" and has been subtly shaped by

five decades of postwar affluence and by the power of television. Its model golfer is the touring pro and its course is the well-watered, upscale, daily-fee or gated community course. Members of the modern party play the game in powered carts. The disputes engendered by the two parties are, in the end, distractions that obscure the fact that people have been, and always will be, drawn to the game by its intrinsic values and by the animal joy of hitting a golf ball well.

Understanding the Golf Community

Contemporary Americans throw the term *community* around with reckless abandon. Recently I met a woman who claimed membership in the poodle-owners community. It seems that just about anything can serve as the basis for a community. The academic discussion of these issues is thick with definitions, debate, and conflict. Within all this noise, however, resides a broad consensus that sometime between the Civil War and World War I the organic and primary sense that Americans lived in stable communities evaporated. Mobility, immigration, industrialization, and urbanization quickly broke apart the village life that gave Americans a sense that they lived in stable, almost timeless communities. Suddenly social and economic relationships that had once been with familiar well-known individuals were often with strangers. A culture of anonymity emerged out of massive historical change.

In this atmosphere, Americans set about the job of creating new kinds of community to replace the small agricultural communities that were quickly becoming nostalgia, that were becoming the stuff of literature about old America. Americans went on a binge of organization building that was, at bottom, an attempt to re-create community and restore order in their lives. Occupations like the law and medicine served as a basis for new organizations, for new communities. Race, ethnicity, and religion served to bind people together in new more formal ways.

Politics, protest, and economic interests also served to unite people. Sport was important in this process. The new city, made up largely of strangers, could come together around the city's new major league baseball teams and later their football and basketball teams. One of the more prominent modern manifestations of this phenomenon is the "Red Sox Nation." Clubs of all sorts were formed to promote sport, exercise, and sociability. It was out of this desire to create communities that Americans began to build golf courses and golf clubs. The rise of industrial capitalism helped by creating dramatically higher levels of discretionary time and income.

For slightly more than forty years, the golf club–country club concept, essentially a special-purpose voluntary association, proved to be an incredibly compelling idea. It was particularly popular among white, Protestant businessmen. These clubs gobbled up old farms, estates, and marginal seaside land. They cut over pine barrens and laid down golf courses. At these courses, "the golfer" evolved as an easily recognizable figure in American cultural imagery. This figure evoked both positive and negative reactions.

Between 1890 and 1930, the golf community created a unique set of roles and organizations. The professional golfer of 1890 evolved into four separate figures: the playing professional, the club professional, the course architect, and the greenkeeper. The professionals created their own community within a community, the Professional Golfers' Association (PGA), in 1916. In the mid-1890s, the game also spawned the United States Golf Association (USGA) that set the rules and helped to define the game for everyone.

By the late 1920s golf had become perhaps the fastest-growing game in the long list of American sports. In 1930 there were approximately 5,800 golf courses in the United States; 4,600 of these were private. There were two million golfers playing on these courses. When the Depression struck, the golf community was among its many victims. The game did not die but it was very sick. There were signs of recovery in the late 1930s but they were snuffed out by the coming of the war. The combination of economic depression and war drove the golf community to its lowest point.

But of course it survived. From the late 1940s to the present day, the golf community has been shaped by generally rising affluence. The number of players and courses grew as wealth and the population expanded; the PGA Tour grew into a popular television sport creating millionaires literally every week. The golf community explicitly recognized that it had created a pantheon of heroes and heroines. National and local halls of fame installed plaques bearing the names Ouimet, Hagan, Sarazen, Jones, Nelson, Snead, Didrickson, Hogan, Wright, Palmer, Nicklaus, Trevino, Watson, and others. Affluence also produced protest and conflict in the golf community. In complicated ways, women struggled to become full members of the golf community. The male professional golfers went through a difficult period in the 1950s and early 1960s, reluctantly facing up to their racist past. Perhaps the most important upshot of all this was the politicalization of golf. This politicalization had deep roots in the past but it came into full flower in the 1950s, during the Eisenhower administration, and has been with us ever since. When an American becomes a golfer he or she, rightly or wrongly, is marked by some as stuffy, old-fashioned, and Republican, as no friend to African Americans and women.

Known 120 years ago only as a game played in Scotland, golf has grown into a large and complex community. Some people at the top of the game like to think of golf as an "industry," and in recent years they have attempted to add up the impact of their industry in the United States. In 2009, Golf 20/20 (a group of golf organizations) created the most concise summation of this history, entitled *The Golf Industry Impact in the United States*. After noting that twenty-eight million Americans play golf and that millions more who do not play enjoy watching the game in person or on television, Golf 20/20 stated that golf "is far more than a game; golf is a leading U.S. industry that makes a wide variety of positive contributions to our society." Golf has created two million jobs held by individuals who collect over $60 billion in wages. By the broadest measure, the total economic impact of golf is $195 billion. The golf industry is larger than the movie and video business and the newspaper industry. The game creates $3.5 billion in charitable contributions annually. The vast majority of this sum comes from local events, with the money going to local charities. Pro tour events also help raise money for good, often local, causes. In 2008, the tour helped raise $135 million. Golf teaches young people important values: "sportsmanship, respect, integrity, honesty, and self-control." Golf courses, Golf 20/20 argues, "provide a vital community service in offering a place to recreate and socialize, serving as a hub of community social interaction."

The golf industry claims that the sixteen thousand golf facilities in the United States provide a vital service to the environment. They are green space in a world that is rapidly being paved over. Almost all courses provide, to some extent, habitat for wildlife. The industry takes pride in the talents of those professionals who operate courses "in an environmentally responsible manner." These courses are maintained using very little water, only one-half of 1 percent of the nation's annual water consumption.

All industries produce public relations documents like this one from the golf industry. It is inevitably defensive in tone, designed to answer criticism of the game. For one thing, many environmentalists have been critical of golf for overusing fertilizers and water. However, the defensive tone is rooted in something even more fundamental. Golf is, after all, voluntary, some would say a frill. The Golf 20/20 document was clearly an answer to critics in 2008–9 who attacked corporate golf outings and golfing in general as inappropriate during a frightening recession.

I would argue that the golf industry is wholly dependent on

the existence of a golf community. Without millions of Americans who are emotionally bonded to the game, the golf industry would quickly evaporate. The question then is how many such people are there and what do we know about them? Between 2000 and 2011, there is little doubt that the community of golfers shrank. The total number of golfers has declined from 30 million to 26 million. The number of people who play more than twenty-five times per year has dropped from 6 million in 2002 to 4.6 million in 2009. In the category of core golfers, who play eight or more times annually, there has also been a substantial decline. The numbers cited come from the National Golf Foundation; these figures are probably a bit high and tend to make the decline look smaller than it really is.

The profile of the golfers in the "avid" category (who played twenty-five rounds or more in 1999) and the "core" group (who played eight rounds or more in 1999) indicate some clear demographic trends. Using numbers from the NGF's *Golf Participation in the United States* report, published in 2000, it is clear that men vastly outnumber women and that most dedicated golfers are older, richer, and better educated than the average citizen. Male, older, richer, educated—let us then call them MORES. In the NGF's avid category, 84.1 percent are male, and almost two-thirds of both genders are over forty, while 22.2 percent are over sixty-five. In the core category, 83.2 percent are male and 55.1 percent are over forty. In the avid group, 28.1 percent are retired. In the core group, 19.3 percent are retired. In both groups, a high percentage reports having some college or a college degree. In the avid category, 84 percent report they had some college or possess a college degree.

It helps to focus on the avid category in the NGF numbers. These players, the MORES, are the substantial core of the golf community. According to the NGF there were approximately 6 million avid golfers in the United States in the year 2000. Can we put this number into historical context? In 2000, avid golfers made up 2.1 percent of the United States population. In 1930, if we put the number of avid golfers at 1.8 million (a reasonable assumption), they comprised 1.8 percent of the American population. Given the expansion of the country, particularly in the South and West, and the large increases in discretionary time and wealth since 1930, one would expect the relative number of avid golfers to have been much higher in 2000, but it wasn't. In 1930, there were 5,800 golf courses, or one course for every 21,100 citizens. In 2000, there were, at most, 17,000 courses, or one course for every 16,500 persons. Again, accounting for increased wealth and the development of new areas, especially in the South and Hawaii, this does not seem like particularly rapid growth. In fact it looks a bit like decline. Remember, I am using numbers from the year 2000, numbers that have declined further in the last decade.

A lot happened between 1930 and 2000. Golf, of course, suffered between 1930 and 1950. But after 1950, while most Americans experienced a long period of prosperity, the golf community, in relative terms, did not grow very much. Of course, the question is why.

Many people argue that the game takes too long and that it costs too much. They note that the modern family, with its two incomes and working wives, is an enemy of golf. Such opinions have been cycled and recycled for the last twenty years. To gain a larger perspective, however, it helps to go back to the first forty years of golf in America. As this book has argued, Americans were confronting the pleasant problem of increased discretionary time and money. The crusade for a shorter workweek was winning a slow-motion victory. The upper classes were the first beneficiaries; but the idea that all Americans could enjoy a forty-hour workweek made substantial strides. The general spread of technology at work and at home seemed to promise that a growing portion of each week could be devoted to leisure. The upper classes were the first to modify their commitment to the Protestant work ethic. They elected to make leisure acceptable, and their behavior served as a model for the rest of America.

Leisure and play were important issues in the 1920s. What would people do with all these free hours? Would the lower classes use them for "amoral" purposes? These and other questions were subsumed under the general heading the Problem of Leisure. Golf and the private golf club thrived in this atmosphere. The club could soak up hours, even whole days, since it provided golf and often swimming, tennis, and other games. The club also served as a hub for socializing and entertaining. The golf club–country club also took up time if you became part of its administration, serving as an officer or on a committee. Finally, a membership often seemed like a good long-term investment.

After World War II, the problem of leisure still existed. But Americans who came to the world of work after 1950 would solve this problem, or have it solved for them, in new ways. Certainly golf was still a part of America's leisure plan, but it was clearly crowded out by new realities. These realities had begun to dawn on some Americans in the 1920s. Some businessmen and economists began to ask what would happen if Americans continued to work less and produce more. The prospect of a stable, or even stagnant, economy clearly loomed on the horizon. In essence, these thinkers began to see a growthless economy in the offing. In simple terms, there would not be enough wages paid to buy the new production. The image of workers, broadly defined, working just enough to provide for a comfortable life and spending the new hours of leisure gardening, golfing, and reading seemed like a prescription for disaster.

The answer to this gloomy forecast was not to increase working hours but to increase consumption. As Benjamin Klein Honeycutt put it, in his 1988 book *Work Without End*, in the 1920s,

> businessmen became increasingly convinced that Americans could be persuaded to buy things produced by industry that they had never needed before and consume goods and services, not in response to some out-of-date set of economic motives, but

according to a standard of living that constantly improved. With this concern for consumption, the business community broke its long concentration on production, introduced the age of mass consumption, founded a new view of progress in an abundant society, and gave life to the advertising industry.

Some business leaders even suggested that a worker's wages should be high enough to buy the products they produced. However, in the 1920s, most businessmen and economists thought that higher wages would motivate workers to demand even shorter hours. In the end, a higher level of consumption was no sure thing but it could be created by higher levels of capital spending on new products, expert marketing and advertising, and by using the consumption habits of the rich as an example to the less affluent.

Certainly the Depression and the war years obscured the shift to this new consumption ethic. After 1950, however, it slowly came to dominate American life. The demand for shorter hours came to a complete halt; in many areas of American economic life workers took on more hours to earn more wages in order to purchase the tidal wave of new goods and services — the European vacation, European wine and beer, the television and air conditioners, and the second and third car. During this period the average American home also ballooned in size to hold all these new products. But the television was a special new product with a crucial role. Americans expended their leisure, in great measure, watching this new device. It was an incredibly cheap way to use one's spare time. As Americans watched more and more, they were trained by television advertising to desire hundreds of new products that were portrayed as essential to the good life.

This was a world in which the number of occasional golfers could grow at a decent rate. The demand for fancy golf vacations, where the middle class could ape the rich for three days and two nights, would rise dramatically. It could all go on the newly invented credit card. It was not a particularly good environment for the production of avid committed golfers. It was not a good environment for the private club, which lost its dominance in the golf world by 1970. Daily-fee and public courses did much better. They were places where golfers could purchase, individually, the three to five rounds played annually. The golf course as an add-on in a real estate development did very well.

Clearly, however, avid golfers do exist. As we noted earlier, they are predominantly male, wealthier, older, and with more years of education. This demographic profile hardly does justice to the golfers we are trying to understand as the heart of the golf community. On at least one occasion, a scholarly investigator discovered the avid golfer, or, more accurately, the avid golfer family. Robert Coles, a child psychiatrist and Harvard professor, in his 1977 book *Privileged Ones: The Well-Off and Rich in America*, stumbled upon the golf-loving family. The following is his take on the game and the family committed to it:

> Golf: a game, but for many a way of life. Some homes are regarded as especially convenient, because near a golf course. The weekends become a marathon of golf, interrupted by a meal or two. The mood of particular parents varies with their game, with their scores. And endless discussions are devoted to experiences in one way or another connected to the sport. Families travel with a certain golf course in mind. Clothing is often geared to what is worn on the links. And to move toward a less sociological and more psychological, even existential vein, some well-to-do men and women openly acknowledge that without golf, life for them would be unbearable, even hard to imagine.

Coles has, without fully realizing it, discovered the heart of the golf community. To his credit he clearly understands that the sociological approach, emphasizing issues of wealth, class, and race, does not exhaust the subject. All through this book I have tried to emphasize that while the social and economic approach to golf is indispensable, in the end, for the truly committed, the choice is ultimately psychological and existential.

We are familiar with the idea that people turn to or turn away from golf for both social and economic reasons. The psychological and existential reasons for loving or hating the game have never been given their due. Perhaps this reflects the profound cynicism of the modern age: Freud, Darwin, and Marx have taught us to think that the openly expressed reasons for any action are rarely the real ones. It also leads to the general view that all games are essentially the same and that their advocates become advocates for economic, social, racial, and class-based reasons. Without denying that these sorts of reasons are very important, I think that it is crucial to ask if golf has some unique features that account for the devoted golfers Coles discovered.

There are some obvious reasons why golf attracts people. There is a considerable literature on this issue, some of which was discussed at length earlier in this book. A classic of the genre that we have not discussed is Herbert Warren Wind's essay "Lure of Golf." In it Wind presents seven of the reasons usually cited as drawing people to the game of golf:

1. Your principal opponent in the contest is yourself.
2. The game is played in varied settings. There are no uniform fields or courts.
3. Golf can be played for a lifetime.
4. The method of scoring—as translated into the accompanying handicap system—is perfect for monitoring progress or decline in skill.
5. The companionship with fellow players is attractive.
6. Devotees can practice and play alone.
7. Golf is a great game for those who like to gamble.

Most dedicated golfers will cite one or more of these reasons to account for their addiction. However, it is my opinion that these seven reasons barely scratch the surface of the game's appeal. If you are going to invest your leisure life in a particular game, you will eventually think more complicated thoughts about your passion than Wind's essay might suggest. You should also suspect that there are other, less obvious, intrinsic aspects of the game that somehow, consciously or unconsciously, bond you to the game. One such aspect is the basic structure of the game. It is, in essence, a spending game. Every player begins with unlimited resources and the final medal score is the total amount spent in the course of play. One confronts numerous choices that call for either risk or caution, and the player has ample time to consider his options. Good golf courses present a number of these choices. Should you attempt to fly the pond and reach the green, or should you expend a shot to lay up short and reduce risk? A good player is able to correctly choose the right path — to take good risks in some cases, and in other circumstances make the cautious decision to use a stroke and avoid a large disastrous expenditure. Golf, looked at this way, resembles a perfect capitalist system. Of course the results are recorded only as bookkeeping entries. There is little physical risk in golf, making it considerably different from other risky hobbies such as skiing or mountain climbing. Gambling for small sums, which is endemic among avid players, does enliven play. In match play, golf remains a spending game. After each hole the competitors compare expense reports; the player who spent the smallest amount is awarded the hole. Win the most holes, win the match.

Another intrinsic characteristic of golf is its nonviolent nature. In this, golf stands as a marked contrast to most other popular American games. It is ironic that the violence of the contact in golf when the club meets the ball is greater than in all other games when all physical contact between players in the course of actual play is strictly forbidden. Certainly this is the case where a player's personality deeply influences the games they choose to play. There are people who truly enjoy the pushing and shoving necessary to capture a rebound in basketball or celebrate the "great hit" in football. Boxing may be the ultimate expression of violence in sport; it may be best understood as pure violence turned into sport. As one grows older, violence becomes less interesting and one turns to golf, happily leaving the violent sports to the young.

Golf in fact goes beyond nonviolence by imposing a strict code of behavior that governs play. For this reason golf has often been thought of as a way to teach general civility and manners. I think there is more to this issue than meets the eye. If one observes a foursome of golfers who have fully internalized the ethos of the game, one quickly realizes that deference of an elaborate sort runs the minute-by-minute play of golf. At each moment of play, when a shot is being struck, those not playing defer completely to the shot maker. They stand still in clearly prescribed positions so as not to annoy the player of the moment. Once that shot is struck, deference passes to the next player, usually the player furthest from the hole.

The centrality of deference is most clearly seen on the green during putting. The player furthest from the hole, and in the poorest position, is deferred to by the others. They take great care not to step in his line or stand in a position that may distract the putter from her task. For example, as a young player I was taught "the belly rule"—you should stand directly behind or in front of the shot maker's belly. If she wishes you to stand somewhere else you should immediately comply. Also as a young player I learned that I was not only responsible for what I did but that I was also responsible for the actions of my shadow.

On the tee, deference is granted to the competitor who is playing the best. The person with the lowest score on the last hole is granted "the honor" of hitting first. The order after that is determined by the players' scores on previous holes. Thus, these deference rules produce an orderliness to the playing of the game. Since the player deferred to changes after each shot, we might name the whole system the democratic deference code.

Deference has had a long and important history in American life. Prerevolutionary America was, in many respects, organized around rules of deference. Those at the bottom rungs of the social ladder paid deference to those above them. Simple farmers removed their hats when addressing wealthy merchants. Voters gave their votes to the elite without much consideration as to how well the elite actually governed. People paid deference up the social scale and expected people below them to do the same.

During the nineteenth century these habits of deference gave way to democratic manners. The common man stopped granting automatic respect to his so-called betters. In general, manners coarsened and Americans gained a reputation as a pushing, even rude, people. Urbanization in the late nineteenth century made matters worse. It's little wonder that the upper classes of the 1890s found in golf a game that embodied the rules of deference and civility that were quickly dying out in society in general. A hundred years later this deferential system clearly rubs the self-absorbed and the narcissistic the wrong way. They much prefer games that put them at the center of the action and keep them there.

All sports in modern American life make some claim to teach good values and behavior. But it seems to me that golf has a more legitimate grip on this task than do most other sports. At the professional level, golf has never produced the brats and thugs that seem too common in other sports. The deferential structure I have described is basic to the experience of golf; deferring, being polite, quiet, and considerate to the other players becomes habitual and profoundly shapes the behavior of golfers off the course.

Of course, related to the deferential system is the honesty and self-policing ethic in golf. We have come to expect rules officials in big televised golf events, and these officials occasionally have to call penalties on players. However, the ethic of the game calls for scrupulous honesty; it is expected that a player will call penalties on himself and be solely responsible for the accuracy of all scores. As with the deferential system, the emphasis on personal honesty and self-policing appeals to some and not to others. If it appeals to you, you are a candidate for membership in the golf community.

Of course, all sports are structured by rules, but golf's rules and rituals seem particularly bourgeois, even Victorian. The emphasis on quiet and self-control, personal honesty and the subjection of self to what seem like old-fashioned strictures, is unique to golf. For example, many clubs and courses ban the wearing of denim and collarless shirts. These same clubs fought the move to allow women to wear shorts on the course, and at many courses short shorts are still forbidden. Then there is the subject of hats. Removing one's hat in the presence of women or in certain venues or at certain times has become a sign of antimodern Victorianism. But many golfers still operate by the old rules. At the end of a round you will see most players, including touring pros, remove their cap and murmur ritualistic comments like "Good playing," "Enjoyed it," "Great day," "I need a drink," or "Suicide is not out of the question." In Scotland I saw eight Americans enter a clubhouse with their hats on only to be confronted by the bartender who barked, "Lids off, gentlemen. This is a golf house, not your everyday bar."

Golf has suffered from this emphasis on rules and rituals. It is one of the reasons, along with its racist and sexist past, that some look upon golf as old-fashioned, stodgy, and repressive. One of the themes of the 1960s was a critique of almost all restraint on personal expression. Liberation of the authentic self from social, cultural, and sexual restraint seemed like the path to psychological health and personal happiness. It was deemed uncool, by some, to point out that the liberation from restraint imposed by rituals and rules has led to some negative consequences, particularly the ugliness and rudeness that characterizes our public space and public behavior.

People who emotionally bond with the game, who join the golf community, fully accept the rituals of the game and, seemingly, tolerate the criticism that this acceptance brings. One of my best friends offered the best explanation of this happy toleration. He had fully enjoyed the liberation of the 1960s, but had also golfed his way through the decade. The game remained a crucial part of his life, an anchor especially during the last thirty years. Golf served him well, and he served it with rare dedication. When I told him that I thought that golf was a form of expression, he brightened and said, "There is no way to truly express yourself without rules. Without rules life is just chaos."

Another important aspect of golf that attracts some is the element of craftsmanship that the game demands. When I was much younger I met an old gentleman golfer who introduced me to the idea that golf was a craft and that as one sought to get better at golf one was taking up a craft. He claimed that golf was much like woodworking, which he also practiced and loved. He had worked out this analogy to a remarkable degree. He said that building a golf game was like building a dining-room table. You needed to develop a number of skills. You had to know how to cut, shape, and attach the pieces, all the while being true to the original design. In golf there is the full swing, but also half and quarter swings, putting, and bunker play—all are separate skills united by a general plan—to build a serviceable game. In both golf and woodworking the better players or practitioners are the ones who have mastered the most skills. The failure to master just one skill (putting!) can ruin the whole endeavor.

The old gent laughed when he asked me if I had ever known a true golfer who did not love golf clubs—the game's tools. Just like a woodworker, the golfer is always, at the same time, deeply in love with his tools and looking for newer even better ones. Finally the old man, who had worked at golf for half a century, claimed that both the master golfer and the master woodworker needed an abundance of the same virtue—patience. Failure was common in both endeavors; one had to face failure and to be patient with one's own ineptitude, believing that eventually you will get it right. In a high philosophical moment my older friend suggested that both golf and woodworking taught one how to deal with inevitable failure. Both endeavors break you down and force you to face your ineptitude straight on. I was deeply impressed by this idea that golf was a complicated craft and that a part of its addictive quality is its demand that you patiently seek something called craftsmanship. In a time when craftsmanship is in decline, labor is increasingly special-ized, and most products are mass produced, it makes a certain amount of sense that we should find in golf satisfactions that come from mastering a complicated craft.

Of course, the game has its great exemplar of this idea. Ben Hogan was a craftsman. He patiently mastered skill after skill. Perhaps motivated by the dark memory of his father, a crafts-man driven from his craft by progress, Hogan sought perfec-tion in a game that, largely by luck, had crossed his path. When his playing skills declined, Hogan turned to making clubs with the same dedication to craftsmanship that he exhibited dur-ing his playing days. Hogan was not the only great player to be-come obsessed by the tools of the game; Arnold Palmer is an-other who tinkers endlessly with his equipment. And whatever else Tiger Woods might represent, he is a tireless student of the craft. As a young man he was asked about his long-term goals, and he replied, "To hit a perfect golf shot."

Inherent in the idea that golf is essentially a craft is the no-tion that true competence comes through repetition. Almost all games demand a certain tolerance for repetition. Baseball infielders take thousands of ground balls in practice so that they can field the ones that count in the game. Tennis players hit thousands of forehands and backhands until they can au-tomatically hit the same shots in a match. Golf is, however, to some extent unique in this regard because golfers can practice alone. A common image in golf is the lone figure on the prac-tice green hitting one three-foot putt after another, or the sol-itary figure on the practice range hitting countless shots, seek-ing a technique that he can trust on the course. Baseball, with its coin-operated batting cages, has created separate venues for repetitious practice. Tennis has invented a machine that will serve up ball after ball. The golf driving range, with its bags and buckets of balls, is a central institution, a crucial space in the game of golf.

This notion that golf attracts players because it is in many ways a craft leads us to the conclusion that avid players have adopted the game because it mimics work. This puts golf in a category of leisure activities that bear a strong resemblance to work. In this group I would put gardening, old-car restoration, sewing, hunting, fishing, boat building, painting, photography and, of course, woodworking. These activities, pursued by millions as hobbies, are or were once deemed to be work, pure and simple. Some were once necessary for survival. Gardening, actual work transformed in modern times into play, may be the most common leisure activity. I would argue that the Protestant work ethic continues to shape the choices many Americans make. For many, if the avocation can be seen as work, or as preparation for work, one can wholeheartedly adopt it without guilt. At least the golfer and the gardener can pursue their passion with the sure knowledge that they are not watching television. I am sure that watching television is not work. It may not be play either. As I have thought about these matters, the line between work and play has become less and less distinct. The touring pro, a fundamental figure and model in the golf community, has turned play into work or some third thing, yet to be named.

Finally, golf more than any other game offers the devoted a long and value-laden tradition. The dominant sports in American life, football, baseball, and basketball, have relatively short histories. These sports also spurn tradition when it seems appropriate. While the major sports make heroic attempts to create a sense of tradition, they simply cannot match certain aspects of golf. The affluent devoted golfer can go to Scotland and play at St. Andrews, where golf has been played for more than five hundred years. One can go north to Dornoch or east to Turnberry. The golf pilgrim, in Scotland or the United States, is very different from the pilgrims of football, baseball, or basketball seeking real contact with the history and traditions of their games. One might go to Yankee Stadium, Fenway Park, or Madison Square Garden, but you almost certainly will not be allowed to play there. Visit Muirfield, St. Andrews, Carnoustie, or Ballybunion and, if you have enough money, you can most certainly play.

To take a somewhat shorter view, it is clear that golf has a tendency to run in families, to be a family tradition. Golf literature in the United States has numerous examples of golf, its values and allure, being passed from father to son. Alas, there is little testimony of the game being passed from mother to daughter. I know that I have come to love golf because my father did. He was a good semipro baseball player, a pitcher with a decent curve. He played golf since his days as a caddie and, when his arm blew out, golf became his sport. I played both sports and remember distinctly the way I felt about baseball and golf. My father *watched* me play baseball; we *played* golf together. It began when I caddied for him; and when I could play decently, we played together. We competed in best-ball and father-and-son tournaments. In some sense, baseball never had a chance. Baseball was and is a great game but I never was going to play much past the age of twenty. My father was the living evidence that golf could go with you deep into life. To many, parents are the embodiment of tradition. In families where this is true, golf can seem like a family heirloom to be treasured and passed on.

As I list these intrinsic qualities of golf, I have also been creating the typical personality that will respond positively to them. This person will have a certain attitude toward spending (parsimony); will be comfortable in an environment based on deference, civility, and ritual; will respond positively to the idea of craftsmanship and the repetition necessary to attain it; and will have respect for tradition. It helps considerably if this person has good eye-hand coordination.

In the last 120 years, this personality type was common in the years between 1890 to 1930. After 1930 this type went into decline. Golf's virtues, if I may call them that, are generally less attractive to the American of the last fifty years.

Golf is a form of personal expression. It is voluntary. In relative terms, the number of people who choose golf as a form of expression is getting smaller, because golf's virtues seem less compelling than they did in 1925. As the historical context changed after 1950, golf's virtues seemed less relevant, less compelling; in many ways these virtues became quaint. The golf community, those tied together by an emotional bond to the game, slowly got smaller.

Against the Wind

Nothing can depress a golfer more profoundly than to stand on the first tee and feel a twenty-mile-per-hour wind in his face. This, however, is exactly the situation golf confronts as it moves into its second century of existence in the United States. The nature of the headwind seems clear—too many courses and not enough players. If only it were that simple. American golf in the twenty-first century confronts a much more insidious and complex set of obstacles than just a supply-and-demand problem. It is too easy to assume that demand will vigorously return when the economy improves. Instead, Americans will return to golf slowly and the recruitment of new players will be beset by a number of problems.

Certainly the supply-and-demand problems are clear enough. Some in the golf industry believe that it must shed two thousand or more courses. This process is well underway. Bradley S. Klein, in a January 2011 *Golfweek* article, notes that "even established private clubs are hurting. Net course closings have averaged 100 annually for five years, and are likely to double in the next five years." Cash-strapped towns are particularly pressured to sell or stop subsidizing their municipal courses. Cheap, often nine-hole public courses are especially at risk. Of the closures between 2000 and 2009, a clear majority (57 percent) were inexpensive, nine-hole courses. These are exactly the kinds of places that beginners seek out as they learn the game.

Demand for golf has dropped significantly. In 1990, 12.1 percent of the American population played at least one round of golf. By 2000 this number had declined to 11.1 percent; and in 2008 it stood at 10.2 percent. Between 2000 and 2009 the number of rounds played plummeted 5.7 percent. It is crucial to understand that the decline in demand was not solely the product of economic distress after 2001, and especially after 2007. Demand, in relation to supply, was dropping in the 1990s. The number of courses increased 20.6 percent in the decade, while rounds played increased only 14.8 percent.

This is a complex story that began in the 1980s. The golf industry confronted the reality that golf, and particularly golf course construction, had become a mature industry, that it could look for little or no growth in the future. The National Golf Foundation and other industry groups launched a study of the situation that urged golf to put its faith and its money on the Baby Boom Generation. It became an article of faith that golf was just at the beginning of a dramatic increase in demand. As the Boomers aged they were going to play a lot of golf. The golf industry was urged to begin building courses for this huge (76–80 million) generation to play on.

In at least two ways the industry got it wrong. In the first place, they built the wrong kinds of courses. Approximately 60 percent of the courses were linked to real estate developments. These courses were inappropriate in two ways. At the high end of these developments, the courses, often designed by a famous designer, were too long and hard for the average golfer. They were impossible for the beginner, especially women. At the more modest developments, the builder often installed a course to fulfill the common requirement of maintaining a certain percentage of the development in open space. Courses met the requirement and produced revenue. The builder did not care much about the course, looking upon it as little more than outdoor carpeting between house lots. Once the lots were sold, the plan was to sell the course and move on.

Second, the industry went deaf to the clear warning that the "golf boom" was not universally popular. This reflects monomaniacal reliance on surveys, demographic studies, and other social-science approaches to understanding the game. They could have listened to John Updike, the novelist and golfer, who by 1990 had heard about the golf boom from articles in the *New York Times* and the *Boston Globe*. Updike had learned to play on Massachusetts public courses that he notes "used to be a breeze to play" but that the golf boom had made them "simply hellish." They were vastly overcrowded and "the old courtesies implode in the crush." He and his pals found themselves in competition with "youthful couch potatoes who scoot around in their carts whacking divots out of the helpless turf and never thinking to replace one." His simple municipal course "isn't just overplayed, it's pillaged." Updike did not like the boom any better at a private club. When he joined his club (Myopia), it was "a shaggy old layout" with no houses on the fairways. For him, "golf's gift to the spirit is space, and the space in this case was organically designed and blessedly, blissfully, underpopulated." But the boom was ruining Myopia as well. The club apparently decided it had to keep up and so replaced the watering system, which required "more trench work than the First World War." Improvements piled upon improvements and all was piled on dues that rose "as irresistibly as tree sap." Perhaps to help cover costs at the club, Updike confronted an increasing number of corporate outings where the corporate elite, "as colorful as jungle parrots," in a huge fleet of carts, "coat the emerald fairways with shiny tire tracks." Nearly his last words on the golf boom are "big-bucks golf-glamour, get lost."

One need not take sides in this contest between Updike and the golf boom. One conclusion, however, is obvious: the boom drove some players from the game and it did less than nothing to provide cheap, easy-to-play courses for novices. Far too many of the courses built between 1990 and 2005 were real estate–related or high-priced, daily-fee layouts that, while nominally public, were far out of reach for the majority of middle-class golfers. Finally, Updike's lament reminds us of similar works written after the crash in 1929. They decried the luxury and expense that grew to mammoth proportions in the 1920s golfing world and yearned to turn back the clock to a simpler, more austere time. Updike, of course wrote his warning long before the crash of 2008.

The crash for golf in the most recent case was not as dramatic as 1929. Demand was slackening even in the economically flush time between 1996 and 2001. When the planes crashed into the Twin Towers in September 2001, golf, along with the rest of the nation, took a fundamental blow from which it is still recovering. It was only a footnote to the attack that golf travel and golf generally clearly declined. The bursting of the tech bubble also hurt but not nearly as much as the financial crisis and recession after 2007. Again, as in 1930, golf's growth was stopped in its tracks by an economic debacle.

The question, of course, is about recovery, about the future. It is my opinion that industry-based estimates of demand are usually too optimistic. If anyone in the golf business thinks that demand will come roaring back as the economy improves they are, for many reasons, wrong.

One reason that demand will be sluggish concerns the Baby Boom Generation upon which golf continues to pin its hopes. In the 1990s the golf industry prayed they would play more golf as they aged. Today the hope is that they will play more when they retire. Born between 1946 and 1960, this ponderous cohort is just beginning to reach age sixty-five. Any hope that they will leave their jobs and march smartly to a golf course and queue up at the first tee is doubtful. First, their ability to retire at sixty-five or earlier is in question. They will not retire with the same comfortable affluence their parents possessed. There will be less money, and their pensions, even Social Security, will be less reliable. A 2011 *New York Times* article claimed that 45 percent of Boomers "are at risk without enough savings to maintain their living standards after they retire." This is also a generation in which significant income disparities have existed. During their working lives too many Boomers have experienced little or no real income growth. Too much of the wealth produced in the last thirty years is concentrated at the top of the economic ladder. There are simply fewer individuals with the economic resources to look forward to a golf-centric retirement.

Many in the generation have relied on rising house prices to partially fund their retirements. Many Boomers tended to look upon their home as a substitute for saving actual money. Today, and for quite a while, they will be lucky to sell their homes even at a much-depressed price. What is referred to in the press as "the housing mess" will influence golf and the golf-centered retirement for a long time. The trade of a northern home for a cheaper home in a southern golf community has been a structural element in American golf for fifty years. If it comes back, it will take a long time.

At the Southern end of this trade we discover the present state of golf-related real estate developments or planned communities. The reputation of these communities has taken a considerable blow and not its first. The poster boy for the collapse of the golf-community development business might well be Edward Robert Ginn, known to his friends and customers as Bobby. During the boom in golf communities he was a super salesman who could sell four hundred lots in a day. During the boom Ginn would build a Versailles-sized clubhouse as the center of a luxury development. At Tesoro, near Port St. Lucie, Florida, he constructed a 116,000-square-foot clubhouse, which cost $48 million. Of the nine hundred lots at Tesoro, only one hundred and fifty have sold. At another Ginn development, Bella Collina, only forty-eight houses stand on a site containing eight hundred lots.

The boom of the late 1990s was not Mr. Ginn's first bite of the apple. In the 1980s he was on Hilton Head Island selling real estate; by 1986 he was selling out to pay his debts and declared personal bankruptcy. In most cases, Ginn was selling quasi-aristocratic status that came with a private development, access to an expensive golf course, and a huge, extravagant clubhouse. One wonders if in the next few decades this approach will ever work again. By 2009, Ginn faced more than thirty lawsuits related to his activities between 1997 and 2008. His problems are merely emblematic of those faced by almost all golf-related real estate development. Even well-established, well-run communities like Amelia Island Plantation in North Florida have filed for Chapter 11 bankruptcy, and they are not alone.

Will golfers ever forget and forgive? Will the excesses of promoters ever slip from memory? Will they ever again flock to new communities that seemed to offer the "golf lifestyle" in the grand manner? Because the retirements of Baby Boomers seem less than well-funded, it is hard to believe that these golf communities will flourish in the foreseeable future.

Golf has problems that extend far beyond unreliable Baby Boomers. All these problems have the potential to suppress demand for golf long into the future. For example, at the other end of the age spectrum, golf has a substantial "kid problem." Between 2005 and 2009, the number of young people between six and seventeen who had played a single round or more of golf declined 24 percent. This has happened despite the fact that the First Tee program has grown substantially. This program can attract children but cannot keep them interested as they become teens. Other sports and other hotter activities win their attention.

Participation levels in various high school sports provide clear evidence that golf does not attract enough young people. In 2006–7, 7.4 million students took part in a high school sport program. Only 225,000 chose golf — 159,000 males and 66,000 females. In comparison, 1.1 million males played football, 556,000 chose basketball, and 544,000 participated in outdoor track-and-field. Among males, golf barely edged out tennis and swimming for last place on the list of popular sports.

Among females, golf was dead last. Almost 30,000 young women chose "competitive spirit squads" (cheerleading) over the golf team.

Golf's problems are deeply rooted in these numbers. In high school young people establish their emotional commitments and begin the process of constructing an identity. Only a very few, in relative terms, take to golf and make it part of their lives.

There are those who believe that the golf community has become antikid, regardless of gender. As courses get longer and harder, young players have a smaller role at many clubs and public layouts. Dan Van Horn, president of U.S. Kids Golf, which sells golf gear for young people, states that "the philosophy of nearly every club right now is that kids get in the way of adult play. The whole industry is set up for the men and the advanced players. A golf course has to be a place for families." If this is true, it does not take a genius to guess the long-term impact. If kids don't learn to love the game now, in twenty or thirty years we will be wondering where all the players have gone. More precisely, golf will be stuck with only those golfers we might call adult-onset players.

In addition to the kid problem, golf has difficulties with women, in other words, a gender problem. In most surveys, for every four or five male golfers there is only one female. Among junior golfers, 77 percent are male. There are some obvious reasons why this should be so. Since the 1890s women have occupied a less than full membership in the golf community. All-male clubs, like Augusta National, have a powerful position in the world of golf. It is, however, too easy to make the gender imbalance in golf solely a political and equality issue. Even with significant progress in the last twenty-five years, women are still not culturally enabled to enjoy sport the way men do. There is some modest evidence that as athletic opportunities open for females, they have shown a preference for team sports and have less interest in individual games like golf. For me the problem of women in golf defies a full explanation, and yet no place on the professional athletic map is more compelling than women's professional golf. It is as if the spirit of globalization has taken up residence inside the LPGA. Other cultures turn out numbers of excellent players — Sweden, South Korea, Mexico, China — while American colleges occasionally find it impossible to find a decent player to accept a golf scholarship. In the end, I don't get it.

Related to the gender problem is the third dilemma that clouds golf's future. The game has a substantial political problem, which tends to overlap all its other difficulties. Golf has become a universal, nonpartisan, political billy club. President George W. Bush, when the nation invaded Iraq, gave up golf for the duration, knowing that playing the game in wartime looked bad. President Barack Obama took a beating from the right and the left for adopting the game. Golf, however, has a poor political image that extends beyond presidents. In the last decade, federal relief measures after a natural disaster have expressly listed golf enterprises as being ineligible for aid. Advocates of gender equality are fond of pointing to golf as evidence of a bias against women. The crusade to get females on the membership rolls of Augusta National no doubt satisfied some, but also hardened the antigolf views of others. When, in August 2012, Augusta National announced that it had admitted two women (Condoleezza Rice and Darla Moore) to membership, there were few positive responses. One side said, in effect, Why did it take so long? While others bemoaned the fact that women had been admitted at all. It hardly eliminated the political lens through which many view golf.

Golf's political problems deepen when we understand that the game is associated with suburbanization and especially with planned, often age-segregated, residential communities. These places are the subject of considerable political and social debate and will remain so for many years. They are often seen, accurately, as strongholds for the Republican Party, and their golf-centric environments make golf look like a Republican sport.

Recent communities have made strong efforts to construct their developments using the best environmental practices. Some of the older ones, however, have justifiably been seen as environmental disasters waiting to happen; they use too much land, too much fertilizer, and too much water, much of it on their golf courses.

The core of the issue is the private nature of these often golf-based, gated communities. Do Americans really want private towns in their midst? Gated fortresses run by developers or property-owners associations? Will Americans accept communities that ban everyone under the age of nineteen from being a resident? The issue will, and has, become political when an adjacent town seeks to annex a private development or when the environmental practices of a private community are questioned. More complicated is the problem of state and federal laws that govern these communities. In many cases, especially in Florida, developer-owners have powers, like the right to issue tax-free bonds, that were once solely the prerogative of more traditional polities like towns, counties, and states. In a larger sense, Americans will have to decide if the right to privacy allows for the creation of private places that are secessionist, that seek to escape the diversity and the dilemmas of the larger community. Golf may not be the main issue in these disputes but it will be fully implicated, like an accessory after the fact. The political bitterness that will inevitably arise as these issues bubble to the surface will deepen the sense among some Americans that golf is a political liability.

It is hard to see how this political problem will work itself out in the coming decades. However, it is not difficult to comprehend that golf as a leisure choice has, and will continue to have, a growing set of challenges in the struggle for discretionary time and money. Among young people, golf competes with Little League and other organized forms of baseball or softball, football, basketball, and soccer. Among grownups, golf competes with fitness programs and the health club. Both young and old look at tennis and golf as competing choices; there are signs that tennis is winning.

The idea that one should participate in some form of fitness training can be traced back at least to the Greeks, if not to the beginning of human history. Modern notions of a fitness regime arose in nineteenth-century Europe as many more urbanites worked at desks and did jobs that were stressful and required almost no physical exertion. Indeed it is one of the defining traits of modernity that we need to voluntarily exercise to replace the exertions intrinsic to an agricultural existence.

In the United States the first crusader of note for systematic exercise was the Harvard-trained doctor George Barker Winship. He was effective in getting men to exercise — or at least he was until he had a stroke at age forty-two. The YMCA and the YWCA added exercise to their programs in the 1860s. In both cases, the rise of a movement called Muscular Christianity, which called for sound bodies among Christians, was very important. The movement was much stronger among men. Women were often discouraged by bad science that claimed that a woman's childbearing capabilities were imperiled by exercise.

The modern health club was born in post–World War II California. Again the focus was on men at the Vic Tanny and Gold's Gyms of the time. By 1980, something that we might call the new "strenuousity" swept America. White-collar workers, especially, took up the idea that systematic exercise could hold off depression, feelings of powerlessness, and, most important, cardiovascular disease and cancer. Following the ideas of a U.S. Air Force doctor, Kenneth Cooper, Americans sought to become aerobically fit. Many Americans eagerly embraced jogging, running, cycling, or any other activity that dramatically increased one's heart rate. Americans, especially the middle-class, upwardly mobile types, became obsessed with their blood pressure, their weight, and their "times" (the time to run a mile, etc.). Each activity, especially running, created its own community, giving the participants both exercise and a sense of belonging. The fitness and health club movement is, and will continue to be, a substantial competitor for golf in the contest for discretionary time and money.

One might doubt the effectiveness of the fitness and health club movement, given the signs that America is in the midst of an obesity epidemic. However, the statistics are impressive. In 2007, slightly more than seventy-six million Americans walked for fitness at least fifty days every year. Over twenty-nine million walked on a treadmill at home or at a club. Approximately twenty-five million did stretching, used hand weights, weight machines, ran, or jogged. The real winner has been the health club. The number of health club members has doubled since 1990, from twenty to forty million. More than twenty-five million Americans have home gyms. At the clubs "classes" are very important. Members assemble for group exercise classes that promise to keep you slim and invigorated. They also provide a popular social experience. Of all the fitness-related activities, the one with the largest growth rate since 2000 is Pilates Training, a popular class at health clubs. It has grown 490 percent in less than a decade. According to the Sporting Goods Manufacturers Association, seven of the ten fastest-growing sports or athletic activities are fitness endeavors of some sort. The only sports with a top-ten growth rate are tennis, lacrosse, and paint balling(!).

Tennis is of special interest. Tennis and golf in the United States have been linked together as upper-crust club sports since just after the Civil War. However, in at least two respects tennis is doing better recently than golf. Between 2000 and 2007, when golf participation was at best flat, tennis grew 30.6 percent. Tennis is also doing much better with kids. Between 2003 and 2009 the number of young people between six and seventeen playing tennis climbed from 6.8 to 9.5 million. During this same period, golf was losing a substantial number from the same age group.

Tennis has created a program that lures young people into

the game and tends to keep them there. The United States Tennis Association (USTA) decided to abandon the role-model approach to growing the game. This theory held that young people would flock to tennis when and if the number of attractive and highly rated American players grew. The USTA instead launched QuickStart Tennis, a modified form of the game played on a smaller court with a lower net and with lighter rackets and foam balls. The court can be laid out on a gym floor, a parking lot, or any hard surface. In effect, the USTA has grown the number of starter courts at the same time that golf is rapidly losing its starter courses. As a follow-up, the USTA has enlisted three thousand high schools in its "no cut program." The organization provides discounts on equipment and training tips in exchange for a promise by the school not to cut any player from the squad. Finally, the USTA has joined five hundred colleges to grow tennis as a club sport. In this way, high school tennis players who cannot make their college team continue competing as intramural players or in matches with clubs from other schools. Tennis has decided to promote itself as a cradle-to-grave fitness activity, something golf has had a hard time doing.

Tennis has several notable, built-in advantages over golf. While not as cheap as many fitness endeavors, tennis is cheaper than golf. Tennis has, to a substantial extent, solved the weather problem. Indoor heated and cooled courts make tennis a reliable year-round source of exercise and competition. Also tennis can make a justifiable claim to be a key part of a lifelong fitness plan. To date, no one has suggested that tennis can be played in a cart. Finally, a set or two of tennis takes much less time than eighteen holes of golf. Tennis seems to fit the schedules of working people who play a bit at lunch or after work or at a club at night. The future of tennis looks brighter than that of golf. If the golf industry wonders why so few women show up at the golf course, perhaps it's because they are at the health club or playing tennis.

Beyond fitness and tennis, golf has additional competition in the struggle for a share of the nation's discretionary time and money. I have argued repeatedly in this book that television is golf's mortal enemy. Even if you are watching golf on the tube, you are not playing the game. Fan and player are decidedly different categories. In the last twenty years things have gotten worse. Television is a screen with pictures. So is your computer monitor. The Internet soaks up such huge amounts of time that no one is really willing to guess how much. The television or the computer screen can also convey video games.

The impact of video games on time use by Americans is hard to estimate. Now that such games are available in so many ways and on so many devices, any appraisal of their impact will be an educated guess. The popularity of video games in general is volatile, often growing explosively after the release of new games or the coming of new technology. The statistics that are available are surprising. The average age of gamers is thirty-four, and the average player has been at it for twelve years. The Entertainment Software Association claims that the average player spends eight hours a week playing games, and that 40 percent of gamers are female. Estimates of the annual revenues garnered by the video game industry vary considerably but they range between $10 and $15 billion annually. This is revenue only from the sale and resale of content; the purchases of consoles and other technology is excluded. The number one console, Sony's PlayStation Two, has sold over 138 million units. Stay tuned, however, because all the numbers above are subject to dramatic change.

The growth of video games in the last twenty years suggests a deeper problem that golf has always faced and will continue to confront. Consumer capitalism, whatever else it might be, is a system designed to produce an ever-increasing number of choices or options for Americans. For golf courses upon which to play, Americans can choose between ten-dollar municipal courses, five-hundred-dollar resort tracks, or private clubs ranging from cheap to very expensive. In equipment, the golfer is presented with an unending array of new balls and clubs that promise deliverance from the difficulties of the game. However, it is outside the game where the tendency of consumer capitalism to endlessly create new options poses the largest problem for golf. The fitness movement in all its aspects eats into the time and money that could be expended on golf, which can no longer make a legitimate claim as a fitness sport. Americans are increasingly glued to screens for information, entertainment, and just to kill time. A recent survey by the Physical Activity Council found that sixty-five million Americans are inactive or sedentary. Thirty-four percent of this number are between the ages of six and thirty-four. The number of inactive kids between the ages of six and twelve has doubled in the last three years. These are bad numbers for golf, but they are much worse if you care about America's future. Consumer capitalism seems unusually good at creating new leisure choices that do not require us to get off the couch.

But what if the inactive among us did get off the couch? What do they want to do? The Physical Activity Council survey asked "nonparticipants" what sports or activities they aspired to take part in, and golf was nowhere to be seen. In all the age groups, from six to sixty-five-plus, fitness activities dominated. Swimming for fitness and weight lifting topped almost all the lists.

Confronted by a world in which golf is losing out to other cheaper, easier, and more time-friendly options, some elements of the golf community have in essence said, the customer is always right, make the game easier and faster. So for those unwilling to wait for the return of demand, or for those who believe that demand will remain anemic, the idea is to change the game, make it more consumer friendly. Let's make golf as easy as walking on a treadmill or as quick and easy as a set of tennis. Important figures in the golf community have made dramatic suggestions about making the game easier. Mark King, the head of club maker Taylor-Made, and Scott McNealy, once the CEO of Sun Microsystems, have proposed enlarging the hole to fifteen inches, allowing preferred lies in all seasons, and granting a number of mulligans or do-overs each round. Jack Nicklaus proposed that courses should be designed so that players could play twelve holes, or one of three sixes, and that it should be easier to play nine holes.

There have been experiments with these sorts of changes. In early September 2011, Muirfield Village, Nicklaus's home course, hosted competitions that featured a twelve-hole course, eight-inch holes, and penalty stokes for exceeding a 180-minute time limit. An event played at Pine Needles Resort in North Carolina enlarged the hole to fifteen inches. There has been almost no systematic reporting on the response by players in these experiments.

Certainly one of the most dramatic attempts to make golf easier is the appearance of the Polara golf ball. This ball employs a dimple pattern that lowers the trajectory and considerably reduces the effect of side spin imparted by an imperfect swing. In short, it cures, to some extent, the slice. Something like the Polara has been around since the 1970s, but in August 2011 its inventor, Dave Felker, introduced a much-improved version. The ball has an arrow printed on it that must be pointed in the intended direction of the shot.

When a *New York Times* reporter took the ball to a New Jersey driving range, many golfers liked the concept while others were appalled. Mr. Felker, the inventor, claimed that the ball would help grow the game, claiming that it's "for people who want to be embarrassed less, play faster, and enjoy it more. I respect the USGA [that outlaws the ball] — they help identify the best golfers in the world, but what about the rest of us?"

This movement to save the game by making it easier and more consumer friendly is misguided. It's like trying to promote mountain climbing by blowing the tops off mountains. Quick fixes, like the Polara ball, will get a few to try the game and maybe a few to stick with it a bit longer. However, these sorts of solutions will not grow the number of lifelong committed golfers.

In fact, any tampering with the traditional parameters of the game may create something worse than a zero-sum game; the game may eventually lose more players than it gains.

Golf is not too hard; but many of the courses built in the last twenty years are. During that time simple, easy-to-play, inexpensive courses where kids, women, indeed all beginners could get started have become too scarce. Golf is caught in a complex dynamic that is stripping starter courses out of the system. Nine-hole, inexpensive courses make up a relatively small proportion of the courses in the United States, but in the last decade 85 percent of the closures were at courses that featured green fees below forty dollars.

The dynamic is simple — these inexpensive courses are often in the hands of cash-strapped towns or private owners. At some point both types of owners realize that selling out for cash is the best bargain. In all parts of America, entry-level courses are closing up and selling out. In Raleigh, North Carolina, Cheviot Hills Golf Course, a fixture since 1930, sold out for $25 million and is now covered with auto dealerships. Courses that were once in rural areas have seen development inevitably catch up with them. As development slowly encroaches, the courses become more valuable as vacant land than as golf courses. Cities recognize that a sale will produce both cash and businesses that will enrich the tax base. Remember, golf is almost always about real estate. This process of turning golf courses into auto dealerships and shopping malls is a big environmental negative, clearly and ironically supported by a politically correct antigolf attitude.

Golf's future looks grim. There are too many courses, and too many of the existing courses are wrong for the future of the game. It seems that the golf community has slowly reduced the size of the entry way into the game. Few courses fit the needs of children, women, and beginners. In the contest for a portion of America's discretionary time and money, golf is faced off against an array of options — some new, some old — that are proving to be more popular than golf. For the foreseeable future, the golf community will get smaller.

What can golf do to counter the wreckage? Some people have made reasonable suggestions. Golfer and entrepreneur Barney Adams has started a movement to move players up to a shorter set of tees, arguing that they will play faster and enjoy the game more. In effect, he wants to change long, hard courses into the short, easy courses that are closing at a rapid rate. Jaime Diaz, in *Golf World* magazine, has struck exactly the right note. He thinks that "longer-term, the greatest opportunity to turn the game back around lies in the way people learn it." For him committed players "started out playing young and on the cheap, usually at a ragtag course where they could go round and round." Diaz would have us contrast this beginner with "the post-boom golfer" who takes up the game later in life, who buys expensive clubs and lessons, and pays huge green fees at courses that are too hard. Eventually this beginner is "the player who walks away, good economy or bad." Golf has to understand that it cannot rely on the adult-onset golfer. They are fickle and quit when they discover how hard the game really is.

Diaz may not know it but he is just a recent recruit to the simplicity wing of the golf community. From the very beginning, a good number of golf people have urged austerity and simplicity as a guiding principle. Their enemy has been prosperity, which produces larger, fancier, more expensive courses, and demands for overwatered green perfection and larger, more luxurious clubhouses. Prosperity, for the moment, has come and gone and, as Diaz represents, we now hear the calls for simplicity, for cheap, easy courses. The problem with simplicity this time around is that it is the simple cheap courses, the pitch and putts, the nine-holers, that are closing in the greatest numbers.

What else can the golf community dream up that might help the game? I am uncomfortable enough writing about the present, so I am doubly uncomfortable about looking into the future.

However, I do have a short, eccentric list of things that I would like to see happen.

First, turn off the water. This sounds simple but involves a major change in American habits. The love affair with expanses of green, weed-free turf is deeply rooted and hugely important. American golf courses should be browner, firmer, and look as if they truly belong on the land they occupy. Southern courses should stop overseeding with ryegrass each winter; this will save water, fertilizer, and labor. It will reduce costs and the courses will be brown in the winter season, as they should be. In essence I am calling for a cure to the "the Augusta syndrome." The perfection Americans see each spring at the Masters has been a profound negative for golf generally. It has led to all sorts of insanity, including the actual painting of golf courses green. People who run golf courses have to get over the fear that Americans will play only on perfect, lushly green courses.

If courses were to make this change, American golfers would quickly learn that playing golf on hard and fast turf is more fun than they ever imagined. Some golfers will wonder why they ever paid to play from one mushy lie to another. This love affair with impossibly green courses has never made sense; it has some of the characteristics of a mass delusion. The same golfers who will not play on a brown golf course in the United States will happily pay high fees to play very brown, very firm courses in Scotland and Ireland.

The odds that the golf industry will switch from green to brown are not good. There is a massive industry, armed with the most sophisticated marketing techniques, that has convinced most Americans that a green, well-tended, weed-free lawn or golf course is a sign of orderliness and respectability. We have been persuaded that to abandon the quest for perfect greenness would suggest not sane environmental policy but rather a capitulation to disorder and a slide toward lassitude and chaos.

Second, we would all be surprised to see the private country club rise again, but it might be a good thing. The game had its best days in the years between 1900 and 1930 as the country club idea spread down the class structure and across the country. The movement was deeply flawed; the people who ran the clubs were so interested in being exclusive and aristocratic that they forgot to be a golf club. The new twenty-first century club should worry only about promoting golf—memberships would go only to those truly desiring to play and advance the game. The sole purpose of the club, then, would be to advance the game of golf. Women and children would have equal access to the course. The local high school team would play for free. The club would follow USGA Green Section advice, and members who made unreasonable demands about course conditions would be expelled. Members who demanded additional amenities, such as pools and tennis courts, would be shot in formal ceremonies on the first tee.

These clubs should do everything possible to encourage family play. This new style of family club would do everything possible to bring families together on the course. All golf courses have to abandon the focus on lower-handicap, affluent males ("golf bullies") willing to pay high fees to play ballyhooed courses. These clubs could make it clear that it was not good enough to merely watch your child play or drive them to their games. The new family club would make it possible for families to actually play a game together. For the private club to rise again will require a wrenching change in consumption habits. I am of the mind that people who buy experiences, like playing golf with your father, are happier than people who buy things. More experiences, less stuff.

The revival of the private club will also require a resurgence of localism. Golf clubs and courses can and should be seen as local resources. As mobility increased over the last fifty years, people cared less and less about the places where they lived and the golf courses they played on. Golf and the private club will benefit if Americans become less mobile and begin to care more about where they live. More local ownership and control of golf courses would help the game a great deal. I am not betting on this one, however.

There is some evidence that wealthy investors see distressed private clubs as a good investment. In North Carolina John McConnell has used some of his considerable fortune to buy clubs in the Raleigh-Durham-Greensboro area, and elsewhere, and market them together. McConnell is a harbinger of what golf might look like in postrecession America. As the recession sinks more private clubs that loaded up on debt during the boom years, one can hope that these clubs will come through the deleveraging process as renewed, well-formed, and golf-centric private clubs. Individuals like McConnell, who has netted a considerable fortune from the sale of two computer-related companies, will be important players as golf reconstitutes itself.

Finally let me suggest that the golf industry and the golf community should reconsider the way it talks about itself and the way it thinks about itself. We play on courses, not facilities. If you try to sell golf as if it were just another product, you will fail. People don't take up a game in the same way they buy a recliner or hand soap. It's not a simple calculation of cost and value. We need simple, affordable, playable golf courses that treat golfers like people, not sheep. PGA Tour officials and Golf Channel commentators should stop referring to PGA Tour events as "the game"—it's show business, it is an entertainment product. The game is a much larger, more complex, cultural and economic reality.

Both the golf community and the golf industry have to wean themselves off a dependence on market surveys and demographic analysis. It was just this kind of dependence in the late '70s and '80s that, in part, caused today's oversupply of the wrong kind of courses and the undersupply of the right kind. Golf has worked itself into a situation where it is increasingly dependent on affluent players willing to pay $150 or more to play on a course that cost $200,000 per hole to build. In effect, the industry is stuck with an unworkable "business model," also a term that they should stop using.

If people in the golf industry stop tracking demographics and give up reading marketing surveys they will have a lot of time on their hands. Let me suggest that they use this time to read the game's best philosophers. At some point, and it will be soon, the golf industry will have to answer the question, *Why does golf matter?* Surveys and statistics will be useless. Since 1970 the game has assembled a huge bookcase of golf books. There are coffee-table books with pretty pictures, player biographies, examinations of life on the tour, detailed portraits of single tournaments, countless guides to golf travel, and many, many instructional books. Down in the lower corner of this bookcase rest four volumes that should have more readers. They are

> Bob Cullen, *Why Golf? The Mystery of the Game Revisited* (2000)
> Michael Murphy, *Golf in the Kingdom* (1972)
> Timothy O'Grady, *On Golf* (2003)
> John Updike, *Golf Dreams* (1996)

I shall present no exhaustive examination of these works. Everyone who cares about golf should read them for themselves. Taken together they provide the best explanation for why golf attracts the truly committed player. These four accessible volumes get at the true heart of the game and why it matters. Golf literature helped create golf's first golden age — maybe these works can ignite something similar. But what might we take away from these four? All four are clearly connected and are linked to the golf literature of the past. There are many references to Haultain and other earlier writers. Updike reviewed Murphy's book in the *New Yorker* and also has a high opinion of Haultain. But what really ties them together is harder to define. We have already seen that Updike had a low opinion of the golf boom in the 1990s. All four would share this opinion. For them golf is not about $10-million courses and $40-million clubhouses. All four would, if possible, vote to ban Donald Trump from the game.

More important, our quartet has a positive case to make: they all in different ways try to get at the heart of golf's attraction. All four deal with golf as a form of personal expression. It is not an accident that modern golf has evolved at the same time as has modern mass society. Life has gotten bigger, more collective, and more corporate; it is easy to lose the feeling that we are unique individuals. The everyday world that we must negotiate is opaque; what happens to us is mysterious, often the product of massive, half-hidden forces. Golf is alarmingly clear; we are confronted with the task of aligning our bodies and minds in a clear eighteen-act drama, quest, or journey. As Shivas Irons puts it in *Golf in the Kingdom*, "In gowf ye see the essence of what the world itself demands. Inclusion of all our parts, alignment o'them all with one another and with the clubs and with the ball, with all the land we play on and with our playing partners." When we attain this nearly perfect alignment, the game rewards us, and it punishes us when we don't. Like all good forms of expression this need for us to be aligned, to be whole, makes golf "a good stage for the drama of our self-discovery."

I am fascinated by the fact that our need to express ourselves so often evolves into a test or a quest. We apparently have a need for the test to be hard. As Updike states it,

> Our mazy progress through the eighteen is a trek such as prehistoric man could understand and the fact that the trek is fatiguingly long constitutes part of its primitive rightness. A more reasonable length — 12 holes, say — wouldn't have the romance, the religious sense of ordeal. It is of the essence that a game of golf can't be quickly over and done with; it must be a journey.

Of course all golfers know that the trek is made up of shots. In Updike, we have the author who elegantly created the most famous golf shot in American fiction (a small category). In *Rabbit, Run*, the hero, Harry (Rabbit) Angstrom, has left his wife and moved in with another woman. At the behest of his wife's family a minister, Eccles, is assigned to lure Harry back to the family circle. Harry tells Eccles that he is looking for something he couldn't find in his marriage or anywhere else in his life — "this thing that wasn't there." Eccles demands to know what this thing is. They carry on this debate on a muddy, springtime public golf course. Harry steps to the tee in the middle of the round and hits his tee shot — "The sound has a hollowness, a singleness he hasn't heard before . . . his ball is hung way out, lunarly pale against the beautiful black blue storm clouds. . . . Rabbit thinks it will die, but he's fooled, for the ball makes its hesitation the ground for a final leap: with a kind of invisible sob it takes a last bite of space before vanishing in falling." Eccles wanted to know what Rabbit was looking for. Rabbit turns to him and says, simply, "That's it."

It is left to Tim O'Grady to provide a formal philosophy of the single golf shot. For him and for all dedicated players, "the shot is the irreducible unit of golf." The single shot seems to be just part of a hole or a round, but for the majority of golfers this single shot is the means by which they define and redefine themselves. Every true member of the golf community has a file of good and bad shots knit into the very fiber of their being. O'Grady claims that "a fine golf shot is succinct. It is simple. It is unambiguous, indisputable, and pure." There are of course good and bad shots. O'Grady is particularly eloquent on the golfer's reaction to a very bad shot: "A violent and enraged self-loathing may enter you like a poison injected into your vein. The excruciating ugliness of the shot has insulted the father who taught you, the years you have played the game, the true abilities you believe you possess. . . . You may feel like tearing your liver out." As golfers attempt to express themselves, things can go well and sometimes not so well.

When things don't go well, you can tear your liver out or you can laugh. Updike points out that golf, and especially golf shots that go awry, are funny and therefore memorable. He gives them amusing names — "the arboreal ricochet," "the pond side scuff and splash," "the stubbed putt," and the "deep grass squirt." Who is not amused by the whiff? Who in golf does not have a memory of some gigantic male, an ex-footballer who has always bulldozed through obstacles, coming to the tee and taking a violent flail that misses his helpless ball by half a foot? Who is not warmed by the memory of these titanic failures?

But they are all expressions, clearly and irrevocably expressions, of who we are. The evasions of this fact are central to the culture of golf. Bad shots are blamed on clubs, caddies, the wife, the husband, the wind, a bird chirp, inferior equipment, and improper course maintenance. But we know. O'Grady quotes Tom Watson, who said, "You cannot persuade yourself that you have hit a good shot when you have hit a bad shot."

The modern world weighs heavily upon us. It really wants us as audience, not as players, as consumers of excellence, not producers. Golf is an antidote to this. Again, as Tom Watson put it in O'Grady's book, "I was silent much of the time. Even the thought of speaking to people I didn't know was something I found paralyzing. But golf was something through which I discovered I could express myself and establish my presence, be somehow acknowledged in the world."

Golf, today, is in a world of hurt. In the golf community all the talk seems to be of loss, course closings, demographics, shrinking demand, and the economics of the game. Golf's problems are rooted in the seismic changes in the economy and the culture of the last forty years. However, if the golf community responds to these changes by dramatically changing the game, by making it shorter, easier, or by changing the rules, it will be a profound mistake. Golf is not best seen as a consumer product; for its adherents it is an essential, a giver of health, meaning, and peace. Golf in the United States has always been an antidote, a form of medicine, for the ills of modernity. There is no reason to believe that this century will be any different.

Golf, Parks, and the American Lawn

Sometimes an appendix is a substitute for writing another book. In this case the book would be about the close connections between golf courses, public parks, and the suburban lawn. My point would be that the three were tied together by a sudden passionate love for grass. By grass I mean long swaths of fine, uniform, weed-free turf. Americans wanted both to play on the stuff and just to look at it.

The public park came first. Central Park in New York was among the first and certainly most famous of the parks. Frederick Law Olmsted and Calvert Vaux completed its design in 1858. By 1876 Baltimore, Boston, San Francisco, and Philadelphia had begun similar parks. These early parks were essentially pastoral with long open fields that ran to a backdrop of thick plantings of trees and specimen plantings. The sweep of open ground could be broken by a single tree or perhaps a pond. The idea was to create a soothing landscape for the overstimulated city dweller to passively enjoy.

By 1890 the rationale for such parks began to change. The people wanted parks that functioned in a new way: they wanted ball fields, playgrounds, pools, and golf courses. Existing parks were retrofitted with these features, and parks created after 1890 had them from the beginning. The public golf course before 1920 was most commonly placed on preexisting park land. The course in Van Cortlandt Park in New York City provided an example for golf advocates in other cities.

At about the same time as parks turned functional, we can detect the beginnings of the modern American lawn. The lawn as we know it was almost unknown in the nineteenth century. Only a very few were willing to spend the time and money maintaining a lawn around their home or in a public space. As the century drew to a close, and as Americans became more suburban, the idea of the lawn took root.

In 1897 F. Lamson-Scribner, an agrologist with the U.S. Department of Agriculture (USDA), included a section called "Lawns and Lawnmaking" in his department's yearbook. The department, devoted to that point to advising farmers, had begun receiving questions about establishing and caring for a lawn. He was pro-lawn. He stated that "nothing was more beautiful than a well-kept lawn" and that such lawns reflected the character of the homeowner. Lamson-Scribner was moved to write what was probably the first definition of the modern lawn. It was "a growth of a single variety of grass with a smooth even surface, uniform color, and an elastic turf which has become though constant care, so fine and so close in texture as to exclude weeds, which appearing, should be at once removed." He warned against using seed mixtures; the ideal lawn should be of bent grass, especially the creeping variety. With this definition we can hear the beginnings of a vast new industry that would provide seeds, mowers, tools, weed killers, and fertilizers to a public seeking the perfect lawn.

At the same time that suburban, middle-class Americans were beginning to establish lawns, builders of golf courses were also seeking methods that would produce the same effect but on a much larger scale. The perfect lawn shares a great deal with the perfect fairway or green. Lawn seekers and course builders turned to the same agencies for help. Seed companies began offering special seeds for lawns and fairways. In 1899 the Vaughan Seed Company was the first to market a variety especially for courses. It was called Vaughan's Golf Link. The USDA, early in the century, began receiving pleas for help from course builders. Not much help was forthcoming until 1912, when Charles V. Piper, an avid golfer and botanist with the USDA, began experimenting with golf turf at the department's farm in Arlington, Virginia. In 1913 he and R. A. Oakley published a helpful series of articles on golf-course grasses in *Golf*. States such as Connecticut and Oklahoma sponsored important turf research that helped the lawn lover and the golf-course builder.

The advent of World War I curtailed all research efforts. This was merely a temporary halt, however. It was clear that the demand for helpful information about nurturing grass was not going to disappear. Course builders such as Macdonald and Crump had wasted small fortunes because they were ignorant about grasses and the establishment and care of proper turf. After the war the demand for helpful research reemerged. The person who got the ball rolling was E. J. Marshall, an attorney in Toledo, Ohio, and the chair of the greens committee at Inverness Golf Club. When he began to prepare the course for the 1920 USGA Open Championship, he learned that he could not draw upon a sound body of information to guide his work. Marshall suggested that the USGA create a national research and advisory body that could help not only the golf community establish courses but anyone wanting to grow grass. Assisted by Charles Piper and R. A. Oakley, the USGA chartered the Green Section, a separate, tax-exempt institution for grass and turf research.

The Green Section has had a rocky but largely positive history. It all but disappeared in the 1930s when grass and lawns seemed less important. But over the years it has done well by the golfing community. It has provided solid, increasingly sophisticated information that has helped the golf community save millions.

This digression into park construction, the rise of the lawn, and grass research suggests a great deal about the history of the American golf course and the golf community. Americans during this period (1900–1915) moved away from a slavish devotion to Scottish and English models. Americans would build the vast majority of their courses away from the seacoast. They also moved away from the idea that courses were basically found, that they could only be laid out on ideal sites. In 1913 Harold H. Hilton wrote that the great British courses had been unplanned because they were set out on land ideally suited for golf. The older courses "were just natural golfing ground, somewhat indifferently nursed by the hand of man." He noted that in 1880 one man looked after the whole of Hoylake. While we venerate these courses, Hilton makes clear that under certain circumstances they were virtually unplayable. Wet, warm weather made them long, thick, and rank. Really more like a hayfield than a playable course. Hilton had noticed a different attitude among Americans. They believe that a good course is merely a matter of money, that "a golf links can be carved out of anything." The agents elected to do the carving were the golf architects. They had to produce not only a place to play a game, but also a uniformly green pastoral look. They had to dramatically alter nature into a new kind of place — a new kind of place where grass was the central attraction.

Finally, the age of grass suggests a profound connection between the golf club–country club and the home. The club was for many an extension of the home. The clubhouse became a collectively shared country house and the course was a really big lawn.

Golf Courses in 1920

Counting golf courses in the United States is not easy. There was no reliable count prior to the late 1920s. I have concluded that there were 1,304 golf clubs in the United States in 1920. This number requires some explanation.

It is taken from the list of clubs in the *American Annual Golf Guide* for 1920. This work was produced by *Golf Illustrated* and edited by W. H. Follette, but exactly how a club came to be listed remains a mystery. It is probable that clubs volunteered to be listed and the editor simply compiled the information. The number of clubs does not automatically equal the number of courses. There were clubs with no course and there were clubs with more than one course. There were clubs that, for whatever reason, did not wish to be on the list. Municipal courses often had several clubs attached to them. The club at Pinehurst had four courses. It is fair, I think, to conclude that the number of actual courses was something like 1,300.

Each club listed provided varying amounts of information. Each listing has the number of holes, yardage, and the type of greens (sand or grass). Clubs usually gave directions to the course and the rules governing play by visitors. It was common for clubs to provide information about Sunday play, the availability of caddies, and the regulations governing play by women. Sunday play by 1920 was widespread, almost a nonissue. Most clubs remain silent on the women issue, but a few reveal their position. Most commonly, women were allowed to play anytime. However, a number of clubs banned women at certain times. The pattern was clear that women were kept off the course at the times that working men could play. This pattern reflects the five-and-a-half-day workweek. Women were excluded most commonly on Sundays, Saturday afternoons, and holidays. Almost no clubs announced an outright ban on play by women. MacDonald's National was one of the few that did.

The list of clubs in the *Annual* for 1920 provides a rough outline of the golf community after three decades. The private club was the most common venue. Public and hotel/resort courses were well entrenched. It was clear that golf had become a vacation-time activity. Golf had arrived in all parts of the Union, but the Northeast remained the critical center of golf. While golf had spread to the South, the number of clubs was relatively small. There were 133 clubs in the South, while New York and Massachusetts had a total of 276. Over time this geographical distribution would change dramatically.

Finally, to provide some perspective, there are today (in 2012) about sixteen thousand golf courses in the United States.

The PGA in 1935

In 1935 the PGA published a small booklet called the *Tournament and Player Record Book for 1935*. It was assembled and written by Robert E. Harlow, manager of the PGA Tournament Committee, which ran the tour; it tells us a great deal about the tour during the 1930s.

Harlow describes the political structure of the PGA that controls the tournament committee. The president was George R. Jacobus and the vice president was Charles Hall. The tournament committee was chaired by Horton Smith and the vice chair was Gene Sarazen. This committee maintained, between May and December, a headquarters in Chicago; during the winter the headquarters moved to St. Petersburg, Florida. While real power lay elsewhere, the face of the tour was Robert E. (Bob) Harlow. Harlow managed every detail from setting the year's schedule to making the pairings and operating the scoreboard at events. In every town, Harlow was the PGA's link to the locals, the sponsors.

Much of the *Tournament and Player Record Book* is given over to describing the tour statistically in 1935. There were a lot of numbers. Johnny Revolta had the lowest scoring average (72.29), with Henry Picard second (72.37). Picard played the most rounds (ninety-five), with Byron Nelson second (eighty-nine). Harlow provides an official list of the year's tournaments. The year began on January 4, with the Riverside Amateur-Pro, and ended on December 24, at the Southern California Open in Glendale. In all, there were forty-five sanctioned events that included a number of sectional PGA championships. The list suggests that the tour was hardly just a wintertime affair. The PGA wanted to penalize players who competed in an event that occurred at the same time as a sanctioned event but had not yet come up with a way of assuring sponsors that big-name players would play in any particular event.

Beyond the statistics, the booklet provides local sponsors with advice about how to run their event. Harlow flogs the notion that having the PGA come to their area is a good idea. He claims that holding "an open tournament" is "rapidly gaining favor as a means of obtaining favorable publicity and fine entertainment for cities and resorts." He adds that the most common sponsor is the Junior Chamber of Commerce and that, in most localities, having a golf event is especially popular among the younger businessmen.

Harlow argues that when staged in a large city, an open golf event can be "self-supporting." When the population in the area is small, such as at a resort like Pinehurst, the cost of the event is usually charged off to the resort's advertising budget. In both cases, Harlow contends that having a PGA golf tournament is "a fine investment."

The success of these events was contingent on a number of factors. Local sponsors had to have the proper attitude and had to take the proper steps to ensure success. Harlow advised local sponsors to realize that once they had agreed to have a PGA tournament, they were "definitely in show business." He urged them to think of the tournament as "a big show coming to your town." Once you take this position, the great imperative becomes selling tickets. No audience, no show.

Selling tickets and promoting the show required that the locals create the best sort of local organization. Harlow clearly has strong feelings about what constitutes an effective organization. The first step is to appoint a general chairman, a business executive with time to devote to the task. Next the tournament needs an "honorary general chairman." This should be someone known and beloved by everyone in the area. As an example, Harlow points to the event in Buffalo where the honorary general chairman was Ganson Depew — "the grand old man of golf in Western New York" and "Buffalo's first citizen." Next the local sponsors should create a number of committees to handle the many details that inevitably arise. The most important committees are concessions, transportation, police, parking, caddies, scoring, and tickets.

The organization's most important job, according to Harlow, is to raise the money to pay prizes and cover the event's other expenses. Harlow strongly suggests that the tournament recruit "underwriters" who promise to pay all expenses. They will have to pay only if the local "crusade" to sell tickets falls short. The tournament should ask local businesses (hotels and restaurants particularly) that will benefit from the event to make outright donations from their ad budgets.

Selling tickets is crucial. Harlow suggests that one-third of the cost of the entire tournament should be covered by advance ticket sales. A big part of advance ticket sales should be "patrons' tickets." Each such ticket should include ten regular tickets that the patron may sell or give away. Clearly, from Harlow's point of view, the big issue was raising the money to pay the players who showed up to put on the show.

Harlow has much to say on exactly how the tournament should be played. Two big issues were who could play and who would play with whom. Obviously it was Harlow's job to get the best field of pros to play each event. At bottom this was an advertising problem. The locals could not promote the event if the field of PGA pros was poor or uncertain. Tournament fields in the 1930s were unstable and exactly who would play was not determined until the last minute. Almost all of the events allowed "post entries" (usually local amateurs and pros) on the day before the event.

A thorny related issue was the entry of high-handicap local amateurs. Harlow accepts the fact that they will play but he insists that they not be paired with the best touring pros. Local players with handicaps below four can be paired with the better players. Obviously one modern solution to this problem was the invention of the Wednesday pro-am in which good local players could be part of the show but not part of the tournament itself.

Harlow and the tournament committee provide a number of suggestions about the actual playing of the event. Groups should go off at six-minute intervals. The round should take between three hours and three hours and twenty minutes to complete. The local superintendent should let the rough grow "fairly long . . . heavy enough so that it is a real penalty." Local greenkeepers should resist the temptation to put the pins in the most difficult positions. This was apparently a persistent problem. Locals did not want the reputation of their course sullied by a barrage of very low scores by visiting pros. Harlow suggests that the course invest in new flags and that they be yellow.

The players cannot bring in "outside caddies." It was a PGA rule that only caddies from the local course and other local clubs were allowed. Harlow also warns against what had apparently become a common problem — the local caddies traditionally jacked up the rates charged to the visiting professionals.

There was much advice from the PGA concerning how to deal with the players off the course. There should be a reserved private space where the players can obtain their meals. Harlow notes that "many players like hot soup." There should be no formal entertainment planned for the players. Harlow states flatly that "the players will not come" to such events since "90 percent of the players will be in bed before midnight."

Harlow, in his little booklet, spends considerable time on the subject of gambling. The PGA asked that local officials "see that no games of chance are permitted in the locker room or elsewhere in the clubhouse while a tournament is in progress."

There was ample reason for this ban. Harlow states that "professional and crooked gamblers have followed the tournament circuit and started games in which both players and club members have been cheated out of considerable sums of money."

Is there any larger meaning we can draw from this little booklet produced by Bob Harlow and the PGA? It's clear that both local sponsors and the PGA were feeling their way toward a system for running what we think of as a "tour event." The PGA had established some solid ground rules, but there remained some key unresolved issues. The most important was the nature and construction of the fields that would play the event. This was largely a matter of discipline. Could the PGA control the players who were, in the end, the whole show? Could they guarantee a field of pros, of "name players," so that locals could promote the event assured that Hagen, Sarazen, Revolta, Picard, and others would show up? Or would post entries and high-handicap local amateurs still be necessary to fill out the event?

However, more than anything else, the *Tournament Player and Record Book for 1935* illustrates the nature of the interface between local institutions and a newly formed national organization. The PGA, essentially a nationwide union of club pros, had spawned a national traveling circus that depended for its success on the considerable efforts of local institutions that were intended to promote the interests, not of the PGA, but of their town or resort. At the same time, the interests of the touring pros were not exactly identical to those of the PGA. Clearly there were three parties involved in putting on an event—the players, the PGA, and the local sponsor. It would take decades to work out the relationships between them. Seventy years later the players have become an independent version of the PGA and the local sponsors have all but completely disappeared. Tour events now garner the most support from large national and international corporations seeking to associate themselves with golf. The local nature of the early tour events is all but dead.

Bibliographical Essay

The point of this essay is to list the sources that have generally informed and influenced the writing of this book. In the text I have made every attempt to provide a guide for the reader who wishes to consult the source being used. A second purpose is to help those who may wish to do further research on American golf.

The notion that a golf community began forming in the late nineteenth century is rooted in Benjamin G. Rader's "The Quest for Sub-communities and the Rise of American Sport" in the *American Quarterly* (Fall 1977). Also very useful is Peter Donnelly's 1981 chapter "Toward a Definition of Sport Subcultures" in *Sport in the Sociocultural Process*, edited by Marie Hart and Susan Birrell.

There are several helpful general histories of golf in the United States. They are George B. Kirsch, *Golf in America* (2009); Herbert Warren Wind, *The Story of American Golf* (1975); Richard J. Moss, *Golf and the American Country Club* (2001), and a book that is both a primary and secondary source, H. B. Martin, *Fifty Years of American Golf* (1936).

For general issues concerning sport in the United States, I have relied on Benjamin G. Rader, *American Sports: From the Age Of Folk Games to the Age of Television* (1999) and, to a lesser extent, Richard O. Davies, *Sports in American Life* (2007).

Club histories are a crucial source. Some are better than

others. As I suggested in chapter 3, H. Craig Miner's *A History of the Wichita Country Club 1900–1975* (1976) is a model of sorts. Local, state, and regional golf associations have produced helpful volumes that present both the association's history and brief accounts of their member clubs. See Bill Quirin, *Golf Clubs of the MGA: A Centennial History of Golf in the New York Metropolitan Area* (1997); and Tim Cronin, *A Century of Golf: The Western Golf Association, 1899–1999* (1998). See also Gary Larrabee, *The Green and the Gold: The History of Golf on Boston's North Shore 1893–2001* (2001).

Biographies are crucial to golf research. The most important are Bradley S. Klein, *Discovering Donald Ross: The Architect and His Golf Courses* (2011); George D. Bahto, *The Evangelist of Golf: The Story of Charles B. Macdonald* (2002); Stephen R. Lowe, *Sir Walter and Mr. Jones: Walter Hagen, Bobby Jones, and the Rise of American Golf* (2000); Susan E. Cayleff, *Babe: The Life and Legend of Babe Didrikson Zaharias* (1995); Al Barkow, *Sam: The One and Only Sam Snead* (2005); James Dodson, *Ben Hogan: An American Life* (2004); and Stuart W. Bendelow, *Thomas "Tom" Bendelow: The Johnny Appleseed of American Golf* (2006). Autobiographies are even more useful. See especially Byron Nelson, *An Autobiography: How I Played the Game* (1993); Walter Hagen, *The Walter Hagen Story* (1956); Robert T. Jones, *Golf Is My Game* (1960) and *Down the Fairway* (1927); Arnold Palmer, *A Golfer's Life* (1999); Glenna Collette, *Ladies in the Rough* (1927); and Gene Sarazen, *Thirty Years of Championship Golf* (1950). Two autobiographies by nongolfers are helpful: Charles B. Macdonald, *Scotland's Gift* (1928); and Fred Corcoran, *Unplayable Lies* (1965).

On specific topics, I have found the following works useful. On the PGA, two works by Al Barkow are important: *Getting to the Dance Floor: The Early Days of American Pro-Golf* (1986) and *The History of the PGA Tour* (1989). Also helpful is an older book by Herb Graffis, *The PGA* (1975). On women in American golf, see Rhonda Glenn, *The Illustrated History of Women's Golf* (1991); and Terri Leonard, *In the Women's Clubhouse* (2000). For African

Americans and race, the most useful works are Calvin H. Sinnette, *Forbidden Fairways: African Americans and the Game of Golf* (1998); and John H. Kennedy, *A Course of Their Own: A History of African American Golfers* (2000). On the Masters, Clifford Roberts, and related issues, start with David Owen, *The Making of the Masters* (1999). All the many works on Augusta National take passionate positions and have some sort of ax to grind. On Pinehurst, see, in addition to Klein on Ross, Richard J. Moss, *Eden in the Pines: A History of Pinehurst Village* (2005); and Richard Mandell, *Pinehurst: Home of American Golf (The Evolution of a Legend)* (2007). On the issue of grass, lawns, and golf courses, see both Virginia Scott Jenkins, *The Lawn: A History of an American Obsession* (1994); and Ted Steinberg, *American Green: The Obsessive Quest for the Perfect Lawn* (2006). There is no good book on golf and American politics and politicians in general. You might consult Shepard Campbell and Peter Landau, *Presidential Lies* (1996); and the best, most ignored golf book, Catherine M. Lewis's *"Don't Ask What I Shot": How Eisenhower's Love of Golf Helped Shape 1950s America* (2007).

Anyone reading this volume will be aware that much of it is based on past journalism. The best source for exploring this journalism is the United States Golf Association (USGA) Library at Far Hills, New Jersey. Much of the library's rich collection, especially for pre-1930 issues, is available as part of the Seagle Electronic Library, which can be found online at http://www. usgamuseum.com/researchers/usga_segl. The USGA magazine *Golf Journal* is an immensely valuable source for the period between World War II and 2004, when the USGA suspended publication. The website GolfClubAtlas.com deals mainly with golf architecture but also has a rich archive on the history of golf clubs and courses. I have found two collections of journalism, in book form, to be especially valuable. Gene Brown's *The Complete Book of Golf* (1980) is a compilation of *The New York Times* reporting on golf from 1895 to 1978. A reader can trace the changing tone of golf journalism, and the book also has great pictures. Mel Shapiro, Warren Dohn, and Leonard Berger's *Golf: A Turn-of-the-Century Treasury* (1986) contains a fine collection of magazine articles on golf from American periodicals between 1895 and 1910.

Golf has had its share of great journalists. Bernard Darwin towers above the rest and collections of his work are easy to find. For me he has something of a rival in Pat Ward-Thomas, who covered golf for the British paper *The Guardian* from 1950 to 1977. A collection of his work called *The Lay of the Land* (Classics of Golf Edition, 1990) has become one of my favorite books because Ward-Thomas writes about the period in which professional golf took center stage but before television ruined everything. He keeps the pros in proper perspective and never fawns, and he can really write.

The National Golf Foundation (ngf.org) publishes an extensive list of reports on the number of players and courses in the modern era. They also publish research reports on other issues of interest to the golf industry, which funds the enterprise. At pellucidcorp.com one can find an independent source of contemporary statistics and commentary on industry issues.

Golf is a game that has been caught up in the powerful currents of American life since 1880. This volume has attempted to put golf into historical context. I have been reading and teaching about American history and culture for forty years, and my sense of post–Civil War American life has been shaped by many sources. The following are some of the most crucial: Thomas Bender, *Community and Social Change in America* (1978); Daniel Bell, *The Coming of Post-Industrial Society* (1973); Edward J. Blakely and Mary Gail Synder, *Fortress America: Gated Communities in the United States* (1999); Lizabeth Cohen, *A Consumer's Republic: The Politics of Mass Consumption in Postwar America* (2003); Lawrence B. Glickman, *Consumer Society in American History: A Reader* (1999); Benjamin Kline Hunnicutt, *Work Without End: Abandoning Shorter Hours for the Right to Work* (1988); Christopher Lasch, *The Culture of Narcissism: American Life in an Age of*

Diminished Expectations (1979); Jackson Lears, *No Place of Grace: Antimodernism and the Transformation of American Culture, 1880–1920* (1981); Stanley Lebergott, *Pursuing Happiness: American Consumers in the Twentieth Century* (1993); William E. Leuchtenberg, *A Troubled Feast: American Society since 1945* (1983); Roderick Nash, *A Nervous Generation: American Thought 1917–1930* (1979); Andrew Potter, *The Authenticity Hoax* (2010); Robert D. Putnam, *Bowling Alone: The Collapse and Revival of American Community* (2000); Witold Rybczynski, *Waiting for the Weekend* (1991); Alan Trachtenberg, *The Incorporation of America: Culture and Society in the Gilded Age* (1982); and Robert H. Wiebe, *The Search for Order, 1877–1920* (1967).

A sharp-eyed reader will notice two things about the this list: the works are generally older (from the 1970s and 1980s), and they are largely history books. My approach to golf has been as an historian of experience, attempting to re-create what it was like to adopt golf as part of an American life. I have found the large and growing literature on sport in general, and especially the works that attempt to apply "theory" to sport, of little use. They are for the most part ahistorical and generally do not shed much light on individual sports. A good introduction to these works, however, is Alan Tomlinson's *The Sport Studies Reader* (2007).

Finally, there is little doubt in my mind that playing golf for sixty years, working briefly at a golf course, and having many friends who are devoted players has had a fundamental impact on what I wrote in this book.

Index

114–15, 313–31; etiquette of, 22, 247, 261, 273, 291–92, 324–26; literature of, x, 20–33, 128, 330, 352–55; politicalization of, 128, 242–51, 315, 339–40; religious aspects of, 18, 129, 178; sociology of, 81–82, 109, 241–42, 304, 321; work ethic of, 45, 74–75, 151, 178, 329

golf courses, 16, 32, 34–60; back-to-basics trend in, 131–32, 142–45, 160–61, 348–50; branding of, 114; at colleges, 43–44, 128, 284, 291, 308, 339; design of, 40, 48–56, 77, 101, 207, 285; professional jobs at, 12–13, 48–49, 71–72, 74, 290–92, 314; ratings of, 59, 97, 108, 302, 307; "stadium," 108, 306–7; statistics on, 200, 204, 207, 209–10, 314, 317–18, 361–62; taxation of, 92–93; typical expenses at, 94. *See also* country clubs

Golf Digest, 59

The Golfer (magazine), 12

Golfer's Magazine, 103

Golf Hall of Fame, 293, 315

Golf Handicap and Information Network, 309

Golf Illustrated (magazine), 60, 64, 73, 361; on golf expenses, 94; on golf professionals, 163; on social inclusiveness of clubs, 103–4; during World War I, 86

Golfing (magazine), 42; creation of, 9–10, 12; on St. Andrew's Golf Club, 6

Golf in the Kingdom (Murphy), 352–53

Golf Journal, 278, 279, 304

golf lessons, 50, 72, 82, 284, 292; Hogan on, 179; PGA-certified, 289; on phonograph records, 88–89

Golf 20/20, 302, 315–16

Golf Writers Association of America, 244

Goodyear Corporation, 263

Graffis, Herb, 157–58

Grand Slam, 116, 119, 138

Grange, Red, 108, 109

Great Depression, 118, 128–52, 199, 314–15, 320, 335

Greenbrier Golf Club (West Virginia), 243

Greene, Hattie, 165–66

greenkeeping, 48–50, 72, 254, 285, 314, 349, 358–59; golf carts and, 254–55; at Pine Valley, 57–58; seeds for, 58, 358; USGA advice on, 80, 278, 304, 305, 350, 359; water use for, 55, 58, 161, 316, 334, 340, 349. *See also* turf science

Greensboro Open (North Carolina), 180, 190, 214

Gregory, Ann, 237–39

Greymont, Walter, 133

Griffin, Marion, 214

Griffith, Thomas H., 46

Grout, Jack, 166, 176

Guelph Golf Club, 89

Guldahl, Ralph, 149

Haas, Lloyd, 170

Hagen, Walter, 72–75, 82, 95, 195; income of, 105, 114; Jones and, 110–11, 114–15, 117–19; Kirkwood and, 112–14, 117; legacy of, 120, 164; lifestyle of, 75, 110, 112, 114, 163–64; nicknames of, 112; Sarazen and, 148; victories of, 110–11; during World War I, 90

Haig Ultra clubs, 114

Hale America Open, 159, 181

Hall, Charles, 363

Hancock, Roland, 107–8

handicap system, 28, 33, 272, 292, 322; gambling and, 279; standardization of, 309; during tournaments, 366

Handmacher, Alvin, 223–24, 230

Hanmore, Merle G., 254

Harbour Town Links (South Carolina), 207–8

Harden, Blaine, 303–4

Harding, Warren, 122

Harding Park Golf Course (California), 215

Harlow, Robert E., 112, 114, 288, 363–67